Old Religion, New Spirituality

International Studies in Sociology and Social Anthropology

Series Editor

Alberto Martinelli (*University of Milan*)

Editorial Board

Vincenzo Cicchelli (*Ceped, Université Paris Descartes/IRD*)
Vittorio Cotesta (*Università degli Studi Roma Tre*)
Benjamin Gregg (*University of Texas at Austin*)
Leo Penta (*Katholische Hochschule für Sozialwesen Berlin*)
Elisa Reis (*Universidade Federal do Rio de Janeiro*)
Madalina Vartejanu-Joubert (*Institut National des Langues et Civilisations Orientales*, Paris)

VOLUME 137

The titles published in this series are listed at *brill.com/issa*

Old Religion, New Spirituality

Implications of Secularisation and Individualisation in Estonia

Edited by

Riho Altnurme

BRILL

LEIDEN | BOSTON

Cover illustration: 'Incense and Bible' by Bildagentur Zoonar GmbH, Shutterstock, photo ID 169009172.

The Library of Congress Cataloging-in-Publication Data is available online at http://catalog.loc.gov
LC record available at http://lccn.loc.gov/2021029049

Typeface for the Latin, Greek, and Cyrillic scripts: "Brill". See and download: brill.com/brill-typeface.

ISSN 0074-8684
ISBN 978-90-04-46113-0 (hardback)
ISBN 978-90-04-46117-8 (e-book)

Copyright 2021 by Riho Altnurme. Published by Koninklijke Brill NV, Leiden, The Netherlands.
Koninklijke Brill NV incorporates the imprints Brill, Brill Nijhoff, Brill Hotei, Brill Schöningh, Brill Fink, Brill mentis, Vandenhoeck & Ruprecht, Böhlau Verlag and V&R Unipress.
Koninklijke Brill NV reserves the right to protect this publication against unauthorized use. Requests for re-use and/or translations must be addressed to Koninklijke Brill NV via brill.com or copyright.com.

This book is printed on acid-free paper and produced in a sustainable manner.

Contents

Acknowledgements   VII
List of Tables and Maps   VIII
Notes on Contributors   IX

1   Introduction   1
    Riho Altnurme

2   The History of the Marginalisation of Christianity in Estonia (1857–2017)   3
    Lea Altnurme

3   The Lutheran Church in Estonian Society: The Impact of Secularisation and Religious Change   29
    Priit Rohtmets, Indrek Pekko, and Riho Altnurme

4   The Orthodox Church in Estonia: Historical and Contemporary Perspectives in the Context of the 2011 Population and Housing Census   45
    Toomas Schvak

5   Secular Society, Secular State: Egalitarian Legislation on Religion?   58
    Ringo Ringvee

6   The Influence of the European Union's Liberal Secularist Policy on Religion upon Religious Authority in Estonia Since 2004   71
    Alar Kilp

7   The Religious Turn in Estonia: Modern Self-understanding in a Flood of Esotericism   86
    Lea Altnurme

8   The Spiritual Milieu in Estonia: Challenges and Opportunities for Studying Contemporary Forms of Religion   118
    Marko Uibu

9 Similarities and Differences between Estonia and the Other 'Most Secular' Countries   131
   Riho Altnurme

Conclusion   150
   Riho Altnurme

References   153
Index   177

Acknowledgements

The project 'Secularization (de-institutionalization and de-christianization): Religion in Estonia from the Modern Period to the Present (2011–2016)' was supported by the Estonian Ministry of Education and Research, Targeted Funding (SF0180026s11). Riho Altnurme's research was also supported by the University of Latvia, project 8.2.2.0/18/A/010. The chapters by Lea Altnurme, Riho Altnurme and Priit Rohtmets also include research done with the support of Horizon 2020 grant 770309 'Religious Toleration and Peace (RETOPEA)'. We are thankful for our supporters!

The anonymous peer reviewers, the *International Studies in Sociology and Social Anthropology* Series Editor Professor Alberto Martinelli and Jennifer Obdam from Brill deserve thanks for their work in helping to make this manuscript publishable. Last but not least – the manuscript was made readable thanks to language editors Tiina Kirss and Jena Gaines!

Tables and Maps

Map

1   Map of Estonia   xii

Tables

7.1   Christian factors based on factor analysis RTE 2014   98
7.2   Factor of the new spirituality based on factor analysis from RTE 2014   106
7.3   Factor of the native faith based on factor analysis from RTE 2014   109
7.4   Factor of the secular intellectuals who appreciate nature based on factor analysis from RTE 2014   109
7.5   Factor of anti-Christian attitudes + 'one's own religion' based on factor analysis RTE 2014   113
7.6   Factor of the beliefs of new spirituality and 'one's own religion' based on factor analysis RTE 2014   114

Notes on Contributors

Lea Altnurme
is an Associate Professor of Sociology of Religion at the School of Theology and Religious Studies, University of Tartu, Estonia. Her research focuses on changes in spirituality on the individual level, new phenomena in the religious landscape, and the role of religion in Estonian cultural history. She is author of the monograph *Kristlusest oma usuni* [From Christianity to One's Own Faith] (University of Tartu Press, 2006), and the founder and Editor-in-Chief of the series *Mitut usku Eesti* [Multireligious Estonia]. E-mail: lea.altnurme@ut.ee

Riho Altnurme
is a Professor of Church History at the School of Theology and Religious Studies, University of Tartu, and visiting Professor at the University of Latvia (2019–2021). His research is concentrated on nineteenth- and twentieth-century church history, in context of church-state-society relations. He is a representative of Estonia in the Commission Internationale d'Histoire et d'Études du Christianisme (CIHEC), member of the Wissenschaftliche Gesellschaft für Theologie (WgTh), co-founder of the International Network of Baltic Church Historians (INBCH) and Estonian Society of Church History. He is the editor of *History of Estonian Ecumenism* (University of Tartu, 2009), a textbook of Estonian church history *Eesti kiriku- ja religiooniluga* (University of Tartu Press, 2018), and co-editor (with Patrick Pasture and Elena Arigita) of *Religious Diversity in Europe: Mediating the Past to the Young* (Bloomsbury, in press). E-mail: riho.altnurme@ut.ee

Alar Kilp
is a lecturer in Comparative Politics at University of Tartu, Estonia. His research specialises in political sociology, religion and politics as well as church and state relations in post-communist Europe. He has co-edited the special issue 'Religion, the Russian Nation and the State: Domestic and International Dimensions' (*Religion, State and Society*, 2013, Volume 41, Issue 3), published papers on religious nationalism, religion and soft power, religion and law in books by Brill and Routledge and several articles in the journals *Religion, State and Society*, *Studies in Church History*, and *Proceedings of Estonian National Defence College*. E-mail: alar.kilp@ut.ee

Indrek Pekko
is a PhD student (MA in Theology) in the School of Theology and Religious Studies at University of Tartu, Estonia and works as a teacher at the Tartu

Herbert Masing School. His fields of research interest are contemporary church history (Protestant churches in Eastern and Central Europe) and sociology of religion (contemporary religious trends, New Age movement, new spirituality, Christian spirituality). His dissertation topic is '(Theological and sociocultural) changes in the Estonian Evangelical Lutheran Church in 1987–2015'. He has already published several articles on the topic. E-mail: indrekpekko@hotmail.com

Ringo Ringvee

graduated with a master's degree from the University of Helsinki as a historian of religions and defended his PhD on the church-state relations at the University of Tartu. Since 1998 he has held a post at the Religious Affairs Department of the Estonian Ministry of the Interior. He is a member of the Estonian Chancellor of Justice's Advisory Committee on Human Rights and sits on the editorial board of the *International Journal for the Study of New Religions*. His academic interests focus mainly on religious minorities and on relations between the state, society and religious communities, including religious freedom issues. His recent publications include 'Stand Up for Your Rights: (Minority) Religions' Reactions to the Law in Estonia', in *Reactions to the Law by Minority Religions*, edited by Eileen Barker and James T. Richardson (Routledge, 2020). E-mail: ringo.ringvee@moi.ee

Priit Rohtmets

is an Associate Professor at the School of Theology and Religious Studies at University of Tartu, Estonia and a Professor of Church History at the Theological Institute of the Estonian Evangelical Lutheran Church. His research interests include religion and politics in the twentieth century, ecclesiastical history of Central-Eastern Europe in the nineteenth and twentieth century (with a focus on Protestant and Orthodox churches), and nationalism studies and the relationship between nationalism and religion. He is an author of monographs on church and state relations in Estonia (*Riik ja usulised ühendused*, Estonian Ministry of the Interior, 2018), religious history of Estonia (*Eesti usuelu 100 aastat*, Postimees, 2019) and his articles have appeared in *Religion, State and Society, Journal of Baltic Studies, Journal of Church and State* and *Journal of Ecumenical Studies*. E-mail: piit.rohtmets@ut.ee

Toomas Schvak

is a church historian and librarian (currently at the Arvo Pärt Centre). He holds a master's degree in Religious Anthropology from the University of Tartu (2009) where he also attended a PhD programme. His main field of research is the modern history of Eastern Orthodox Church in the Baltic region. He has authored texts for textbooks and encyclopaedias, published two monographs on the history of Estonian Orthodox congregations and several research articles in English, German, Russian and Estonian. E-mail: toomas.schvak@gmail.com

Marko Uibu
is a lecturer of Communication Studies at the Institute of Social Studies, University of Tartu. His academic interests pertain to diverse aspects of social change, from religion and health to the potential of (co-)creating social change. Marko has an interdisciplinary background: he has master's degrees in Media and Communication Studies and in Sociology and Social Anthropology, and a PhD in Religious Studies. He has published studies on medical pluralism (in *Anthropology and Medicine* and the *Journal of Ethnology and Folkloristics*); contemporary religiosity (in *Implicit Religion* and the *Journal of Baltic Studies*); and health and social change (in *BMC Public Health* and *Health Policy*). E-mail: marko.uibu@ut.ee

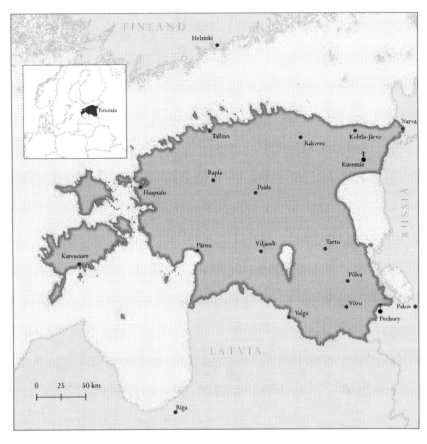

MAP 1   Map of Estonia
CREATED BY AGO TOMINGA. WITH KIND PERMISSION BY THE UNIVERSITY OF TARTU, DEPARTMENT OF GEOGRAPHY.

CHAPTER 1

Introduction

Riho Altnurme

This book answers two important questions about Estonia. The first question – why is Estonia so secularised in terms of de-institutionalisation and de-christianisation? – is the thread running through of all the chapters, from the historical discussion to the contemporary situation. The second question pertains to the consequences of secularisation: what is the link between Estonia's secularity and today's picture of individualised religiosity in the country? The results of this research project[1] provide fresh results from surveys, archival work and analysis by experienced researchers and doctoral students.

Sociologists have described Estonia as one of the most secularised countries in the world. In this context, secularisation has two meanings. In terms of de-institutionalisation, secularisation is the decline of institutional religion – a decline reflected in surveys from Gallup or the World Values Survey. It also means that Christianity has lost its former place in society, and therefore we can speak about de-christianisation specifically rather than about religiosity in general. The Christian mainstream churches have also changed, as we can see when we take a closer look at the religious ideas of their members. This spiritual milieu has influenced all of Estonian society.

The approaches and hypotheses to be presented in the book are:

1) De-christianisation is discussed as a result of the intellectual clash with modern ideologies, including nationalism, atheism, and Marxism. Estonian nationalism was often anticlerical, and this is one reason why Estonian national identity is not associated with a religious identity. Still, there are other examples of the connections between religious leaders and political activity. Was atheism a serious ideological competitor for Christianity? How has the liberal understanding of social structures and legislation influenced the position of churches?

2) De-christianisation is discussed as a result of social changes, including urbanisation, immigration, and industrialisation. In Estonia, this development is tightly connected with the Soviet period, when one can observe

---

1 Secularization (de-institutionalization and de-christianization): Religion in Estonia from the Modern Period to the Present (2011–2016), Targeted Funding (SF0180026s11) by Estonian Ministry of Education and Research.

industrialisation, immigration of industrial workers to towns in Estonia and rapid urbanisation. Today's urban population attends church more than the rural population does. Is this the result of the closer connection of the Russian population (which is concentrated in the cities) to religion? Religious dynamics among the country's Russian- and Estonian-speaking populations sometimes follow different paths. In this case, the hypothesis is that social changes have unexpectedly created cells of religiosity.

3) De-christianisation is discussed as a result of the inner secularisation of church organisations – secularisation on the meso-level of organisations (Dobbelaere 1999). Is there any tendency toward secularisation in the history of churches? Have the actions of churches been sufficient to avoid secularisation? Has the competition between the Lutheran and Orthodox churches since the 19th century contributed to secularisation?

4) De-christianisation is discussed as a current transformation of religion towards a remarkable growth of individual religiosity and the New Age (i.e., new spirituality). From the beginning of the 20th century, some religious pluralism was possible, and this process has accelerated since the end of the 1980s. What were the factors that enabled the relatively easy transformation of religious views and practices? How does this picture fit into the frame of a secular society?

No book has yet been published on the topic of religiosity in Estonia. This book focuses on the most important theme in research on the contemporary religious situation of Estonia, not only giving a deep insight into the Estonian case but also casting light on comparable developments elsewhere in Europe. Estonia is an interesting example of religiosity, as other books describing the contemporary religious situation in Europe often fail to understand the situation in this kind of Eastern European country.

The authors hope that this book finds enthusiastic readers among postgraduate researchers, university lecturers, and everybody interested in the interaction of secularisation and religiosity!

CHAPTER 2

The History of the Marginalisation of Christianity in Estonia (1857–2017)

Lea Altnurme

In this chapter,[1] the marginalisation of Christianity will be approached as a part of the secularisation process. By marginalisation we mean a decrease in the political and sociocultural importance and influence of Christianity, as effected by bearers of competing ideologies and worldviews who Christianity it a negative meaning. In addition to the societal macrolevel, secularisation – the decrease in the importance and influence of religion – also comprises the meso-and microlevels of religious organisations and the individual, as well as processes that go beyond the competition between ideologies and worldviews (Dobbelaere 1999: 229–247). In this chapter, we will focus on the marginalisation of Christianity, in the context of a broader secularisation process in Estonia over the last 160 years.

Religion is a multifaceted phenomenon. Its importance and especially its meaning depends on the culture and the era one is looking at, and on the perspective of the observer. Ordinarily there are several conflicting meanings in use simultaneously, depending on whether they are expressed by socially dominant or marginal groups. Importance can be defined as something that can be assessed in the population as expressed support, on a scale of 'valuable' to 'not at all valuable'; meaning is what participants in social interactions attribute either to representations, phenomena, individuals, or narratives in the process of interpretation or understanding.

As with any other phenomenon, as soon as religion becomes a topic of public discourse, it is mediated by social representations: collectively constructed imaginations, often rigidly stereotypical. This is often done based on a value system or ideology, knowledge that usually seems (to bystanders, at least) to be taken as truth, and which is very resilient (van Dijk 2005: 153). Such truth reflects the ways people represent beliefs about themselves and the social world based on what is important to them (van Dijk 2005: 155), relying on answers to questions which constitute the fundamental structure of ideology: who we

---

[1] This is the elaborated version of an earlier article, published in Estonian (Altnurme 2013a).

are, where we come from, what we stand for, what our values and resources are (van Dijk 2005: 154).

This chapter offers an historical overview of the marginalisation of Christianity in Estonia from 1857 to 2017. How have the meaning and importance of Christianity changed in this process? The focus shall be on Lutheranism, the most widespread confession among ethnic Estonians. The Brethren movement, Russian Orthodoxy, and free congregations will be mentioned in cases where their functions or meanings appeared distinct from Lutheranism.

It should certainly be mentioned that in all historical periods, individual understandings of religion have been significantly more differentiated than social representations which arise in conflictual or labile situations; the latter primarily reflect functions of religion relevant to a particular moment, whether these are understood as positive or negative.

Due to the 150 years to be examined, our account of the marginalisation of Christianity will be rather schematic. The selection of materials covered for specific time periods was made retrospectively, in relation to the present situation. Periodisation is based on political history, because changes of regime were accompanied by changes in official and dominant ideologies, which subsequently had a determining role on new social representations of Christianity. The temporal point of departure is the year 1857, when the concept of the *Estonian people* (*eesti rahvas*) emerged alongside the previous designation of people of the land (*maarahvas*), later generalised as *the Estonians* (Zetterberg 2009: 325). Thus this date marks the beginning of the movement of Estonia's national awakening. In 1857, the majority of Estonians belonged to the inferior rank of the peasantry. The higher estates were composed of German nobles and clerics. Estonia's geographical territory was part of the Russian Empire.

1 Christianity as Self-evident (1857–1918)

When Johann Voldemar Jannsen (1819–1890), in the premiere issue of the first Estonian-language weekly newspaper *Pärnu Postimees* greeted his readers with the much-anthologised words 'Terre, armas Eesti rahwas! [Hello, dear Estonian people!]', the national awakening still lay ahead. In the opening editorial, Jannsen wrote:

> Thanks to God, spring has come again [–], every farmer has sown his field with seed with hope in his heart, and if he knows God and fears him, he has taken off his hat after he finished the ploughing and sighed, Lord! Now all is in your hands and in your power. I ploughed and sowed,

now you must water and raise the grain; for your glory and my strength. In this time of sprouting and blooming the Postimees starts gathering its seed together for sowing [–] Yes, the Lord has sent us many and varied things. We have seen fear and trembling, sadness and anguish; we have also tasted joy and good fortune, all according to which you have done what is good toward us, if we remembered to thank you for your mercies and kissed the rod of punishment [–] Our merciful Lord Emperor, may God extend his days, has made peace again and the bloodshed is over [–] Fear God and honour the king and may we continue to live in our dear Evangelical Lutheran faith, as is the duty of every pious Christian! [–].

PERNO POSTIMEES 1857

Clearly, this passage reflects the official ideology of a society of rank and privilege, based on Christianity, and there is no reason to doubt that Jannsen, who had a pietist background, and his readers believed in its legitimacy. Though secular thinking (in the sense of secular explanations about the world and secular ideologies) had been possible since the beginning of the 18th century (Sommerville 2002: 367), and it had become more widespread, Jannsen himself expressed doubts about his own faith in a wave of despair (Salupere 2001: 17). Among the Estonian peasantry, secular thinking was rare until the middle of the 19th century. The temporality of rural people's ordinary lives remained attuned to the rhythms of nature (Viires 2001: 20), reinforced by magical observances marking the beginning and end of seasons of agricultural labour, and holidays of the church calendar. Rural Estonians' heritage did not pass down memories of the violent christianisation carried out by German crusaders in the 13th century (Viires 2001: 20), nor did they transmit knowledge of Estonian pre-conquest freedom and ancient religion, though village Christianity may have preserved some beliefs and practices from that time. The popular consciousness was shaped by sacred Biblical narrative, stories of events that had happened in distant times and places, which were also relevant to the here and now (Viires 2001: 20–21), giving a conceptual scaffolding to ordinary life. Such knowledge was transmitted orally at church services and in school lessons (Viires 2001: 22).

Beginning in the Swedish era, the church had promoted spiritual culture among the peasants. At the same time, the network of local schools expanded (Jansen 2007: 323), where great emphasis was placed on catechism and church hymns (Jansen 2004: 87). Attending church services and Christian customs and rituals were definitely a part of Estonians' ordinary life (Jansen 2004: 87); the pious custom of reading aloud from the Bible on Saturdays or Sundays, under the direction of the head of the household was widespread, and parents recited evening prayers with children (Jansen 2007: 324). Until the end of the 19th century, most of the printed material available to peasant families was spiritual – the hymnal, the catechism, the New Testament. More families than ever owned the full Bible (Jansen 2007: 323). The expanding selection of secular printed matter – appendices to almanacs, newspapers, and belles lettres, not to speak of schoolbooks – was permeated by the spirit of Christianity (Jansen 2007: 324). After a Christian upbringing in the home and in school, young people underwent instruction preparing them for confirmation and reinforcing their religious knowledge; confirmation marked the beginning of life as an adult (Jansen 2007: 327). As the institution that ritually marked and officially registered births, marriages, and deaths, the church could not be bypassed.

In sum, Estonians were still living in an environment where it was difficult to think about life and the world without using religious language, let alone express oneself on a level transcending everyday tasks and activities. Of course this does not mean that individual faith lacked variety. There was the magical Christianity of the village, scripturally based church faith, the moral hero's struggle and the childlike heart-centred spirituality of pietism, ritual-based Orthodox faith – the diversity was probably even greater. Nor does this mean that the power of reflection or doubt was lacking; however, opposition to religion took the form of upside-down religion or blasphemy. A memory was reported from South Estonia as late as the beginning of the 20th century, when it might happen that 'farmers blasphemed against God if it rained on their hay-making. One stupid farmer even angrily tossed pitchforks full of hay angrily toward the sky, saying "Eat! Eat! Take and eat it all!"' (Altnurme 2006: 121). Likewise, it should be observed that anticlericalism and critique of the clergy did not automatically signify atheism. If criticisms were made, they never targeted the clergy as a whole, but were directed at the arrogant and violent behaviour, greed and profit-mongering of individual pastors, who were described as 'not good enough Christians' (Jansen 2007: 327). Christianity had no available alternative identity.

New ideas – liberal, nationalist, or drawn from the natural sciences – initially spread in ways harmonious with Christianity, or at least not in opposition to it. The first Estonian theoretician of nationality was the Lutheran clergyman Jakob Hurt. Understandably, given his profession, he associated national-mindedness with Christianity: God has created different peoples, and only the Creator has the right to decide their birth and death. Therefore violent imposition of a different nationality was an inexcusable human intervention in the divine world order (Karjahärm, Sirk 1997: 213).

When the national movement gained momentum in the middle of the 19th century and schools began teaching the history of Estonians, the violent christianisation of their forebears was made conscious. Jakob Hurt tried to exonerate Christianity in relation to the developing national myth, arguing that the Christianity forced on the people in the 13th century was not the true faith, but papal superstition in the Latin language (Kukk 2003: 101; Viires 2001: 24; 26–27). He claimed:

> First, the gospel was not preached purely, as it stands in the Bible. The candle of clear religion did not even illuminate the Catholic church, so how could it shine on others. [–] In addition, the wrongful teachings of the popes were preached. These wrongful teachings could neither bring clarity to reason nor warmth to the heart; besides little heed was paid to teaching people at all.
> HURT 1879: 81

Hurt considered the Lutheran church the 'spiritual mother' and 'teacher of the Estonian people's spirits and hearts', (Hurt 1939a: 202) arguing that it was the Lutheran church, alongside the Estonian language that would help prevent russification (Hurt 1989a: 48). He fervently defended the primacy of 'the evangelical credo of our fathers' in shaping the Estonian spirit, over and against Russian Orthodoxy (Hurt 1989a: 60), free congregations (Hurt 1907: 131), pantheism, materialism, and every other kind of –ism (Hurt 1989b: 70).

The growth of national self-consciousness and efforts toward autonomy began to lay a path for secular thinking. The more education the people received, the greater their acceptance of the idea that the Baltic 'noblemen's church' was a foreign body. At first, distinctions were made between faith and the organised church. This attitude was facilitated by Baltic German enlighteners and Estonian intellectuals, who took a critical position with respect to the church (Jansen 2004: 88), but acknowledged the evangelical teaching of salvation. The split between national-mindedness and Christianity was made wider by the German clergy. In the 1870s, when the Estonian national movement began to expand, it was opposed by the consistoria of the Lutheran church as well as many local pastors. Baltic German clergy found the national movement to be contrary to reason, a manifestation of rebellion, not cultural enlightenment, as the Estonian nationalists saw it (Jansen 2007: 335–336).

Conscious opposition to the Baltic nobility and its church was articulated by Carl Robert Jakobson, a leading figure of the Estonian national movement, on the pages of his newspaper, *Sakala*; Jakobson's intention was to create a new phenomenon: Estonian public opinion (Jansen 2007: 327). In contrast to Lutheran clergyman Jakob Hurt, who spoke of the need to transform the colonial church led by the Baltic Germans into the people's church (Saard

2000: 200–201), with the participation of clergy who not only needed to speak Estonian, but explain the Gospel to Estonians in a way they could understand (Hurt 1939b: 89), Jakobson regarded the local church as an institution of a society based on rank and its privileges. Representatives of this church crossed the acceptable boundaries of power and hindered Estonians' spiritual progress and their efforts toward equality (Jakobson 1959: 165–180). Jakobson's positive view of the Orthodox faith led to the participation of Estonian Orthodox clergy at events of the national movement (Laar 2005: 242).

Gradually, the spread of scientific knowledge brought about the acceptance of a scientific-materialist worldview among the emerging educated elite, and at the end of the 19th and the beginning of the 20th, an opposition was set up between science and religion (Jansen 2007: 329–330). In letters sent to the national-minded newspapers, some anti-Christian views were published, such as the claim that Biblical religion did not fit the science of the new era (Jansen 2007: 329).

To sum up, at the beginning of the 1857–1918 period, the ruling, legitimating ideology was Christian (Russian Orthodoxy in the Russian empire; Lutheranism in the provinces of Estonia and Livonia); this ideology represented those who were in power and executed it as the guarantors of a divine social order and its laws. Lutheranism was part of Baltic Germans' identity and the symbol of Protestant culture (Jansen 2004: 87). Those representations pertaining to the social level were dominant among various possible alternatives; in other words, this entailed an understanding of religion as responsibility before God, rulers, and fellow human beings, expressed by the fulfillment of Biblical commandments as divine will, and by repentance. Throughout the period, the emerging national ideology remained connected to Christianity and held within its bounds. However, opposition to the church did emerge, with the church seen as an institution of power that supported a social order based on rank. Indeed, until the end of this period Christianity remained the primary framework of meaning within which the world was conceptualised; as such the importance of the Christian faith cannot be overestimated.

2   The Struggle for Morality (1918–1940)

In 1918, the independence of the Estonian Republic was declared. The creation of statehood would take another few years, led by political parties that carried left-wing and nationalist ideologies.

At the beginning of the 20th century, educated Estonians were increasingly influenced by a positivist worldview based on the natural sciences, accompanied by achievements in the empirical sciences. Evolutionary theory was used not only to explain development in the natural world, but also in society and culture; a belief in progress emerged. Positivist ideas and Social Darwinism, particularly in Herbert Spencer's version – which explained people's, nations' and states' struggle for survival and their efforts toward fulfillment – had a strong influence on Estonian nationalist thought (Karjahärm, Sirk 2001: 218–220). At the beginning of the 20th century, nationalist and socialist ideology gained public dominance. The spectrum of nationalism was politically pluralistic and richly nuanced, spanning both liberalism and socialism (Karjahärm, Sirk 2001: 221).

Socialist ideas had come to Estonia at the end of the 19th century, but they blossomed in the Russian revolutions (1905, 1917). With the exception of Bolsheviks, Estonian socialists were nationally minded and fought for Estonian independence. The Estonian state was created by collaboration between nationalists and socialists (Karjahärm, Sirk 2001: 219).

As Christianity was no longer the only ideology or way of explaining the world, the opportunity arose to regard religion not as of divine, but rather human origin; the self-evidence of Christianity disappeared. Along with left-wing ideology and faith in science and progress, doubts with respect to existing religious traditions were expressed publicly. Close ties between church and state in Europe, and, of course, in Estonia added an anticlerical edge to left-wing critiques of power. In the early years of Estonian statehood, the question arose of teaching religion in the schools. Debates took place in newspapers, public meetings and education congresses, the Founding Assembly (*Asutav Kogu*) and Parliament (Valk 1997: 18–26), all of which foregrounded important changes in representations of religion. According to the decision of the Founding Assembly, religious instruction was abolished in schools, based on the law of public elementary education (1920) (Valk 1997: 24) and public secondary education (1922) (Valk 1997: 26). The main arguments against religious instruction in the schools were based on positivist-natural scientific and left-wing worldviews.

In opposition to science, religion (Christianity) was regarded as a fallacy, an imposture, and a false teaching, especially its account of the creation of the world. The creation story was presented as a compulsory fairy tale that distorted the understanding of life, prevented human development, and led to harmful behaviour (Cf AK 1920: III ij, v 374, v 897, v 898; AK 1920: IV ij, v 3–4, v 6, v 21; Eesti II Hariduse kongress 1918: 17, 21). The counterargument was that science itself was not infallible, that it was continually changing and could not answer existential questions about human life, thus creating an unconceptualised void that religion could fill. In response to these arguments, the social democrat Karl Ast stated at the Founding Assembly:

> ... who dares to prove that religion is at all necessary in our times, when science has already made it this far? That in our time there could be any talk of some kind of use for religion to fill a void – I find it impossible to believe such a thing. I think there is no longer any such use, because the epoch of the development of religions has come to a halt and petrified; religions have turned into the church and its petrified dogma.[–] The creative human spirit is no longer active in the realm of religion. Nowadays the creative human spirit has gone over to science.
>
> AK 1920: IV ij, V 70–71

Based on understandings influenced by Marxist ideology, religion was represented as a reactionary medium of propaganda to ensure the power of the nobility, which blinded and poisoned the people, on the principle that 'everyone must submit to the rulers, for the rulers are ordained by God'. The goal of religion was regarded primarily in political terms (AK 1920: III ij, V 373; AK 1920: IV ij, V 7, V 20, V 22, V 26; Põld 1917: 208). For example, social democrat Emma Asson claimed:

> But the Christian religion, threatening those rising up against the holders of power with the pains of hell, while promising great bliss to those who suffer on earth, forced the people to live in misery; by such an influence [Christianity] has paralyzed the forward-moving power of peoples and caused them suffering.
>
> AK 1920: IV ij, V 310

Opponents of religious instruction in the schools interpreted freedom of religion and the absence of a state church to mean that religion belonged only in the private sphere or in the purview of religious organisations; it must not be a matter of the state or the community (AK 1920: III ij, V 372; IV ij, V 17). Despite increasing public demand to continue teaching religion in the schools, the left wing maintained that this was unnecessary. In the words of Johannes Semper:

> It is understandable that children should be raised for the sake of culture and not continue eternally to follow the same path as their parents. [–] Why can the state not plough the field of culture, in the knowledge that in the future this [the abolition of religious instruction from the schools] will be deemed the right thing to do? [–] This is a place where the state

must intervene and eliminate this evil, and not trust that religious instruction will, in and of itself undergo a natural process of deterioration.

AK 1920: IV ij, v 5–6

The debates over religious instruction created moral panic in worried parents, grandparents, and citizens who saw religion as the articulator and guarantor of rules which brought order to common life and established a basis for moral formation. For example, the following resolution was sent to the Founding Assembly by a public meeting on 3 March 1920 in the Estonia concert hall:

> The school's responsibility is not only to provide knowledge, but above all to raise people firm in character;, good people, loyal citizens. Life has shown that a people without a moral foundation cannot withstand the storms of history. Morality without religion has no vitality. [–] A school that lacks religious instruction has a destructive impact on children mentally, morally, and physically; therefore parents can have no trust in such schools.
>
> AK 1920: III ij, v 904

Religion as a guarantee of morality was the best-laid argument in favour of religious instruction (Cf Eesti II Hariduse congress 1918; Põld 1917). As Jaan Tõnisson, Prime Minister in the Founding Assembly stated:

> So long as we have nothing better, and as long as we have close at hand the whole history of Christian culture, with its relative abundance of great figures, we can find models for our children's spirits there. Try and find another source of such personified idealists!
>
> AK 1920: IV ij, v 38, cf also v 316

Tõnisson's view was that it would be democratic to consider the opinion of the majority 'who want to raise children in the spirituality that they deem best, that they wish to pass on to their children' (AK 1920: IV ij, v 38). The comments of People's Party representative Johan Ploompuu on religion that has been learned in school is worth passing on to subsequent generations:

> ... a human being may ask for God's help and then expect it if he or she has completely lived up to their own responsibility. Fulfilling one's responsibility was the first priority. It was also taught that if a person has erred, they need not despair, but rather expect forgiveness, provided that they do not continue in their error, that is, if repentance has taken place.

> It was taught that there is no need to worry about anything if one has fulfilled one's responsibilities. Worry belongs to the Almighty; all a person has to do is faithfully fulfill their responsibilities. Children were told that they are always under the protection of the Almighty, and that they have nothing to fear. I think the last of these principles has been a great resource for raising peaceful people with healthy nerves.
>
> AK 1920: IV ij, V 33

Agricultural Union representative Jüri Uluots added, '… the questions you are discussing here are not of a trivial nature; they touch a person's deepest roots, and these roots are tender, especially when we start cutting them, which may lead to bad results' (AK 1920: IV ij, V 317).

Moral counterarguments were presented by speakers like the social democrat Mihkel Martna: 'Like Mr Kann, they consider religious instruction to be a regulator of virtue! [–] Our legion of moonshiners have all come up through the good, old religious instruction! And yet it hasn't had any influence …' (AK 1920: IV ij, V 29). However, most people were not convinced.

The moral dimension was also emphasised in the ideology of the nationally minded, as initiated by Hurt. Morality was derived from religion, which according to Hurt was 'the mother and nourisher of any serious morality'. Being Estonian and nationally minded was not a choice, but a moral norm, a responsibility, and a high moral ideal, toward which every Estonian must strive. The ordering of social and personal life had to grow out of nationalism which was ethically motivated and shaped into a norm; for example, rigorous Protestant morals were required in relations of marriage and family, sexual chastity, sobriety, and thrift (Karjahärm, Sirk 1997: 215). The construction of the Estonian people's character was to be founded on Lutheran values, such as hard work, seriousness, goal-orientedness, and a sense of responsibility (Altnurme 2006: 91).

After the passing of the elementary education law in 1920, by which religious instruction was omitted from the curriculum, the Christian People's Party began a successful petition campaign to repeal the law. In 1923 the religious instruction question was submitted to a referendum. Almost three-quarters of those who voted supported religious instruction in the schools (71.9%) (Valk 1997: 28–33). The curricular goal of religious instruction in the elementary schools was to awaken, develop, and deepen religious-feeling, to lead children to a religious-moral understanding and develop an understanding of Christian morality (Raud 1936: 5). After the referendum, the religious instruction that had been removed in the interim was quickly re-established in all schools, and although it was an elective subject, 86.3% of students (Valk 1997: 38) enrolled.

Those who declined were either children of Jews or members of free congregations (Valk 1997: 70). The few nonparticipants were liable to be mocked as 'pagans' (Altnurme 2006: 102). An explanation of why intellectuals enrolled their children in religious instruction was given by Marta Lepp-Utuste, an activist for the Taara religion, based on neopagan and nationalist ideology:

> '... in their atheism, rationalism, individualism, and liberalism they have stayed within the boundaries of Christian dogma. They might ridicule the Bible for its "naive" legends, criticize Christian dogma, refuse to drink Christ's blood and eat his flesh, but at life's major events – being born, dying, and marrying, they feel a need for religious rituals. They invite a pastor or priest to marry them, baptize them, bury them. [–] They let their children learn the same Christian teachings that they despise, because it is necessary, after all, to give children a moral foundation. Finally, they pay their church tithes, too, and go to their graves marked with a cross.
> ESIMENE ÕHTU 1933

The referendum on religious instruction showed that religion remained important in the first half of the 20th century, and that it was seen as a norm guaranteeing the cohesion of society on the basis of Christian values. The 1934 census asked everyone to give a religious preference. The result showed that 78.2% of the population affiliated with Lutheranism and 19% with Orthodoxy (the religious preference of children under the age of 16 was marked according to their parents' statement). Thus 97.2% of Estonia's population designated themselves as belonging to one of the two largest confessions. The total number of Baptists, Adventists, Methodists, and Evangelicals was 1.5%. Only 0.7% reported having no religion (Reiman 1935: 126). The census indicates that almost 100% of the population confirmed its alignment with one Christian confession or the other. Though the majority of them did not attend religious services regularly, their connection to the church was considered natural; given that almost 100% of those living in Estonia preferred one of the two largest churches, there is no reason to conclude that this religion was merely nominal. This is also supported by the fact that neither the constitutionally established freedom of religion nor the 1925 Religious Societies Act, according to which 'membership in a religious organization or removal from such membership shall be decided upon by each person individually' (RT 1925c), resulted in a significant decrease in membership in either the Lutheran or the Orthodox Church.

Although Christianity and especially Lutheranism played an important role in the nationalist ideology of Hurt's lineage, it did not become a part of the national narrative, which was based on historical myths, and rooted in the Marxist basis of class struggle. Estonian nationalism was framed by anti-German attitudes: for centuries the clergy had been German and upper class (and opposed to the Estonians' national movement). Since lines formerly drawn along differences of rank later merged with ethnic boundaries, the church was associated with Germanness. The national narrative based on historical events was already taking shape in the 19th century, but as a coherent narrative, it was adopted into Estonians' consciousness in the 1920s and 1930s. Its content was the struggle against the Germans and for independence. All of the most famous uprisings, battles, and wars were linked in the Great Battle (Tamm 2003: 64), which had begun with the struggle against German crusaders. The idea that the Baltic Crusades represented the local peoples' fight for freedom derived from the Baltic German publicist Garlieb Helwig Merkel, who was drawn to the Enlightenment ideal of the free, noble savage. Estonians heard of 'this idea, borne by anti-nobility, anticlerical sentiment, the exaltation of ancient peoples and the understanding of the Middle Ages as a time of darkness as popularised mainly by Carl Robert Jakobson in his first "Speech to the Fatherland"' (Selart 2003: 110). Authors of historical fiction instilled this national myth (Tamm 2003: 66). The nationalist narrative contained the argument that the Christianity, shaped by German theology – perhaps even Christianity itself – had been an ideological means of justifying the power of the ruling class to conquer the Estonians and hold them in bondage. All in all, it had been imposed upon the Estonians' ethnic character, to which it was foreign. Thus it is understandable that the need to 'Estonianise' Christianity would be discussed (e.g., Jakob Hurt, Johan Kõpp, Uku Masing), and steps were indeed taken in this direction. By the end of the 1930s, the goal had almost been achieved, but the process was interrupted by the Second World War. Connections between Christianity and nationalism were not tight enough to be incorporated into the nationalist narrative (Altnurme 2006: 52, 56–61).

Christianity was not integral to the projects to found the Estonian people and its state, because it did not form a unified package with modern values, such as progress, science, education, and culture. Even if Christianity remained important in its moral aspect, it began to retreat from nationalist self-understanding.

Culture became the central and highest value of nationalist ideology. Quoting Toomas Karjahärm and Väino Sirk, we can agree with that

> in Estonian intellectual history, culture continued to be a central, even a magical concept throughout the ages. Culture has been the reason and

> purpose for the existence of Estonianness, its real god; 'the unifying concept for all that is good' (A. Annist), 'a small people's reason for existence' (G. Ränk). From the beginning of the era of awakening, Estonian leaders drew up extensive and detailed projects for educational and cultural work [–] What has been determinative is the belief in the force and greatness of culture.
>
> KARJAHÄRM, SIRK 2001: 229

To summarise, national and socialist ideologies were predominant from 1918 to 1940 (granted, the influence of socialism decreased after the Bolsheviks' attempt to overthrow the government in 1924, but it did not disappear among the ideas circulating on the social level, for instance concerning religion). New ideologies brought along new representations of Christianity. Nevertheless, national ideology helped preserve images current in the previous period – that religion was a guarantor of order and morality. The national narrative was influenced by socialist ideology, whereby Christianity came to be represented as a foreign imposition, a means of manipulation and exploitation in the hands of the ruling Germans. This was the beginning of the marginalisation of Christianity. Estonian nationalism was constructed in opposition to the Germans, and by drawing upon historical facts (e.g., violent christianisation, the opposition of German pastors to the Estonian national movement), nationalism came to be seen as antithetical to Christianity. When set alongside culture, the core nationalist value, religion was judged as erroneous in relation to a positivist worldview based on the natural sciences; a fairy tale, a relic which obstructed progress and hindered the development of the people. However, such representations primarily characterised the educated elite. The people continued to value Christianity based on previous understandings: the debate over religious instruction in the schools showed that religion remained important.

3 From Norm to Alternative (1940–1991)

The Soviet Union occupied Estonia in 1940, and again in 1944 as the Second World War approached its end. During the Soviet period, the official ideology was Marxist-Leninist, intolerant of other ideologies and ways of explaining the world. Socialist ideology was cultivated in political form, as a state religion (Gentile 2000: 23–25), with the goal of providing a substitute for Christianity. The myths, institutions, rituals and symbols of the state religion became the medium for expressing loyalty as well as evaluating and controlling citizens.

The content of the Marxist myth was class struggle, in the course of which a messianic proletariat would seize power and abolish social injustice, freeing the oppressed masses from the slavery of exploitation and building a socialist society with the final goal of a communist paradise on earth. Christianity was regarded as an ideological medium of the ruling classes to force the working classes into submission: the narcotic effect of religion seduced workers into a world of illusions and diverted them from a class-conscious understanding of their situation. Therefore religion was seen as a dangerous relic that had to be combated.

The central Marxist myth was filled out with ideologically constructed narratives of great persons and historical events, which were meant to confirm the myth's validity and to give it a Soviet face: for example, stories of the great Lenin and the Communist Party that continued his work, the Great Socialist October Revolution and the Great Patriotic War. Maarja Lõhmus has called these stories the creation and existence myths of the Soviet system, supported by myths of achievement that determined norms of behaviour and thought. Myths of achievement were stories about the family of the Soviet republics and their allies; the free, happy new Soviet person; and the ongoing rapid growth of the Soviet economy (Lõhmus 2004: 704–705).

Consistent with the Soviet myth, rituals of the state religion coincided with celebrations of significant holidays and anniversaries. May 1, workers' international day of solidarity, and November 7, the anniversary of the October Revolution were celebrated with parades. On the individual level, new customs and observances began to be established in the late 1950s, with the goal of casting aside Christian ones. For example, to interfere with the traditional Christian practice of confirmation, summer youth gatherings were organised, modelled on similar practices in the German Democratic Republic. In addition to entertainment, young people listened to lectures on politics, behaviour, health, and, of course, atheism. Weddings and funerals imitated church ceremonies with, as expected, the elimination of Christian content (Altnurme 2006: 70).

The symbols of state religion included images or sculptures of Party leaders, flags and crests of the USSR and the socialist republics, such as the hammer and sickle and the five-pointed star; slogans printed on obligatory red banners to signify ideologies or a current campaign. Every institution was required to have a 'red corner', inspired by the icon shelf of the Orthodox Church, and this became a site where ideological events were organised. The emotions cultivated in connection with these practices ranged from awe to fear.

Estonians never supported the Soviet state religion. Though leftist ideas had been widespread among the intelligentsia in the first period of independence,

Stalinism hit society with discursive shock. Educated people, who had acquired their culture in the key of liberal humanities found it difficult to become accustomed to unquestioned authorities, worshipped teachers, and a world of absolute truths (Ruutsoo 2000: 40–41). The brutality and violence of the Soviet regime frightened them away from the new state religion. As it had been created on the model of Orthodox faith, the state religion seemed all the more foreign due to a discrepancy in mentalities; its pathos failed to awaken Estonians' religious emotions. A deep contrast prevailed between high-blown rhetoric and the reality of everyday life. The hold of state religion began to diminish at the end of the 1950s, even in the USSR, and ten years later the central government no longer expected it to exert a unifying spiritual power (Kangilaski 2002: 17). Though officially it remained in place, it had to be shored up with steadily augmented russification.

Estonians opposed the official ideology with their folk culture. In itself, the national narrative based on the Marxist paradigm of class struggle, hostility to Germans and the church was consistent with official Soviet ideology. However, this narrative was ideologically amplified (Selart 2003: 117–118) at public events following the principle 'socialist in content, nationalist in form', performing the message of the friendship of nations in the 'brotherly family' of the USSR. Nevertheless, nationalism had another, much more important meaning in Soviet society. Eve Annuk wrote:

> Resistance was 'inscribed' in the hidden discourse of Estonian nationalism during the Soviet era: resistance to the Soviet occupation in order to preserve one's language, culture, and national identity; resistance to Soviet ideology and the state; resistance as a way of survival, as a way of being Estonian.
> ANNUK 2003: 29

The era of interwar Estonian independence lived on in the Soviet era in the secrecy of memory and in hidden objects, banned literature and the blue-black-and-white national flag. Participating in national or folk culture, such as choirs and music ensembles (Siemer 2003: 146), folk dance groups, the Nature Preservation Society, the Book Association, the local history movement (Aarelaid 1998: 234) offered inner dignity and satisfaction.

Even though Estonians never supported the official Soviet ideology, the regime's anti-religious politics was not without impact. The regime persecuted religious people by thwarting their efforts to acquire an education or find an apartment or a job. The regime could also sabotage a new career. After 1963, the activities of the religious were under the observation of surveillance committees adjunct to the *raion* executive committees (Remmel 2011b: 85–104). Special attention was paid to any work being done with youth or children. Those whose activities or devotion made them a possible threat were invited to a 'conversation' (Plaat 2001: 211–215) where coercion admonitions and temptations were used to try to convince them to stop.

Feelings of shame and fear toward religion were cultivated and used to shape negative public stereotypes; religion began to be associated with stupidity, weakness and violence. Accordingly, the faithful were described as deceived, misled and uneducated, or even crazy. The representation of nonconformists as mentally ill and their forced medical treatment was a practice used intermittently in the USSR (Kaasik 2011: 79–96); they were victims of amoral, clever, greedy deceivers and power-hungry manipulators. Based on one such case, the Estonian Evangelical Lutheran Church Consistory protested in 1947 to comrade Arnold Veimer, chairman of the Estonian SSR Council of Ministers, against the means used in anti-religious propaganda to stigmatise clergy and religious people as 'crazed believers' (EELKKA 1947). From 1958 to 1964, anti-religious propaganda took the form of an organised campaign (Remmel 2011a: 33–49). While in the first independence period children who did not participate in religious instruction had been called 'pagans', in the Soviet era the children of religious parents were persecuted.

Since confession of one's religion meant trouble with the regime and social disapproval, Estonians who had been shaped according to a Lutheran mentality – for whom struggling ahead, obedience to the law, a sense of responsibility and loyalty to the government were values – disconnected themselves from the church for fear of losing their dignity and standard of living. Children were kept away from religion to safeguard their futures. During the first independence period, the mark of a trustworthy member of society had been affiliation with the community of Christians; under Soviet rule, a good citizen did not go to church. If the state condemned religion, the responsible, submissive person was not religious. People adjusted to the existing order (Altnurme 2006: 72).

In addition, an important role was played in the diminishment of religion – Christianity – by changes in the realm of individual morality in the 1960s both in western culture and in western-oriented Estonia. Women had a prominent role in the development. Both Enlightenment philosophy and conservative Christianity had regarded morality as a foundation of social cohesion. From the Romantic era, when religion began to be individualised – and also feminised – women assumed responsibility for serving as ethical role models and guarding morality (Brown 2005: 195). It is not known exactly when religion began to be feminised in Estonia, but at the beginning of the 20th century, the religious teacher at home was usually the mother or grandmother, in addition to the instruction provided in school and confirmation classes offered by the church. For example, in the debate over religious instruction in the schools, Mihkel Martna claimed that 'religious instruction can only be given by role models, by virtuous living. And this has to happen in the child's home, at mother's knee, in the atmosphere where the child is being raised' (AK 1920: IV ij, v 18). It was a widespread opinion, particularly among proponents of left-wing ideas, that religion was more a woman's matter (Valk 1997: 31).

The woman's gender role was based on Christian values and norms, as mother and wife focused on the family and home, watching over the morals of husband and children. This cultural role model began to break down with the spread of leftist ideas and the rise in women's education and employment, but it remained in place in the West until the 1960s (Brown 2005: 175–180). The same happened in Estonia. Women's emancipation had begun in the first half of the 20th century, and in the Soviet period it was augmented by state politics and official ideology, accompanied by a positivist worldview grounded in the natural sciences. Women's increasing level of education and participation in work life (which became equal to that of men by the middle of the 20th century, at the time when women in most developed countries were just beginning their struggle for equal employment with men) led to the feminisation of sectors such as trade, health care, and education (Tiit 2011: 141). Here too, the conceptualisation of women's role according to a new worldview took place in the 1960s; confirmation classes remained large in the 1950s, as the atmosphere of fear began lifted after Stalin's death (Altnurme 1998: 227–228).

Of course, there were other reasons for the enlivening of church life in the 1950s and the subsequent decrease in the importance of religion in the 1960s, but women's part in this process should be taken into account. If women reconfigured their role as members of society under new social circumstances and rethought their relationship to their bodies and sexuality, then they were no longer doing so on a religious level. Both in the West and in Estonia, as Christian culture lost its function of conceptualising life and what it meant to be a woman (Brown 2005: 179–180), Christian understandings went into decline. Women distanced themselves from Christianity and no longer socialised their children in a religious manner, even though this could still be done in the Soviet era in the privacy of the family circle – just as nationalism was used in opposition to official ideology. Groundbreaking changes in constructing women's role did not affect all generations at the same time, but targeted those who were coming of age in the 1960s.

Along with the reconceptualisation of the woman's role, great changes took place in the area of individual and personal morality. Christian attitudes lost their authority in questions of premarital or extramarital relations, divorce and abortion. What had been traditionally religious and collective became secular and individual (Halman 1995: 422–423). In Estonian society Christianity had rested primarily on the argument of morality. When that disappeared, rapid secularisation began.

Reasons for secularisation should also be sought in the destruction of agrarian culture (which upheld religious traditions) by deportations and forced collectivisation of agriculture, and the increased pace of urbanisation during the Soviet era. While in 1934 the urban population was 31.3% (Tiit 2011: 105) of the total, by 1970 it had increased to 64.7% (Tiit 2011: 54) and in 1989, it was 71.5% (Tiit 2011: 58).

Under the combined influence of several factors, Estonian society underwent strong secularisation in the Soviet era. The Lutheran church dominated the religious sector, accounting for 78.2% (Reiman 1935: 126) of the population in 1934, and losing over two-thirds of its paying members – most likely even more of those who were not formally connected with the church – by 1977 (Plaat 2001: 213).

The availability of religious services reached a nadir in 1978 (Paul 2003: 210); this was also a low point for the other East European countries (Tomka 1998: 187). Religious socialisation had been interrupted, since religious organisations were forbidden to work with youth and children, engage in diaconal or missions work, or publish religious literature (Kiivit 1995: 104). As already stated, most homes abandoned their religious traditions (Altnurme 2006: 286). Alongside the home and the church, the school had been an agent of religious socialisation. Before the Soviet occupation, 86.3% of children (Valk 1997: 38) received religious instruction in school – despite the fact that this was freely chosen by their parents (Valk 1997: 34). By the 1970s, a second generation was reaching school age, deprived of the opportunity for religious education. If participants in a 1990–1991 research project were asked, 'Have you been raised in a religious manner?', 85% of the Estonians answered that they were not (Dogan 1995: 411). It should certainly be taken into account that among the 15% who answered affirmatively, some had grown up before the Soviet occupation. Thus the church was banned and religion lost its broader meaning as a norm as well as its unifying function (Altnurme 2006: 283–285); the significance of Christianity decreased drastically compared to 1918–1940.

In the 1970s, after religion had ceased its normative function, it gradually acquired a new meaning in the alternative (Rittersporn et al., 2003: 443), or unofficial public sphere, which emerged in the field between the public and private spheres where leisure-time activities (Jõesalu 2006: 94) took place and people interacted with their friends and acquaintances. In this area, views opposed to the official ideology spread, and most of them were derived from nationalist, cultural or religious strata. Religion, which had previously had a normative meaning, became an alternative, an opportunity for nonconformism; in addition to Christianity it embraced eastern religious philosophies and esotericism (Altnurme 2006: 74–79). In this new meaning, religion began to attract adherents, particularly young people from secular families, who were looking for ways of thinking and living differently from what was prescribed by Soviet norms and rules, which emphasised collectivism and uniformity. Originality and being different from others became new values. As distinct from the older religious generation that had kept a low profile, these young people were not afraid of social condemnation. As a religious person, one could get attention, and this could even be pleasant and intentional; activities at the boundary of the permitted and forbidden were adventurous. These youth became interested in religious organisations that supported thinking differently, if only because the state ideology had forced them into an oppositional role, quite an unfamiliar situation for the Lutheran and Orthodox churches in Estonian history. Free congregations did better under these circumstances, because they already had an oppositional history. The alternative-seekers expected attitudes and activities from religious organisations for which the latter were unprepared, since their main membership was composed of people whose religious convictions derived from the independence period (either directly acquired at that time, or through family traditions; in the Lutheran church these older believers still made up the largest age group in 2000 (Hansen 2002: 41)) and their interest was to maintain the status quo. The inwardly focused church gave older believers a fortress and shelter, helping preserve the lost Estonian era of their childhood (Altnurme 2006: 283). Young people brought a different mentality to congregations, creating a generational rift in the conservative atmosphere, and this split was exacerbated by the ways of interpreting and expressing the religious message that the newcomers had learned from western Christian youth movements (Altnurme 2006: 76). At the beginning of the 1980s, the process by which religion changed from norm into alternative did not include mass joining of congregations, but it helped overcome the low point (Paul 2003: 210). Little by little the number of baptisms and church weddings began to rise, but not enough to offset the steady decline in church membership (Altnurme 2006: 75).

Unlike Western Europe, Christianity in Estonia remained conservative, as it had been in the 1930s. Among the Christian confessions, Catholicism grew in popularity among young people in the 1980s, following the example of the Polish resistance movement, where nationalism and Christianity were closely connected. This resulted in reinforcement of the conservative angle.

Although on a social level the dominant socialist ideology lost its credibility, the representations of Christianity it had cultivated were reinforced and widely disseminated – from intellectuals to the common people. Christianity was marginalised with the help of the ruling ideology. The understanding of Christianity as a guarantor of morality lost its social basis on the individual level because its foundations had been changed by the reconstruction of women's gender roles during emancipation. The importance of religion decreased markedly, particularly among the generations that had been educated during the Soviet period. The government's anti-religious politics influenced the creation of a new representation of Christianity (and other religions and religious worldviews) as an opportunity for nonconformism. Nevertheless, this had little ground for support.

4 Christianity: Keeper of Cultural Memory and Vicarious Religion (1991–2017)

During the turbulent years of the Singing Revolution (1987–1991), when the Soviet regime collapsed and the Estonian Republic was restored, nationalist ideology returned to the fore. This has been called 'the second era of national awakening'. It was accompanied by a religious boom, including not only Christianity, but Eastern religions, esoteric religion and New Age.

There were many reasons for this sudden popularity. Under Soviet rule, nationalism and religion had had the functions of nonconformism and spiritual resistance; both returned to the agenda. In addition, the social crisis created insecurity: the regime that had been seen as unchangeable had collapsed, but nothing was there to replace it. The future of the land and its people – and the future of each individual – was unknown, a situation which has traditionally occasioned a rise in religious activity. In those years, tens of thousands of people had their children baptised, primarily in the Lutheran church; in retrospect one might even speak of a baptismal movement. The religious boom has also been linked to the distribution of humanitarian aid through the churches, and it has been claimed that the hope of material aid brought people into congregations. If some people came with such a motivation, this cannot be considered the main reason for the peak of religious activity, for the boom not only affected the Christian congregations that were distributing aid. Besides, humanitarian aid did not peak until after the restoration of Estonian independence in 1991, and by then religious enthusiasm had declined. This is another sign that the religious boom arose from the crisis. In 1992, Estonians' interest in religious questions also began to decline, and religious activity markedly diminished (Altnurme 2006: 80–83). As Soviet-era resistance and the complex of nonconformism collapsed, religion lost its corresponding meaning.

During the first independence period, the national narrative and the collective self-designation on which it was based stood in opposition to the Germans; in the Soviet era a turn took place, in which the opposing term came to be the Russians. At first, of course, this affected unofficial historical and national discourse. In opposing the Germans, the Lutheranism that was held in common was not mentioned; in opposing the Russians it was brought out again (Altnurme 2006: 90).

Such a turn had taken place earlier in among exiles. It is a well-known phenomenon of the sociology of religion that refugees or immigrants feel (at least temporarily) more than average support for the traditional religion of their country of origin than do their compatriots who remained at home. Even when their religious and national identities had been separate, this finding confirms refugees' and immigrants' national identity. Riho Saard has cited a range of examples of the sermons and miscellaneous writings of exile clergy in which Lutheran and national ideologies are interwoven and directed against the Soviet regime, in hopes that God would direct the people to the road to repentance and save Estonia from occupation (Saard 2007: 1432–1436). Estonian exiles maintained the 1930s tendency to bring nationalism and Christianity together.

Beginning with reindependence in 1991, Germany's centuries-long contribution to culture and Lutheranism came to be evaluated more favourably; these important aspects of Baltic German identity became an argument for Estonia as part of Europe. Journalism introduced and propagated Christianity as a free person's natural worldview and a marker of being European. Efforts were made to restore the Estonian Republic in its entirety; thus the Lutheran church and Christian traditions became associated with the rebirth of the nation. According to sociological questionnaires, support for the Lutheran church remained high throughout the 1990s; in 1998, 45% of Estonians considered themselves Lutherans but only 14% considered themselves religions (keep in mind that the word 'religious' had negative connotations in Estonian society, given the influence of modernist attitudes). However, this did not help reverse the trend of declining church membership since 1992. Neither Lutheranism nor Christianity became part of the national narrative, though the baptismal movement during the Singing Revolution had set a precedent (Altnurme 2006: 90). The Lutheran church was disappointed in its hope to regain its status as people's church (Pikkur 1997: 1). National and Christian identities remained separate; no connection was forged between them, as had been the case for Russian Orthodoxy. The position of Lutheran and Orthodox churches will be discussed in more detail in the next two chapters.

The most articulate segment of educated people involved with culture and the arts, that segment which shaped public opinion, remained loyal to the national narrative which was hostile to Christianity. This became apparent in the 2008 design competition for the War of Independence monument in the shape of a Latin cross. Even though the quarrel did not involve the cross as a religious symbol, there was a sentiment that it signified a foreign religion that had been forced on the Estonians. Soon after the monument was raised, Kalev Kesküla wrote:

> ... we are Europe's most unbelieving people. For us the pagan Kalevipoeg has always been closer than the cross brought by the men with iron helmets. According to our national mythology, Toompea was the burial mound of Old Kalev, its stones carried into a heap by mother Linda. Should the hero return from the gates of hell and desire to visit his father's grave and his mother's statue, he would be tripped up by the cross. We fear that he will have the impression that he has been fighting for the wrong side – like so many other Estonian men.
> KESKÜLA 2009

Once again, the debates over religious instruction in the schools are useful in clarifying understandings of religion, particularly Christianity and its role in society. During the second period of independence, there were many such debates. The debate was especially vitriolic in the spring of 2003, when newspapers published information about the compulsory incorporation of religious instruction in the schools (which did not happen). In the autumn of 2005, at the initiative of the leading skeptic Martin Vällik, petitions were circulated against such instruction. Some confusion was created since some of the participants in the debate had not understood that the study of religion was not the same thing as religious instruction; some argued about the latter as others did about the former. In these debates, religion was equated with Christianity, especially by opponents of the policy. Supporters of the policy included people who expressed their support for children's need to learn about world religions. Those who were against religious instruction decried it as a means of disseminating Christian ideology or as crypto-apologetics (Barkalaja 2001; Kivirähk 2003; Lõhmus 2003); they were opposed to the teaching of Lutheranism as a traditional religion, claiming that it no longer reflected today's circumstances (Kaplinski 2001). As an alternative, these opponents proposed the introduction of neopagan native faith to support national ideology (Vaher 2003). Similarly, instruction in various worldviews or philosophy was proposed as an alternative to religious instruction (Kaplinski 2001; Veingold 2003). In the speeches of opponents to Christianity one can see the tendency to represent it according to its negative stereotypes as instilling hypocrisy or championing an erroneous imagination of the world (Kändler 2003; Kivirähk 2003; Lõhmus 2003).

In the debate over school religious instruction at the beginning of the 21st century, the most often repeated and most convincing justification was the argument for the value of education and culture, in other words, the supervalue of Estonian national ideology. Almost all of the participants in the discussion mentioned this caveat. The latter set forth their reasons for being opposed to religious instruction, but did not fail to add that from the perspective of education and cultural knowledge, it was necessary to be informed on the subject of religion. According to the writer Jaan Kaplinski:

> Knowledge about the Bible and church history certainly belong to the minimum of basic education, not to speak of an education in the humanities. An art historian or a scholar who specializes in medieval history must definitely be able to orient themselves in theology.
> KAPLINSKI 2001

Here it is important to point out the changes that have taken place: at the beginning of the 20th century an argument based on culture would be aligned with opposition to religious instruction, rather than the justifications for its inclusion. Based on an LFRL 2010 survey, 68% of Estonians thought that religious instruction should be taught as a high school elective; 10% believed it should be compulsory: this accounts for three-quarters of the Estonians polled. The younger the students, the less support for religious instruction. Thirty percent of Estonians agreed that the subject should be taught in the elementary grades. Results of the survey should be understood in such a way that knowledge about religions is valued in the context of cultural education, but children's religiosity is to be feared. Therefore there is no general support for provision of religious instruction in the lower grades. Based on the discussion and surveys concerning religious instruction, it can be argued that Christianity was considered important mainly as a carrier and preserver of cultural memory, and something valuable enough to be transmitted the following generations.

During the first interwar independence period, the main argument in defence of religious instruction was the need to raise children to be trustworthy, moral members of society. This argument was also presented at the beginning of the 21st century, particularly convincingly by the oldest generation, who had had religious instruction as part of their own education:

> Thus the lack of education in religious matters has occasioned a fearsome decline of morality in Estonian society. [–] It is regrettable that at present only a small minority of students have religious instruction available to them, yet growing up to be citizens who comply with the law depends on the organization of religious instruction in the schools.
> KRIIK 2005

In the first decade of the 21st century, those opposed to religious instruction stood staunchly against this argument. After the cultural turn of the 1960s, the understanding of religion as a guarantor of social morality continued to decline, but as can be seen from this citation, it had not disappeared.

At the beginning of the 21st century, the meaning of Christianity as a preserver and carrier of cultural memory was socioculturally acceptable, but its importance, as seen in popular support, had become marginal. Some changes were occasioned by the 2014 debate over the cohabitation law. Among other goals, this was intended to give homosexuals a way to legalise their living together. The debate involved hostility among conservatively inclined people, who did not consider same-sex relationships moral (55%); who did not support the recognition by the state of same-sex couples as families (67%), nor giving them the legal right to adopt children (73%) (TNS Emor 2014). On the social level, liberal and left-wing journalists and politicians as well as representatives of LGBT people spoke out. Opponents of the laws, primarily conservative Christians, also spoke out using moral arguments. The discussion culminated on 4 October in the 'Demonstration in defence of the family and democracy'. To some extent, the activity of conservative Christians was recognised by opponents of the cohabitation law, though not all of these considered themselves Christians. Attitudes toward Christianity shifted. Nevertheless, this was not accompanied by a growth of the number of Estonians who described themselves as Christians. Instead of reversing the continuing decline, this became associated with the spread of vicarious religion. As Grace Davie explained:

> ... the notion of religion performed by an active minority but on behalf of a much larger number, who (implicitly at least) not only understand, but, quite clearly, approve of what the minority is doing.
> DAVIE 2007: 22

Davie equates religion with Christianity. In Estonia, in addition to those wanted to see the preservation of Christian moral norms, those who hoped that there would be a religious service each Christmas Eve, and lovely Christian rituals on the occasion of the birth, marriage, and death, there were those who had begun to hope for Christian argumentation in favour of traditional family values and gender roles. From 2015 onward, in connection with the refugee crisis, an additional demand was issued to Christianity to be a shield against encroaching Islam. In 2017, only 16% of Estonians indicated an affiliation with Christianity, while 62% believed that European culture should remain Christian (Religio 2 2017).

Characteristic of this period is that if Estonians have felt threatened as a people (e.g., during the outbreak of the Georgian and Ukrainian war), they have sought reconfirmation of their nationalism; since the years of rupture (1987–1991), however, religion has not been connected with these causes. From 2014, one can observe the rapprochement of Christianity and nationalism on the basis of conservative values. How and in what way these two ideologies will join cannot yet be predicted.

Though at the beginning of this period nationalist ideology and a politics of restoration obtained a dominant position, by means of which attempts were made to elevate the status of Christianity, the ruling nationalist narrative did not become any friendlier to Christianity, which did not become a part of national identity. However, Christianity was still valued as a preserver and carrier of cultural memory. At the end of this period, the significance of Christianity grew somewhat, particularly in the form of vicarious religion as the protector of conservative values. On this basis a new rapprochement of nationalism and Christianity has taken place, although on an individual basis, most Estonians have distanced themselves from Christianity, which remains in a marginal position.

5   Conclusion

This chapter has provided an overview of questions on changes in the importance and meaning of religion, especially Christianity, and the factors explaining these changes over the past 160 years. In the 19th century, Estonians were not particularly different from their neighbours in their religiosity, but today they are one of Europe's the most secular peoples, at least in terms of institutional Christianity. In Europe, on the social level, the determining factor for Christianity's continuation has been its connection to national ideology and identity. The stronger this association, the stronger the preservation of Christianity. In Estonia, the decisive factor in the diminished importance of Christianity was the overlap between social classes and ethnicity. Since the national narrative was created in both social and cultural opposition to the Germans, the Marxist myth of class struggle was implicit and, and thus

Christianity began to be regarded as a means of manipulation on the part of the German ruling classes toward the subjection of the lower (Estonian) classes. In the Soviet era this version was amplified as the official version of ideology (unofficially, opposition toward the Russians continued to grow). Nevertheless, until the 1960s, Christianity's preservation of its position was maintained by its association with nationalism along the lines of morality and values. As it had been formerly, the national character of the Estonians was constructed – and significant values and moral norms confirmed – with the aid of Christianity. When this association disappeared, rapid secularisation took place, which came to a halt at the beginning of the second independence period, when there was a religious boom. Sporadic attempts were made in the second independence period to unite nationalism and Christianity, but they have borne little fruit. As a preserver of cultural memory, traditional religious customs and moral norms, the church continues to be valued, but it has commanded little individual support and connection. The social importance of the church remains low. As a result, Estonia has become one of the least Christian of the European lands.

CHAPTER 3

The Lutheran Church in Estonian Society
The Impact of Secularisation and Religious Change

Priit Rohtmets, Indrek Pekko, and Riho Altnurme

As the previous chapter described and explained the marginalisation of Christianity, this chapter explains how this process affected the public profile and membership of the majority Estonian Evangelical Lutheran Church (EELC) and how the Lutheran church acted and reacted to maintain control of secularisation.

Estonia has been a Protestant area since the Reformation, but the Estonian national church, is only 100 years old. In the 20th century the church has tried to find its own Estonian Lutheranism and Lutheran identity among major Scandinavian and German traditions. Although the statistics show the decreasing influence of the Lutheran church (mainly in terms of shrinking membership) over time, Estonians still love to speak about their Lutheran identity. Many of these people could probably be called cultural Lutherans; often, however, they have a poor knowledge of the tenets and language of Lutheranism (Ketola 2009: 226). This is also supported by the fact that more people identify themselves as Lutheran than as believers.

The Lutheran identity in Estonia still has a strong historical and cultural value, which has influenced the society not only by means of religious categories or ideas but in a much broader sense. Besides religious questions it values education. One important result of the Reformation was the translation of the Bible from Latin into local languages. Over the following centuries, dissemination of the written word made it possible for Estonian peasants to become literate. Education made it possible for them to read the Bible on their own. This then led to many other individual practices (such as praying), but also to the general idea that one can believe whatever one wants to. Catholic and orthodox religiosities differ from protestant religiosity in the high value they place on authorities. Instead, the protestant way is to be seek answers on one's own.

'Work hard, then love will come' – this famous quote by Estonian writer Anton Hansen Tammsaare expresses the Estonian work ethic, which again is profoundly protestant. Achieving a high standard of living through success and hard work is essential. Today's problem is that although these traditional values are remain important, they are often no longer recognised as Lutheran.

© PRIIT ROHTMETS, INDREK PEKKO, AND RIHO ALTNURME, 2021 | DOI:10.1163/9789004461178_004

The religious situation is so profoundly affected by secularised society that what is Lutheran has turned into the secular in an unnoticed way. We can trace this historical development.

1 The Beginning of Independence

In 1917, a democratic and independent Estonian Lutheran church was established. The leaders of the new church, who were elected in 1919 and all of Estonian descent, declared that the church was now free to organise itself as it wished (Rohtmets 2011: 1135–1178). Thus, close ties between the state and the church were considered something to be overcome, and by the mid-1920s the goal had been achieved, at least in principle (Brandt 1928: 33–39).

The model of the separation of church and state, often mentioned by the political left, was the law in France and in some parts of Switzerland (Rohtmets 2018: 23). Representatives of socialist and communist parties also claimed that in addition to the Lutheran religion the institutional Lutheran church, which had been ruled by the nobility and represented the social order of the nobility, now certainly belonged to the past. It was quite difficult to argue against this; the argument that the Lutheran church was a German affair rose occasionally even at the end of 1930s, after two decades of Estonian independence (Masing 1938: 5–9; Salumaa 1938: 306–310).

After a failed communist coup in 1924, communist parties were outlawed and the socialist position became weaker. In the 1930s, Estonian political life was dominated by centre and centre-right wing parties – the Farmers Party, the National Party and the National Centre, and finally the National Christian Party. Even so, the lines of new religious policy were drawn between 1919 and 1923 and although the centre and right-wing parties altered some aspects of the legislation, the principle of strict church and state separation remained intact.

The new policy meant that the church lost nearly all of its public functions, and the parliament withdrew financial support from the church. In the 1919 land reform, the church lost most of its properties in rural areas, because these were considered equivalent to Baltic German manors and nationalised (RT 1919). This considerably weakened the church's position. Financially, the church now functioned only with the support of its members and their voluntary annual fees. The system of compulsory tax and regulative tax, with landowners financing the church was abolished. Now the state helped to collect the tax (RT 1920b). For that reason many pastors had to take on a second job and this of course limited their ability to focus exclusively on their congregation (Raudsepp 1982: 35).

In the 1920s the society went through a period of transition to secular institutions. Thus, from the second half of the 1920s, the church ceded its duties of registering births, deaths, marriages and divorces to the state. In the Russian empire this has been the responsibility of the church; now it became the responsibility of the state (RT 1922; RT 1925b). However, the clergy retained the right to register births, marriages and deaths as civil servants, without being paid by the state. In 1929, after protests by the church, the parliament passed a law establishing a pension fund for clergy who worked as civil servants (Rohtmets 2018: 54–55, 109).

The new policy of handing duties over to secular institutions certainly affected the number of church weddings and the number of divorces. A 1937 report by the Lutheran church claimed that there were more than 1000 divorces per year in Estonia. According to a law enacted in 1926, cemeteries, previously owned by parishes, were declared public, and congregations lost the right to deny burial to people who were not members of their congregation (RT 1925a).

In 1925 a new Religious Societies Act was passed, defining congregations as religious societies and the church as a union of religious societies. The law was so ambiguous that it did not even use the terms 'church' and 'congregation'. Religious societies were registered through the central boards of the churches, but if the church's government did not send the statute of a congregation to the Ministry of the Interior for registration, the congregation had the right to turn to the Ministry. A congregation that had been registered in this way remained part of the church to which it had previously belonged. The law also gave the congregation the right to leave the church with its assets if two-thirds of its membership supported it. With the law the state withdrew from any kind of direct supervision of religious communities. Since the law introduced a congregational approach, in the ensuing years the churches suffered from the lack of regulations to control their position as a governing organisation (Rohtmets 2012: 480–481).

Religious adherence and the percentage of participation in church services decreased steadily over the two decades. In 1937 a questionnaire was distributed in a comprehensive school for girls in Tallinn. Out of 491 students from 14 to 18 years of age, 9% had attended church on Sundays; 29% had listened to radio broadcasts, and 62% had done neither. Thirty percent of the respondents said that they had not attended a Christmas service (EELK 1938: 24).

The same pattern can be found in the statistics, where all the numbers decreased over these two decades. Only the number of official church members remained almost unchanged; however, there had been 16,629 baptisms in 1923 was 16,629 and by 1937 this number had dropped by approximately one-third, to 11,437. In their reports, clergy stated that children were usually baptised at the age of two and sometimes all of the children of one family were baptised together. Confirmation, as a religious ritual for adolescents to become adults, showed the same pattern. In 1923 the number of confirmands was 14,731; by 1937 it had dropped to 10,530. Although in the 1920s the sacrament of the Eucharist was celebrated on several Sundays a month, attendance showed a consistent decrease. In 1923, 262,149 people had taken communion; by 1937 the number had decreased to 208,145. Taking into account the number of church members, which according to 1922 census was 867,137 and according to the 1934 census, 874,026, only a quarter of church members took communion (Rohtmets 2018: 27).

In his 1936 report, Bishop Hugo Bernhard Rahamägi expressed little doubt that Estonian people were living in a time characterised by secularisation (this was the first report to use the term 'secularisation') and that religiosity and religious behaviour had become shallow. The bishop complained that most church members did not even take Sundays seriously anymore. Instead, shops were open on Sundays, and there were fairs and social meetings; because the working classes had no time to for these public events on during the week, they were able to enjoy them on weekends. Among the upper middle class and clerisy, Sunday did not mean anything at all, so for example it was normal to play cards on Sundays (EELK 1937: 24). Even the German deanery stated that while the youth were searching for religion, they were bothered by hearing the Christian/Lutheran sermon and service. There seemed to be a gap between the present day and the World of God.

Even before the establishment of the Republic of Estonia, Estonian clergy had an expectation for reforms to adapt the church to a modern and democratic society. Estonians were looking for a new and different form of Christianity, and now Estonians could govern their church. However the Lutheran church as the majority church resisted social change by trying to control its course, and the Lutheran church itself was far from united. After the the first congress of the newly established church in May 1917, two factions emerged. The divide only widened exacerbated at the start of the 1920s. One group of clergy and church numbers were keen to get rid of the Baltic German past and bring the church closer to its members. The other group wanted to rid the church of 'nominal Christians', and to include only those who valued the church because of its eternal message and foundation (Rohtmets 2012: 475).

When the Republic of Estonia was established, Baltic German pastors outnumbered Estonian clergy. By 1920 there were already more Estonian pastors working in the church, and by the end of 1930s the number of Baltic German pastors had dropped to a quarter of the entire clergy (Aunver 1953: 76). During the establishment of the Estonian Lutheran church, the most influential of its pastors wanted to overcome the image of a Baltic German past. In fact, the Estonians responsible for reorganising the church at the beginning of the 1920s did everything they could to free the church and Estonian Lutheranism from anything that resembled the *Landeskirche*, the church of the nobility (Rohtmets & Altnurme 2018: 229–230).

The nationality question was related to mentality, theology, and the way the church wanted to deliver its message. After the Baltic Germans were ousted from their leading position in the church, and limited to a German deanery, a fairly liberal position mixed with Estonian national sentiment prevailed (Ketola 2000: 68–69). The key question was how to establish a new and uniquely Estonian approach to Christianity. However, while there had been some elements introduced from Finland, Scandinavia and, in the 1930s from the Church of England, Estonia's general theological profile remained almost unchanged.

In connection with a new start, a new approach to theological research and authority was introduced. In 1920 the liberal pastor Theodor Tallmeister sent a letter to his colleagues proposing the formation of a society to promote Christian values. For a short time the society and Tallmeister's views were successful. He expressed his sadness that the educated class was rather hostile to the church, because there was so much ignorance about religion in Estonian society. With education and social activity this could have been overcome. Soon Tallmeister with a few other colleagues formed a liberal faction, and defended the views of 19th century German liberal theology (Rohtmets 2012: 477–478).

Tallmeister's opponent was the conservative faction, formed even earlier than the liberal one, whose leader, dean Harald Põld confronted the historical-critical approach to Biblical research and promoted a dichotomy between science and religion. He also criticised the national stance the church had taken in the beginning of 1920s, declaring that with nationalism and liberal theology the church lost its convincing position and had become a society with no theological seriousness, in other words, an institution that organised ceremonies just to get the attention of the educated class (Avalik sõna 1925: 192). In the 1920s these two factions clashed, forcing some congregations to leave the Lutheran church.

Bringing educated people to the church was a constant topic for discussion. In 1930, a promising young theologian, Hugo (Uku) Masing published an article about the ignorance and hatred of religion among educated Estonians. He also criticised the superficiality of Estonian literature. Estonian writers were also critical of religion. Masing claimed that literature was more concerned with who kissed whom, or had there been any kissing, and did not dig deeper (Masing 1930: 8–10). Not everyone shared his opinion, and so Masing's article received criticism from people like the journalist Georg Eduard Luiga those who did not value religion very highly. This critique focused on the old way the message was delivered and the conservative theological profile, which made it difficult to make any changes in connection with church life (Luiga 1930: 43–45).

In fact it was the theological heritage which made it difficult to create a new religious profile for the church. Thus it comes as no surprise that the theological profile was criticised by the educated class in the Estonian media, where the Lutheran church was accused of preserving the 'German' theological profile and thus remaining a German affair. At the same time, the church found it difficult to adopt a sustainable domestic form of theology which would have satisfied the educated class. It must be emphasised that the church itself wanted to create a more positive narrative, one that placed the Lutheran reformation, Lutheranism and the Lutheran church in the best light. The church was said to have brought spiritual freedom to Estonian peasants, and religion had made Estonians the most educated nation in the Russian empire by the 20th century. However, for most of the period, this positive narrative was challenged by the theological and historical controversy around Lutheranism.

Urbanisation became an issue for the church, not so much in small towns where new churches were being built, but certainly in Tallinn, the capital of Estonia. In the 1920s and 1930s Tallinn's population continued to grow, reaching 137,792 by 1934. However, not a single Lutheran church had been built in the capital since the end of the 19th century. In 1937 the Peeteli church in Northern Tallinn was consecrated; this was the only church built in Tallinn during the interwar period (Tamm 2001: 10).

The congregations in Tallinn were predictably overcrowded. In a report of the Lutheran church's activity in 1930, Bishop Jakob Kukk stated that it was good if a person went to a service at least once a month, and going once in two months was satisfactory. In Tallinn, where the congregation of Kaarli (Karl) had 57,000 members and the congregation of Jaani (St John) had 37,000, this would have meant that on Sundays there would have been more than 10,000 (in Kaarli) or a slightly fewer than 10,000 (in Jaani). As the bishop said, it was impossible to imagine holding services for such a crowd (EELKKA 1930). This also meant that people were attending the services seldom, if ever, and that they simply observed.

As a consequence of church overcrowding, congregants were moving back to their countryside homes for the sacrament of confirmation, which was still to be an important rite of passage into adulthood. In a 1934 report submitted by the acting church leader (Bishop Kukk had died in 1933 and his successor Hugo Bernhard Rahamägi was elected in 1934) it was observed that that although people were moving back to the countryside to get their adolescents confirmed, they did not have a close relationship with the rural congregation or its pastor (EELKKA 1934). It was therefore impossible for a city dweller to have a strong relationship with a rural parish. This also meant that church rituals were still considered important, but they were carried out wherever and whenever it was considered necessary.

2 Towards a Closer Cooperation

Under the authoritarian regime of President Konstantin Päts, which lasted from the 1934 coup until the Soviet occupation in 1940, the prestige of religion and religious organisations in society rose, with the support of the state. Päts wanted to use religious institutions to promote national unity. Religious life, from academic theology to Sunday sermons, focused on the Estonian national cause. A normative form of religion, suitable to Estonian souls and minds, was most often sought by different religious groups (Rohtmets 2016: 148–149).

This new approach went hand in hand with new legislation. In December 1934 the regime enacted a new Churches and Religious Societies Act, which corrected most of the points that the Lutheran and the Orthodox churches had criticised. Churches (Lutheran and Orthodox) with more than 100 000 members, were given special status. Church leaders could fire pastors and congregation councils could alter their decisions; church courts had the right to discuss such matters, and their decision was considered final even from the state's point of view. The state did not collect the membership tax for the church, but according to the law, the state had the right to demand church members to pay the tax (RT 1934b).

The 1938 constitution granted the heads of the two largest churches a seat in the upper house of the parliament. The constitution also stated that if necessary, the larger churches could be granted public status. However it it was declared that there was no state church in Estonia (Vihuri 2008: 226), and no public status was officially given to any church. In September 1934, Konstantin Päts approved a law to pay compensation for church land, which had been nationalised under the 1919 Land Reform Act.

Having mentioned all the benefits that the churches were granted after 1934, one should not overlook increased state control over religious institutions. Such control came to violate the freedom of religion. This was a marked contrast to the previous period, when religious institutions had been autonomous.

Now several religious associations were closed down and clergy removed from office.

Hugo Bernhard Rahamägi, elected bishop of the Lutheran church in 1934, initiated a structural reform in accordance with the state's centralising reforms. However, Rahamägi's reform caused fervent reactions from the conservative side in the church, which was opposed to 'clericalisation'. Rahamägi wanted to divide the church into eparchies and appoint bishops, which would have made him an archbishop (Vihuri 2007: 127–149). On the positive side, new ways of delivering the church's message (radio broadcasts, children services, evening services, increased youth work) were implemented during his tenure (Vihuri 2007: 205–218).

Not all pastors supported the new authoritarian regime, and certainly were not in agreement with the church's changing position in society. Younger theologians were especially critical of the centralisation of power. Consequently, the end of the 1930s was characterised by a growing discomfort with the Lutheran church, which was accused of being German-minded, untrustworthy, and unable to become a truly Estonian church (Salumaa 2010: 435–438). State representatives expressed their criticism too, because there were pastors, who were not obedient to the new regime (Vihuri 2007: 355–358).

Most of the time the clergy publicly defended the new regime because of its conservative moral stance, which was in accordance with Christian morality. However, in his annual report for 193, Bishop Rahamägi claimed that the shallowness of modern times had affected religious and moral life, and especially the family. The bishop cited a report claiming that the Christian home was disappearing, because the outside world was coming in and a disproportionate influence on youth (EELK 1937: 24). Religion had become a private matter by the end of the 1930s, making it easier for the Soviet authorities to interfere with the church's activity and social position in the 1940s.

3   Under Hitler and Stalin

By 1939, the numbers of ordinary members and clergy of the Estonian Evangelical Lutheran Church (EELC) had started to decrease. Among 11,500 Germans 'called back to Germany by Hitler' in that year were 53 members of clergy (28 of whom had also served Estonian congregations). The remaining ten German ministers left during the second wave of repatriation in 1941 (Ketola 2000).

In the first Soviet year of Soviet occupation, 1940–41, 15 Lutheran pastors were deported to Siberia, two were murdered, and seven were conscripted into the Soviet army. The former bishop of the EELC, Hugo Bernhard Rahamägi was arrested and executed in Russia in 1941. Bishop Johan Kõpp was able to remain in office. Nonetheless, the churches continued their work and there was no significant decrease in its activity. The number of participants in confirmation ceremonies even increased, as parents of adolescents feared that confirmations would be banned.

The German occupation that began in the summer of 1941 reinstated many of the churches' rights. The main problem for the Lutheran church was a shortage of clergy; nearly one-third of the congregations did not have a pastor in 1943. The National Socialist regime had confiscated bells and other ceremonial items made of precious metals for the war effort. This was a source of tension between the authorities and church leaders (Samoldin 2007).

Even under the Nazi occupation it is difficult to find expressions of hostility against the Jews from representatives of the Lutheran Church. It is true that Soviet oppression served to blunt the earlier hostility against Germans and thus make the Nazis seem like liberators. Clearly, this was sufficient to turn the Lutheran clergy against the Jews (Ketola 2003: 126). Still, one should point out that there were neither protests nor active resistance to the persecution of the Jews. The only exception is the renowned Estonian theologian Uku Masing, one of only three Estonians who, along with his wife, was listed in the Yad Vashem Book of the Just. Masing and his wife provided forged documents, shelter and food to one of his Jewish students and gave false testimony to the Gestapo. He also salvaged Jewish cultural and religious artifacts (Yad Vashem).

A new church policy was enacted after Estonia's reoccupation by the Soviet troops in 1944. The Soviet policy of religion had changed during the war, because church support of the church was necessary for victory. In the western territories of the Soviet Union, the church had remained intact; the authorities hoped to use it to advance their imperialist policy, and the Western Allies demanded toleration of churches in exchange for relief efforts.

The EELC was in a bind. Many members of the clergy (and many church members) had left Estonia– the 70,000 Estonians who escaped to Sweden and Germany in the autumn of 1944 included 72 clergymen (including Bishop Johan Kõpp) and 12 candidate ministers and theology students. During the war, the Estonians abroad established a church in exile uniting the congregations in different countries. After the church members and the clergymen had escaped to Sweden, the Swedish congregations and the deanery in Western

Estonia were disbanded. Twenty-four church buildings were destroyed and 79 damaged during the war.[1]

Before his escape, Bishop Kõpp had compiled an emergency succession list. On this basis, Assessor Anton Eilart assumed the responsibilities of bishop in Estonia in September 1944. He did not hold this position for long: on 25 November he was ordered to appear before the security services for interrogation. After being permitted to return home for the night, he and his wife tried to hide from the Soviet authorities. He was captured and imprisoned in March 1948. His disappearance broke the line of succession of church leadership.

The Episcopal Council of the EELC elected a temporary Church Council on 29 November 1944 in Tallinn. This was to be a temporary substitute for the Consistory. The Episcopal Council reconvened on 17 January 1945 and elected August Pähn, Assistant Pastor of the Episcopal Dome Congregation of Tallinn, as acting Bishop. They also elected a temporary consistory. On 5 July 1945, the Consistory issued a circular relieving all clergymen who were no longer at their posts in Estonia of their duties. This left around 80 clergymen.[2] In the meeting of the first Episcopal Council, participants had to declare their willingness to collaborate with the government (Altnurme 2001: 192).

According to Soviet registration policy, only congregations with their own minister – pastor or preacher – were permitted. This was the why the EELC permitted ordination of pastors with incomplete theological educations but who had the ability to serve a congregation. Women also received more rights. The first Episcopal Council after the war had permitted women to work as preachers, and the ordination of women was authorised in the 1960s. Laine Villenthal, the first female pastor in Estonia, was ordained on 16 November 1967 (Käärde 2006).

Church ceremonies were quite popular after the war, so the authorities had to be careful in their dealings with the church. The number of confirmations in the EELC in 1947 was higher than in any of the subsequent occupation years. However, in the first months of 1947, after consultations with Moscow, the state commissioner prohibited confirmations of people under the age of 18. In 1945, people under 18 had accounted for 35% of all persons confirmed. Confirmation classes were banned in 1949. The pastors were notified of this decision in the Consistory circular of 7 June 1949. In subsequent years the number of confirmations dropped, partly as a result of the fear caused by mass deportations

---

[1] There were 195 church buildings in use by the Lutheran church in Estonia at the end of the 1930s.

[2] There were 209 Lutheran pastors in Estonia at the end of the 1930s.

and collectivisation. The ban on confirmation classes gravely influenced the religious education of the next generations.

The year 1949 was as a turning point in the mentality of the Lutheran church. The church seemed to have come to terms with the Soviet state. A break from the past was evident in the adoption of Soviet jargon (and doublethink) (Aarelaid-Tart 2000: 755–773). After Acting Bishop August Pähn was arrested on 12 April 1949, church leadership was replaced. A total of 23 Lutheran pastors were arrested between 1944 and 1953. On 23 October 1949, the extraordinary General Synod of the EELC elected the former Acting Bishop, Jaan Kiivit as the new Archbishop. Using the title 'Archbishop' instead of 'Bishop' was thought to facilitate relations with the churches abroad, but this was a demand by the authorities. The Synod also adopted new church statutes (based on the those of the Latvian church), which governed the church's activities in accordance with Soviet laws. The church now also took part in 'patriotic' endeavours: special services were held on public holidays and the Consistory sent out classified circulars instructing the clergy to promote the participation of congregation members in state elections. The most important 'patriotic' activity promoted by the state was the 'fight for peace'.

4 Rise, Fall, and New Rise in Church Popularity

The pressure on the churches was relieved after Stalin's death in 1953. The statistical records of the Lutheran church even indicate that this was a kind of heyday for the church – all indicators improved after the return of the deportees from Siberia following the amnesty of 1955. There was a certain 'air of liberation', at the end of the 1980s. Several clergymen were also permitted to return and take up positions in the church, though only in rural congregations.

In the middle of the 1950s, the EELC developed active contacts with the churches abroad. In 1955, the Archbishop made his first international visits – to Finland and Great Britain. The Soviet authorities allowed such contacts to demonstrate the freedom of religion in the USSR and to collect information on foreign religious organisations (Altnurme 2006). This opportunity to restore contacts with foreign churches and ecumenical organisations was used mainly by the EELC, but to a lesser degree by the Baptists, the Methodists and the Orthodox. All visits were under strict KGB scrutiny, and everyone who travelled abroad, including church officials, had to submit reports.

Khrushchev's era can be associated with militant atheism in 1958–1964, which might have eased later in 1960s, but its effects lasted for many years. In the same period, general participation in church activities dropped. The statistical indicators concerning church ceremonies and membership numbers of the EELC continued to decrease into the 1970s. A few members of the clergy participated in anti-Soviet activities, particularly at the beginning of the 1980s, by delivering dissenting sermons, writing critical texts on the relations between the church and the state/society – occasionally publishing them abroad (e.g., Harri Mõtsnik, 'Confronting Atheism' or Vello Salum, 'Church and Nation') – and organising youth camps (ed Velliste 2011). The summer camps for Christian youth in Häädemeeste, organised by Villu Jürjo, are probably the best-known example. The authorities naturally responded with sanctions, but only one Lutheran pastor, Harri Mõtsnik was arrested between 1955 and 1987. He was pardoned and released soon after the court verdict – 3 years in prison for anti-Soviet agitation and propaganda, having expressed public regret for his sermons and writings. However, religion was suppressed through a variety of administrative means, and religious convictions could have repercussions. Nevertheless, the role of the Lutheran church in the resistance movement remained modest (Niitsoo 1997: 112–116).

Between 1987 and 1991, nascent political changes enabled religious associations to act more freely. The Lutheran church was accepted as a carrier of non-Soviet ideology. Church attendance became a trend. Still, many people (often adults) who were baptised and confirmed in these years did not participate in church activities so there was no significant increase in the number of active church members. The number of participants in church ceremonies of the EELC peaked in 1991. Politically, the Christian Democratic Party and the Estonian National Independence Party were the most popular among the clergy, and some of the pastors were elected to parliament. However, Kuno Pajula (1987–1994), the last Archbishop of the EELC to be elected to office under Soviet rule, declared that the church would remain politically neutral.[3]

5   Religious Change and the Estonian Evangelical Lutheran Church

After regaining space for action, the Lutheran church could resume the old traditional discussions and problems inherited from the long past of this protestant church. However, the church had to acknowledge that several surveys had shown that the people of Estonia placed the the lowest priority on religion

---

[3] A longer version of the story of the Lutheran church life in 1940–1991 can be found in *History of Estonian Ecumenism* (ed. Altnurme 2009: 109–125).

in the world. Nevertheless, spiritual ideas enjoyed great popularity, especially when are not labelled as religious (Uibu 2016: 257).

As this new spirituality has grown in significance, it also come into contact with the churches, including Lutheran church. Indeed, sooner or later churches will have to take clear positions and opinions on this topic. This will not be easy given the various forms these the new spirituality has taken.

One characteristic of Estonians since the 1990s is their readiness to believe in things which are not related to traditional Christianity. All sorts of paranormal phenomena were and remain popular, even among Christians. In 2010, overtly non-Christian beliefs held by Lutherans included healing through prayer (42%), intuitive healers (88%), horoscopes (66%), magical rituals (witchcraft) (56%), and the transmigration of souls (reincarnation) (45%) (see Jõks 2012).

In today's Estonia, new spirituality is as widespread as the historically dominant Christianity. Spirituality is usually not regarded as a transmittable religion. As the subculture uses the vocabulary of science, education, and medicine it does not often conflict with the mainstream scientific-materialistic worldview. Therefore, new spirituality blurs the borders between religion and other spheres of life by bringing in a new religious sensibility (Altnurme 2013b: 190). Here, members of the Lutheran Church are in a similar position to those outside.

6   Perspectives for the Future

The history of the 20th century with its ideological hostility to religion brought a new angle to the religious landscape: the conviction that churches must stick together. This understanding has developed into a form of ecumenical work among different churches as fulfilled in the institution of the Estonian Council of Churches (ECC), established in 1989. The best examples here are the good bilateral connections between the Orthodox and Lutheran churches (and between the western and eastern traditions), as well as the remarkably friendly ties that have developed between the Roman Catholic Church and free churches. The ECC is in the process of organising ecumenical pastoral care system in state institutions.

In some respects the religious situation in Estonia is ahead of other European countries, meaning that in the near future Estonian developments will probably manifest in other countries. As the EELC's Archbishop Urmas Viilma likes to greet delegations from other churches, 'Welcome to the Future!' (Viilma 2016: 419).

In structural terms, the EELC is an episcopal-synodal church, meaning that the oppositional duality between the episcopal and synodal wings, supporters of high- and low-church mentalities is already pre-programmed into the system. Both sides have their special spiritualities and vary in their attention to theological questions, as expressed through the attitudes and acts of the clergymen. There are also many other political and spiritual factions and parties (in 2016 the church had 214 clergymen, 43 of them women and 171 men: 5 bishops, 173 priests and 36 deacons). Thus the EELC is not very coherent – either in its theological views or in the parties preferred by clergy. Indeed, the historical background of this opposition dates from the early 1930s.

This situation has both positive and negative sides. It is positive that different opinions, practices, and spiritualities are allowed and accepted; that there is a place for everyone. The motto 'united in diversity' is well known and often used by archbishops and the leading clergy. On the negative side, these differences often lead to arguments and fights. Since there are not many employees in the church, those few know each other very well, and disagreements can turn into offensive and insulting personal attacks. One 'burning' discussion is over liturgical reform. The purpose of this longlasting EELC reform has been to modernise the church and make it more attractive to today's people. However, it has caused many conflicts since these changes have not been universally accepted, and thus the church has split into two factions. When the church is not cohesive, it is even more difficult to face further secularisation.

Besides these opinions and disagreements, the biggest challenge for the EELC today is its ageing and declining membership. Today more than 70% of EELC members are over 50 years old, not to mention that many of them have a very tenuous connection with their parishes and with the church. After 1992, the membership of the EELC entered a period of steady decline. Here are two examples: In 1992 there were 76,132 contributing and active members who donated to the church; by 2016, there were only 28,204. In addition, if in 1992, there were 10,777 baptisms, in 2016 there were only 1659. Thus the number of paying church members is less than half what it was at its peak; christenings have decreased even more. Basically, we could say that this is a general question with regard to the existence of the church, which is losing around 1000 paying members each year. This situation illustrates secularisation on an institutional level – survey statistics show that there are fewer members; that religion is decreasing in importance; that there is a declining interest in religion and religious organisations. Understandably, due to its decreasing membership the church is losing its social position.

How has the EELC reacted to these issues? Some reactions were conservative and others were more liberal. The reaction to the diminishing membership, declining financial resources and dwindling societal influence has been intensifying moral and theological conservatism on issues such as women's ordination, abortion and homosexuality (Ketola 2009: 238). The church has also become more critical of liberal society and government, customs, and relationships. This means as 'keepers of tradition', churches have not adapted as well to this changing environment as they had hoped. Instead, the outcomes of these developments and today's situation are the decline of membership, financial problems, different opinions of the church and the people concerning values and morality, along with the emergence of other contemporary religious trends, such as the new spirituality and the individualisation of religion. Perhaps a smaller membership facilitates trends towards more fundamental and conservative ideas and high church traditions. Some members of the clergy insist on keeping only the truly faithful in the church, a common view that considers conservative ways of thinking and acting as the best solution to church problems. When viewed through the prism of sociology of religion, which distinguishes three types of religious institution – church, denomination, and sect – a development toward the sect is apparent.

On the other side, there are opportunities for the Baltic churches. In the future, churches may have a more deeply committed membership, one that inspires others to join on the strength of their personal example. Churches may also be pushed to pool resources and increase cooperation at all levels, thus creating a sort of 'practical ecumenism' and a reduction of old theological enmities (Ketola 2009: 238).

Another possibility is to be more welcoming and to speak to the people in their language. The EELC's development plan for 2008–2017 states that the values for church development are holiness, Christ-centredness, communion, consideration, visibility, openness, activity. This means that the church should be receptive to new people, ideas, and spiritual diversity, while keeping its traditions alive.

One example of this kind of openness has been New Age breathwork groups held a few years ago at St. John's Church in the town of Tartu. The participants in these breathwork sessions, both members and non-members of the Lutheran Church, claimed that these sessions strengthened their inner faith. They valued doing these exercises in the church. These exercises were also combined with Christian elements, like blessings and the reading of common prayers (see more Pekko & Koppel 2013). Other examples of this openness can be seen in social activity; EELC is one of the few organisations to offer refugees and survivors of war victims places to live and assistance with joining the community. This sends a strong, direct message to society that the church stays with the people.

Both liberal and conservative reactions can be problematic. But one thing is sure – this non-religious situation offers a broad field for missionary/missions work and activities; churches cannot simply stay in their comfort zone (which is weak anyway), but they have a constant need to work hard. This field of work is wide – a large part of the population has scant knowledge of Christianity and Christian beliefs. Traditional European culture in general, but especially Estonian society has forgotten its Christian roots.

There is an urgent need to reexamine the missionary strategy of the Lutheran church. Although the church has a special individual unit – the Mission Centre – its effectiveness outside the church is small. Its events such as mission days draw followers and attendance mostly from among the small circle of churchgoers. The events are not interesting and attractive enough to attract people outside of the church.

7 Conclusion

There are many types of spirituality and religiosity inside and outside the church, and as we can see, the religiosity of the people need not decline, only change. The Lutheran church has had to fend off attacks by atheist regimes and the general decline of interest in organised religion. It is easy to suggest that the church should translate its message from 'Canaan language' into modern language, so that today's 'spiritual but not religious' people will understand it. The old institution struggles to preserve its traditions in a changing world.

CHAPTER 4

The Orthodox Church in Estonia

Historical and Contemporary Perspectives in the Context of the 2011 Population and Housing Census

Toomas Schvak

The 2011 population and housing census marked an important change in the Estonian religious landscape. For the first time in Estonia's history, Eastern Orthodoxy supplanted Lutheranism as the majority religion. In the public discussions that followed the publication of the census results in 2013, several questions were raised, ranging from what this would mean for the traditional understanding of Estonia as a Lutheran country to why Eastern Orthodoxy had become so popular. Several popular articles trying to explain this change were written, with some authors claiming that Estonia was on its way to becoming an Orthodox country (Bender 2014; Lõhmus 2013; Ringvee 2013; Rohtmets 2013; Saard 2014). This chapter offers a short analysis of the census results, looks at how the social and political conditions in Estonian history have influenced today's Orthodox Church, and draws attention to some contemporary problems that make it impossible for Eastern Orthodoxy to realise its full potential as the largest religious denomination in Estonia.

The census results reflected larger socio-demographic processes in Estonian society, not mass conversion. As the initial adoption of Eastern Orthodoxy by Estonians in the 19th century did happen through mass conversions, there might be a temptation to ascribe this change from a Lutheran to an Orthodox majority to mass conversion. The mass conversion resulting in the emergence of a native Estonian Orthodox community, however, took place in the 1840s and was mostly limited to Livland, the southern and western parts of present-day Estonia. As a result, approximately 17% of the province population changed their religious affiliation; in areas such as the counties of Pärnu and Saare the number of converts exceeded a quarter of the population, almost 70% on the island of Muhu (Kruus 1930: 342–344). Historians have long debated the reasons for this movement. Baltic German scholars have stressed the economic aspects and claimed that the Russian government had initiated a systematic campaign to spread Orthodoxy. In contrast, pro-Russian authors, particularly those affiliated with the Orthodox Church, have stressed the possible religious motives (see Aleksius 2009: 209–210; Harless 1869: 37–42, 111–112;

© TOOMAS SCHVAK, 2021 | DOI:10.1163/9789004461178_005

Leisman 1907: 18–25; Samarin 1889: 134–158; Tobien 1911: 114–116). Estonian and Latvian authors have been more circumspect, ruling out religious motivation while admitting that there were other reasons in addition to the hopes for land ownership via conversion – a popular narrative used to explain the conversion movement (see Gavrilin 1999: 66–67; Gavriļins 1988: 40–51; Jansen 2010: 318–320; Kruus 1930: 402–410). General dissatisfaction with Baltic German domination in the economy, legal matters, and religion was likely an important factor in facilitating conversions (Kruus 1930: 18). On the one hand, the protest movement took the form of religious conversion because of disillusionment with the German-dominated Lutheran Church; on the other, because the Russian Orthodox Church (ROC) was a state church and its proximity to the Emperor seemed to promise freedoms and protections not extended to Lutherans.

Another wave of conversions from Lutheranism to Eastern Orthodoxy in the 1880s took place in the province of Estland, which had been untouched by the wave of the 1840s. This wave was much smaller and added fewer than 10,000 people to the number of Orthodox believers. Its motives are similarly unclear, but compared to the earlier wave it received much more support from the Russian civil authorities and the ROC (Plaat 2001: 127–130). Although it is an interesting phenomenon that has not yet been sufficiently researched, the conversion movement as a phenomenon cannot be expanded beyond its original time frame of the 1840s to the 1880s. Nothing comparable has occurred in Estonia since then, so mass conversion is not a tenable explanation for the changes of the 21st century.

Most of the changes took place inside the religious part of the population. Compared to the 2000 census, the share of people self-identifying as Eastern Orthodox increased from 12.8% to 16.2% while the share of people self-identifying as Lutheran decreased from 13.6% to 9.9%. Comparing these numbers with statistical data from the interwar period of Estonian independence (1918–1940), the share of Orthodox believers is now approaching the percentage of that era; according to the censuses of 1922 and 1934, the Orthodox made up 18.9% of the population (Risch 1937: 121–122, 133). The changes are even more worrisome from a Lutheran perspective when looking at the composition of the two main denominations by age. Nearly half (48.3%) of Lutherans are 65 years old or older but only 8.8% are under the age of 30. Among the Orthodox population, 25.2% are 65 years old or older while 16.3% are under the age of 30. This seems to indicate that the share of the self-identified Orthodox population will continue to grow in the years to come through natural demographic processes of mortality and fertility.

Then there is the ethnic aspect. The number of ethnic Estonians who profess a religious affiliation continues to decline while number who claim to be non-religious share continues to increase. This means that the growth among the religious is sustained mostly by ethnic minorities; in the case of Eastern Orthodoxy, this is primarily the Russian-speaking minority. The 2011 census shows that only 11.6% of Orthodox adherents are ethnic Estonians while the three major Russian-speaking ethnic groups (Russians, Ukrainians, Byelorussians) comprise 85.6% of the Orthodox community. At the same time, among Lutherans the share of ethnic Estonians is 96.5%. This indicates that as younger Estonians become increasingly non-religious and the older, more religious generations pass away, the number of Lutherans continues to decline. At the same time, younger Russian-speaking people have started to identify more with religion, ensuring the sustainability of growth in the Orthodox community for the near future.

However, this does not say anything about their religious commitment. Sociological studies in Russia have shown that a substantial increase in religious affiliation does not lead to an increase in church attendance or belief in God (Pew Research Center 2014). At the same time, Eastern Orthodoxy is one of the major markers of Russian national identity and the Orthodox Church has been one of the most trusted institutions for Russians in the Baltic states since the early 1990s. The rise in religiosity therefore does not necessarily reflect actual changes in beliefs or customs (Laitin 1998: 310–312).

Nonetheless, the situation is interesting because Estonia's largest religious denomination is now mostly comprised of ethnic minorities, yet, when looking at the whole population, this denomination is itself a minority in a mostly non-religious society. We now explore the historical roots of this situation.

The past and present of the Orthodox Church in Estonia cannot be separated from the political history of the country. It is characteristic of Orthodox churches, particularly the ROC to act in close cooperation with and to depend upon the state. Therefore, we see that all attempts to introduce Eastern Orthodoxy to Estonian territories before the 19th century were undertaken in concert with Russia's territorial expansion. The fortified settlement of Yuryev, established in 1030 and considered in popular tradition to be the location of the first Orthodox church in Estonia, was established only as a result of a military campaign by Yaroslav the Wise, Grand Prince of Kiev. There is no archaeological evidence of Orthodox churches in Yuryev (now Tartu), so its role as the potential centre for the Orthodox mission in the 30 years it existed is contested. However, it certainly was an outpost of an Eastern Orthodox power (Plaat 2011: 9–10).

The first documented baptism of Estonians by Orthodox priests in 1210 took place in the course of a military incursion by Mstislav Mstislavich, Prince of Novgorod, and his brother Vladimir Mstislavich, Prince of Pskov (Henry of

Livonia 2003: 95). The first Orthodox monastery and eparchy in Estonia were established around 1570 during a military campaign by the Tsar of Muscovy, Ivan the Terrible. They only existed for a short period, as in 1582 the Russians ceded the territories under their control to Sweden and Poland, bringing an end to Orthodox church structures in Estonia (Selart 2009: 46–55).

Although the mass conversion movement of 1840s was not initiated by the Russian authorities, it would not have been possible without the Russian victory in the Great Northern War as a result of which the territory of Estonia transferred from Sweden to the Russian Empire, finalised by the Uusikaupunki peace treaty in 1721. At the same time, Peter the Great instituted church reforms that saw the elimination of the office of the Patriarch of Moscow, and the ROC reduced to a department of state (Pospielovsky 1998: 105–106). Although this proximity to the Russian state fuelled the conversion movements of the 19th century, it later became a major liability for the Orthodox Church.

The Estonian national awakening, which took place under Baltic German cultural influences in the second half of the 19th century, created a national discourse where Russian culture and religion were seen inferior to its Western counterparts (as discussed in the first chapter). In the 1880s and 1890s Emperor Alexander III carried out the 'Russification' of the non-Russian provinces of the Empire (for more information see Polunov 2001). Aimed at better assimilation of non-Slavic ethnic groups, the ROC became one tool in the service of this aim. However, the policies created a backlash, whereas the ROC came to be seen as a tool of state repression, tied to unpopular reforms like the introduction of Russian-language education in Estonian schools. The close relationship of the church and state only reinforced the understanding of the Eastern Orthodoxy as the 'Russian faith' among the majority of ethnic Estonians. Toomas Schvak has summarised the tensions between the Estonian Orthodox community and the wider, predominantly Lutheran society in one of his articles (Schvak 2016).

There were tensions not only between the larger, non-Orthodox segments of the society and the church, but also within local church structures. Even though most of the believers in the Eparchy of Riga, in charge of the Eastern Orthodox congregations in present-day Estonia and Latvia, were ethnic Estonians and Latvians, both ethnicities were sidelined in the local church hierarchy. In the 80 years of its history there were no Estonian or Latvian bishops. Moreover, most of the bishops in Riga did not even speak the local languages and the theological seminary in Riga never had an Estonian or a Latvian rector or a vice-rector. At the same time, from 1847 to 1918 at least 663 ethnic Estonians studied there, training to become clergymen and schoolteachers (Raudsepp 1998: 25–26, 60). These ethnic tensions and frustrations were visible before the collapse of the Russian Empire. When finally, at the end of 1917, in the changed political environment an ethnic Estonian, Paul Kulbusch, was consecrated the Vicar Bishop of Tallinn, this was a cause for celebration among Estonian Orthodox believers.[1]

After the founding of the Republic of Estonia in 1918, the ethnic Estonian clergy attempted to disassociate the Orthodox Church in Estonia from everything Russian, trying to shed the label of the 'Russian faith'. Its modernisation programme included the adoption of the Gregorian calendar instead of the Julian calendar used in the ROC; changes in liturgical music and texts aimed at encouraging congregants to participate more actively in the church services and shortening the services; introducing Estonian Orthodox names instead of Russian ones; modernising the appearance of the clergy and encouraging participation in social and political life. On the canonical and administrative level, the full independence of Orthodox congregations in Estonia was desired. The semi-autonomous status granted by Moscow in 1920 was deemed insufficient. The process was completed in July 1923 when the Estonian Apostolic Orthodox Church (EAOC) obtained the status of an autonomous church in the canonical jurisdiction of the Ecumenical Patriarchate of Constantinople. The latter step was justified using the political conditions in Russia that had led to the imprisonment of Patriarch Tikhon and various other kinds of repression of the ROC. Although the Estonians had desired full canonical independence (autocephaly), this proved impossible, so autonomy from Constantinople was accepted after negotiations with the patriarchal synod (Rimestad 2012: 84–96; Schvak 2015: 49–54).

In 1919 and 1920 when the first local Orthodox church councils were held in the newly independent Republic of Estonia, it quickly became clear that Estonian and Russian believers had very different ideas of how the church should operate, ranging from religious customs to the form of church government. Most Russian believers were opposed to the reforms proposed by the ethnic Estonian clergy. Therefore those first councils articulated the need for the Russian congregations to conduct their business autonomously from the Estonian majority; several consecutive institutions for the self-government of Russian congregations were introduced in the early 1920s until finally, in 1924 a separate eparchy for Russian congregations was established, headed initially by

---

[1] Paul Kulbusch, consecrated under the name Platon, was the first known Orthodox bishop of ethnic Estonian origin. Consecrated on December 31, 1917, he was also appointed caretaker of the Riga eparchy in January 1918 but was murdered on January 14, 1919 by the retreating Bolsheviks. Bishop Platon was canonised in 2000 by the Ecumenical Patriarchate of Constantinople and the Patriarchate of Moscow. (For more biographical details see Poska 1968.).

the former Archbishop of Pskov Eusebius (Grozdov), living in exile in Estonia (Rimestad 2012: 96–104, 145–154, 194–199; Saard 2008: 1568–1576). Despite serious problems between the two communities throughout the 1920s and 1930s, this helped to maintain the nominal unity of the Church, although in practice the Estonian and Russian congregations operated largely independently from each other. While maintaining the unity of the church in Estonia, this system also laid the foundation for the separation of the two ethnic communities of Orthodox believers. Although this is a common principle of organisation in the modern Orthodox Church, the practice of church administration based on ethnicity is contrary to the original church canons which only indicates geographical units of church administration (Walters 2002: 360–361).

Although the EAOC conducted a modernisation programme that was intended to bring Eastern Orthodoxy closer to both church members and those outside the church, it was less than successful. The numbers for church attendance and membership dues remained low while those outside the church still labelled Eastern Orthodoxy as a 'Russian faith' – a name used for Eastern Orthodoxy in vernacular Estonian even today – even though 59% of Orthodox believers were ethnic Estonians.[2] The reasons for the rather weak ties of many ethnic Estonian Orthodox believers to their church were historical and can be traced to their weak religious identity. As discussed earlier, the conversion movement of the 1840s was mainly a socioeconomic protest movement, not an actual religious awakening. As the converts failed to achieve their social and economic goals, there was widespread disillusionment with the Orthodox Church. In the 1850s and 1860s, a growing number of disappointed converts desired to reconvert to Lutheranism: however, the laws of the Russian Empire did not allow conversion from Orthodoxy. This caused a large segment of people to see their new church as another formal obligation, not a true spiritual home. Many people also became secret Lutherans, remaining nominally Orthodox, but performing their religious rites in Lutheran parishes (Gavrilin 1999: 195–198, 233–237; Ryan 2007).

---

2   There is as yet no comprehensive study on religious commitment, but complaints about low attendance and little interest in church matters were present in the reports of parish priests from the second half of the 19th century. Based on the parish files in the archive of the EAOC Synod (National Archives of Estonia, RA EAA.1655), the numbers from the parishes of two deaneries – the Harju deanery in northern Estonia and the Tartu deanery in southern Estonia – were compared by Toomas Schvak over the period of 1921–1937. He discovered that of the registered parish members in Harju deanery, an average of 29% took communion and paid their dues, while in Tartu deanery the share of communicants was closer to 25% and the payments of membership dues below 20%.

If such attitudes were also handed down to the next generations, weak religious identity and the lack of religious commitment are not that surprising. The situation was exacerbated by the seeming incompatibility between the emerging Estonian national identity and the 'Russian faith' which made the ethnic Estonian Orthodox believers feel like incomplete Estonians because of their religious background. The attacks on Eastern Orthodox symbols in the public sphere started in the early 1920s[3] and culminated in the attempt to demolish the St. Alexander Nevsky Cathedral in Tallinn in 1928 (Ketola 1996; Lääne 2009), reinforcing the understanding of Orthodoxy as alien to modern Estonian society. All of these factors may have contributed to why the ethnic Estonian Orthodox population secularised and de-Christianised much faster than its ethnic Russian counterpart during the ensuing Soviet occupation. If for Russians Eastern Orthodoxy was an important markers of national and cultural identity, for Estonians it was a source of tension with their national identity.

The World War II years continued to build on the foundation of ethnic separation laid down during the years of Estonian independence. The first year of Soviet occupation (1940–1941) had seen the elimination of the autonomous EAOC and the return of its structures brought into the ROC, despite protests by both clergy and laypeople. In the nine months from May 1940 to March 1941, 76 clergymen resigned, usually citing family issues or ill health (Schvak 2015: 58–61; Sõtšov 2001: 33–35). After the start of the German occupation (1941–1944), the military authorities allowed two parallel church structures to register and operate independently from each other: in October 1942 the Estonian Metropolitanate under the Ecumenical Patriarchate was restored, while most Russian parishes continued operating as the Narva Eparchy of the ROC, registered by the German authorities in November 1942 (Schvak 2015: 61–62).

The defeat of the Germans in World War II and the ensuing Soviet occupation (1944–1991) made the division of the Orthodox community into two separate canonical jurisdictions permanent. In 1944 several clergymen and laypeople, including Metropolitan Alexander (Paulus), emigrated from Estonia and operated in exile as EAOC under the jurisdiction of the Ecumenical Patriarchate. However, the local church structures in Estonia, were once again brought under the control of the Moscow Patriarchate and demoted to a single

---

3   The main wave of attacks began in the form of a series of articles on the pages of the daily newspaper *Vaba Maa* in January 1922, calling for the demolition of the small water benediction chapels in Tallinn. Soon the newspaper started a fund for the demolition works and advised removal of the Orthodox cathedral. See: *Vaba Maa*, 28.01.1922, 10; 30.01.1922, 6; 31.01.1922, 6; 2.02.1922, 7; 13.02.1922, 6; etc.

eparchy. The reintegration into the ROC took place from March to April 1945 (Schvak 2015: 62–63).

The Soviet occupation changed the religious landscape in four ways. The antireligious legislation restricted public expressions of religion while cutting off religious communities' sources of income and imposing heavy taxes on them.[4] A campaign of atheistic propaganda and education directed at children and youth hollowed out future generations of believers. Extensive industrialisation and urbanisation uprooted rural residents and sent them to towns and cities where the role of religious communities was significantly diminished. Finally, Russian-speaking workers from other areas of the Soviet Union were settled in Estonia to expand the industrialisation programme and assimilate the native population. This had a permanent effect on the ethnic composition of Estonia: the share of ethnic Estonians in the population continued to decrease, from 88% in 1934 to 74.6% in 1959 and further to 61.5% in 1989 (Eesti Statistikaamet 1995: 56–57). As a result, many ethnic Estonian Orthodox parishes in the countryside (and some in cities) were closed. Between 1950 and 1964 at least 45 parishes were closed, but this number does not include the churches that were already destroyed in World War II and where parishes were never reopened, even though they were not officially closed. An additional 18 parishes had become part of Russia when the borders of the Estonian SSR were changed in 1946. Closing of parishes continued at a slower pace through the 1970s and 1980s. The remaining parishes were often not served regularly due to the lack of available clergy (Schvak 2015: 65). In the cities many previously mixed parishes became almost entirely Russian-speaking with the influx of Russian-speaking immigrants. The ethnic Estonian part of the Orthodox community dwindled. The Soviet occupation destroyed the small achievements of the 1920s and 1930s in improving the public image of the Eastern Orthodoxy and reinforced its image as a 'Russian faith'. Even though the ROC and its local structures were often more heavily persecuted than the Lutheran Church, to many Estonians the Orthodox Church became the occupier's church.

When at the end of 1980s people began returning to organised religion, the Orthodox Church also experienced a growth in membership. Although Eastern Orthodoxy mostly attracted Russian-speaking people, some ethnic Estonians were also discovering Orthodoxy. One group was comprised of those who had discovered their Orthodox roots and decided to return to the church of their parents or grandparents; the other, quite significant group of people, including

---

4   For more information and specific examples, see Andrei Sõtšov's studies on the Soviet policies on religious communities in the 20 years after World War II from the Estonian Orthodox perspective (Sõtšov 2004; Sõtšov 2008).

many future priests, came to Eastern Orthodoxy through Eastern spiritual practices – Buddhism, Taoism, Yoga, martial arts and various strands of New Age (Eek 2015: 103–104).

However, the re-independence of Estonia in 1991 tore open old wounds related to nationality and politics. While many ethnic Estonians in the Orthodox community were interested in restoring, along with the political independence of the country, the independence of the local church from the ROC, most Russian-speaking believers were happy with the *status quo* – a situation similar to the years 1918–1923. However, compared to the early 1920s, the situation had changed. Back then the Estonians had been the majority in the church, now they were a tiny minority. The ROC was also in a different position – if in the 1920s it had been a persecuted community in the antireligious Soviet Union, in the 1990s it was a respectable social institution enjoying the respect and support of the Russian government. The ROC also carried an unpleasant Soviet legacy – many clergymen had been recruited as KGB agents in the Soviet times and they continued to hold positions in the higher hierarchy of the church. Also, in 1990 the Metropolitan of Tallinn and Estonia Alexy (Ridiger) had been elected the new Patriarch of Moscow, meaning that the head of the ROC took a personal interest in church matters in Estonia.[5] All this made the Estonian project of transferring the local Orthodox Church back to the jurisdiction of the Ecumenical Patriarchate complicated – but in the eyes of many this was necessary, as the connections could have given the Russian authorities an opportunity to use the church to assert its influence on Estonia (Heljas 2003).

This caused a schism in the Orthodox Church of Estonia and a return to the World War II era where there had been two canonical jurisdictions in Estonia. With the help of the local ethnic Estonian clergy, the EAOC, having spent almost 50 years in exile, re-established its presence in Estonia in 1993, and was declared by the courts to be the legal successor to prewar EAOC. Its autonomy had been suspended in 1978 under diplomatic pressure from the Moscow Patriarchate, but it was reactivated by the Ecumenical Patriarchate in 1996 (Rohtmets & Tēraudkalns 2016: 655). For years the parishes in the jurisdiction of the Patriarchate of Moscow refused to register under any other name than the EAOC, spending almost ten years in a legal vacuum, and only registering in 2002 as the Estonian Orthodox Church – Moscow Patriarchate (EOC-MP) as

---

5 Alexei Ridiger was born in Tallinn in 1929, consecrated into priesthood in 1950, elevated to Bishop of Tallinn and Estonia in 1961, elevated to Metropolitan in 1968 and transferred to the see of Leningrad and Novgorod in 1986, remaining also the head of his previous eparchy. He was allegedly recruited by the KGB in 1958 (see Sõtšov 2008: 122–126).

a result of a compromise mediated by the Estonian government. The details of these developments have been covered in many studies (see Rimestad 2014: 295–302; Ringvee 2011: 125–164; Rohtmets & Tēraudkalns 2016: 633–665; Schvak 2015: 68–80). Almost all ethnic Estonian parishes, along with the large Russian parish of Dormition in Tartu joined the EAOC. The EOC-MP became predominantly an ethnic Russian church with just a few mixed parishes.

As we have seen from the demographic data, most of today's Orthodox believers are Russian-speaking people, thus making the EOC-MP the larger of the two churches (170,000 members compared to 30,000 in the EAOC). The EAOC has 65 parishes; the EOC-MP has only 32, many of which are small or even inactive rural parishes (Eesti Kirikute Nõukogu 2017: 7; Schvak 2015: 80–82). There are no official contacts between the two churches, as each considered itself the sole legitimate Orthodox Church in Estonia. The relationship has worsened in light of the conflict over canonical jurisdiction in Ukraine in 2018–2019 that resulted in a complete rupture between their mother churches, the patriarchates of Constantinople and Moscow (Rohtmets 2019).

This situation does not allow the church in Estonia to realise its full potential as the largest religious denomination. Although the growth in membership over the last two decades has been statistically significant, this growth is divided between two church organisations. As the two jurisdictions are divided along ethnic lines, each speaks only to its respective ethnic community. It is worth taking a look at how inclusive or exclusive they are in their everyday activities.

The EOC-MP operates not as a self-sustainable church but a proxy of the ROC. It sees its role as serving the local Russian-speaking community and relies on its mother church. For example, it does not have its own institution of clerical education, meaning that all candidates for priesthood must study abroad, usually in Russia. It employs seven ethnic Estonian priests but most of them entered the clergy before the schism and no new ethnic Estonian priests have been consecrated since 2001 (MPEÕK 2019). Two out of three bishops in the EOC-MP originate from Russia and had not served a day in Estonia before their appointment to the country. This is true both for the head of the church, the Metropolitan of Tallinn and All Estonia Eugene (Reshetnikov) who served as the Rector of the Moscow Theological Academy prior to his appointment in 2018, as well as for the Bishop of Narva and Chud Lazar (Gurkin) who was archimandrite of a monastery in Mordovia, Russia, prior to his appointment in 2009.

Church services in Estonian are rare in the EOC-MP churches, even in churches with ethnically mixed parishes. In St. Alexander Nevsky Cathedral in Tallinn, the seat of the Metropolitan, Estonian services are held on Saturday morning. On Sunday the services are in Church Slavonic with only the major prayers recited in Estonian. The EOC-MP publishes its newspaper, *Pravoslavnyi Sobesednik,* and almost all other official publications from church calendars to religious books only in Russian.[6] In today's political climate, where Russia is perceived as a potential threat to the Baltic States, the EOC-MP's almost exclusive care for the local Russian-speaking community and its full dependence on its mother church, ROC, continues to tarnish its reputation among ethnic Estonians. Its close relationship with the Estonian Centre Party, which derives a large part of its support from the Russian-speaking minority has drawn the church into a public scandal.[7] The EOC-MP positions itself as the church of the Russian-speaking minority and does not feel any need to engage with the wider society.

At the same time, it is remarkable that some ethnic Estonian priests and laymen belonging to the EOC-MP are working hard to change the situation. Associations established by the members of the EOC-MP such as the Orthodox Publishing Society of St. Issidore produce religious literature in Estonian (more than 20 books since 1999), but although they seek approval for their publications from their church authorities, none of this work is carried out by the official publishing department of the EOC-MP. More literature than ever is being published by the St. John the Evangelist School Foundation, established in 2012 to maintain and operate the only private Orthodox school in Tallinn, the St. John the Evangelist School (Püha Johannese Kool 2019). Again, although operating with the blessing of the Metropolitan of the EOC-MP, this school was established as a private initiative, not under the aegis of the church. This confirms that all attempts on the side of the EOC-MP to bridge divides between ethnicities, languages and canonical jurisdictions have been unofficial. Furthermore, most of them can be traced to just one ethnically mixed parish: the Nõmme St. John the Baptist Parish located in a suburb of Tallinn.

The EAOC has always tried to be ethnically inclusive, as it has a large Russian parish in its structure: its newspaper *Metropoolia* is published in two languages. The EAOC has some experience in publishing some of its books in

---

6 The online version of *Pravoslavnyi Sobesednik* is located at http://www.orthodox.ee/sobesednik.html. Until August 2017 it was called *Mir Pravoslaviya* and its archive is available at http://www.baltwillinfo.com/mp.htm.

7 At the end of 2010 it was revealed that the chairman of the Estonian Centre Party Edgar Savisaar had tried to obtain money from Russia for his party under the pretence of acquiring funds for the construction of the Church of the Icon of the Mother of God "Quick to Hearken", built by the EOC-MP. After the scandal, the EOC-MP was accused of being overly politicised and using its influence among the Russian-speaking community to guarantee political support for the Centre Party (Tarand 2013).

two languages.[8] Initially the EAOC was interested in maintaining the official dialogue between the two churches and with the Ecumenical Patriarchate proposed a model integrating the two Orthodox communities in Estonia into one church. The model was based on the canons of the ecumenical council of 691 and resembled the autonomous Russian parishes of the interwar period (Papathomas 2007). Since according to this model the Russian parishes would have been subject to the Ecumenical Patriarchate, the Moscow Patriarchate rejected the proposal and the dialogue ended. As an ethnic Estonian church the EAOC sees itself as an integral part of Estonian society and has made serious efforts to ensure its self-sustainability. It has tried to manage the property that was returned to it as the legal successor to the interwar EAOC and used the income to fund its other activities. As the historical Pühtitsa convent in Kuremäe, northeastern Estonia, remained in the jurisdiction of the Moscow Patriarchate, the EAOC has established its own convent on the island of Saaremaa. Founding a monastery has been a work in progress for several years. A key accomplishment was the opening of the chair of Orthodox theology at the Theological Institute of the Estonian Evangelical Lutheran Church, an uncommon example of ecumenical cooperation in the Orthodox world. This serves as the base of education for the EAOC clergy. The church has also published a theological journal *Usk ja Elu* (Schvak 2015: 81).

In the interwar period, the Orthodox Church in Estonia aspired to be recognised as a people's church (from the German term *Volkskirche*). In Estonia this term has been historically applied to the Lutheran Church which used to count most of the Estonian population as its members. However, Lutheran theologian and bishop Johan Kõpp has stated that every church that performs a serious and influential role in the life of people can claim the name of a people's church (Kõpp 1940: 147). Despite its ambitions to depict itself as the natural, voluntarily accepted religion of ethnic Estonians and therefore as the true people's church, in contrast to Roman Catholicism and Lutheranism that were imposed on Estonians by Germans – the Orthodox Church of the 1920s and 1930s failed. Now, as the largest religious denomination, it is better positioned to live up to this claim. However, the prerequisites for this are internal unity and the ability to speak authoritatively in one voice to all people of Estonia, of every ethnic background and political viewpoint. Both of these prerequisites are currently lacking.

---

8 Copies of the newspaper *Metropoolia* are available at the URL http://www.eoc.ee/mteropoolia/ At least three books published between 2007 and 2019 by the EAOC have been printed in parallel in Estonian and Russian.

To summarise, the latest census shows that the Orthodox Church has indeed become the largest religious group in Estonia and is demographically well positioned for further growth, even though Estonian society can be characterised as non-religious. However, the Orthodox community is burdened by its complicated history, which underlies its division into two separate canonical jurisdictions, largely along ethnic lines. The lack of dialogue between the two churches has turned them both inwards, to their respective communities. This is particularly true of the EOC-MP, which sees itself as the pillar of identity for the local Russian-speaking minority and makes very little effort to reach out to ethnic Estonians, even those among its members. The reluctance of the Moscow Patriarchate, the mother church of the EOC-MP, to open itself to humble dialogue and concessions, also visible on an international level makes any hopes for bridging the divide inside the Orthodox community of Estonia unlikely.

CHAPTER 5

Secular Society, Secular State
Egalitarian Legislation on Religion?

Ringo Ringvee

1   Introduction

Estonia is one of the most secularised societies in the world, if we measure secularisation on the scale of affiliation with organised religion, participation in religious services, the importance of religion in everyday life or general indifference to religion (Population Census 2011; Ringvee 2014; EUU 2016; Remmel 2017; Berger et al. 2008: 57). Surveys and reports on religious freedom also show that Estonia is characterised by low-level state-imposed restrictions on religion and a high level of religious freedom on the legislative level and in practice (Pew Research Center 2017; Freedom House 2016).

In its basic principles, the Estonian legal framework on religion, religious associations and religious freedom is egalitarian. Besides this egalitarian legal framework which applies similar regulations to similar associations and does not differentiate among religious associations according to their religious tradition, there is also a place for religious lobbying in policy making (Ringvee 2015a; Kilp 2015: 122, 126).

2   Some Historical Background for the State and Religion Relations in Estonia

For the sake of clarity, it is good to start with a historical overview of the changes in the legal background. Estonia was declared an independent democratic republic in 1918 after centuries of foreign rule. In the ensuing years, for the first time in their history, Estonians could define relations between the independent state and organised religion. The first Constitution of the Republic of Estonia was adopted in 1920, and besides equality among citizens it stipulated the principles of freedom of religion and conscience quite similarly to today's international standards for the freedom of religion or belief (RT 1920a). Under the 1920 Constitution there is no state religion in Estonia. In the first years of independence, the two largest churches, the Evangelical Lutheran Church and the Orthodox Church, had become independent and self-governing institutions; they were separated from the state and thus lost the privileges they had had in the Russian Empire (1721–1917). According to the 1922 population census, 98% of the population defined themselves as religiously affiliated, 78% as Lutherans and 19% as Orthodox (Eesti Riikline Statistika 1924: 138–139).

In 1925 the Parliament (*Riigikogu*) adopted the Religious Societies Act to set a legal framework for religious associations or religious societies as legal entities (RT 1925c). The 1925 Act was egalitarian and treated all religious communities on the same grounds, with no privileges conferred on any religious tradition. This egalitarian and liberal approach began to change in 1934. In January 1934, a new Constitution, adopted by national referendum in 1933, took effect (RT 1933). The 1934 Constitution gave more power to the head of state, referred to from then on as the State Elder. On 12 March 1934 the State Elder imposed the State of Emergency Act and established an authoritarian regime (RT 1934a). In 1935 the State of Emergency Act was used to close down the Watchtower Bible and Tract Society (Jehovah's Witnesses), which had been accused of the activities harmful to Estonia's foreign policy and deemed a threat to public order (Ringvee 2015b, 24–27). In December 1934 the State Elder approved the Churches and Religious Societies Act to replace the 1925 Religious Societies Act (RT 1934b).

From 1934 to 1940 governmental control over religious activities increased while the government's cooperation with the Estonian Evangelical Lutheran Church and the Estonian Apostolic Orthodox Church became tighter. The 1934 Churches and Religious Societies Act introduced new terminology to legislation by using the term 'church' instead of the former categories, 'religious society' and 'union of religious societies.' According to the 1934 Act, the government of the republic approved the statutes of the churches with more than 100 000, while the statutes of other churches, religious societies and their unions were approved by the Minister of the Interior. The 1934 Act gave the state the right to intervene in the autonomous sphere of religious associations. The State Elder had the right to demand a change of candidate for the head of the church or the union of religious societies if the candidate was not considered appropriate. The internal regulations of a church or a society had to be approved by the Minister of the Interior, who could also demand the discharge of clergy who did not fulfil their legal duties. The Minister also had the right to forbid the clergy to perform his duties should this be necessary for the state or the public order. According to § 20 the Minister of the Interior had the authority to ban religious associations if their activities were considered a threat to the state or the public order. This option was used once in 1939 when the Minister of the Interior suspended the activities of the Bishop, General Synod and the

Consistory of the Estonian Evangelical Lutheran Church over an internal dispute over the bishop's divorce (Vihuri 2007: 358–360).

On 1 January 1938, a third Constitution came into effect in Estonia in which the State Elder was titled as the President (RT 1937). While the 1920 and 1934 Constitutions had stipulated that there was no 'state religion' in Estonia, § 14 of the new Constitution stated that there was no 'state church.' The public position of the Estonian Evangelical Lutheran Church and the Estonian Apostolic Orthodox Church was given greater power; according to § 84 (1) of the Constitution, the heads of the two large churches became *ex officio* members of the Upper House of the Parliament (*Riiginõukogu*). The Constitution also noted that the 'larger churches' could operate under public law; however, the meaning of this principle remained unclear (Kõpp 1940: 141–143).

The 1939 Molotov-Ribbentrop Pact between Germany and the Soviet Union assigned Estonia and the two other Baltic States to the Soviet sphere of interest. The Soviet regime took control of Estonia on 21 June 1940, and a month later, on 21 July 1940 Estonia, Latvia and Lithuania were incorporated into the Soviet Union as Soviet Socialist Republics. From then on restrictive Soviet legislation and policies were enforced. The Soviet authorities liquidated the pagan association *Hiis* (the Grove), and closed the theological faculty at the University of Tartu; the Estonian Apostolic Orthodox Church, which had been under the canonical jurisdiction of the Ecumenical Patriarchate until being incorporated into the Moscow Patriarchate and then liquidated in 1944 (Rohtmets & Tēraudkalns 2016).

During the Second World War, the Soviet occupation was replaced by German occupation between 1941 and 1944. Soviet anticlerical policies and atheist campaigns had serious consequences for religious communities. From 1945 until 1990 religious life in Soviet Estonia was supervised by the Commissioner of Religious Affairs of the Council of Ministers of the USSR. From 1945 to 1965 there were two commissioners in Estonia – one for the Orthodox Church and the other for all other denominations. The Soviet legislation and governance policy on religion was marginalising. These policies remained in effect until the late 1980s unti *glasnost* and *perestroika* helped to usher in a national reawakening. After 1988, restrictions on religious life were loosened, and religion began to enter the public sphere. Clergymen of different churches, especially the Estonian Evangelical Lutheran Church, were active in the emerging social and political movements. At the same time, official religious institutions were modestly neutral, not showing a preference for any particular political movement (Rohtmets & Ringvee 2013). As in other parts of the USSR, in Estonia there were discussions and demands for new legislation on religion.

In March 1990, the religious affairs commissioner's office in Estonia was liquidated. Henceforth the registration of new religious associations took place in accordance with the 1989 Estonian SSR legislative act 'On Civic Associations' (RT 1990). On 16 May 1990, the Supreme Council of the Estonian Republic adopted an act laying out the basics of the interim governance of Estonia, according to which religious freedom was guaranteed (ENSV ÜVT 1990). On 20 August 1991 Estonia's independence was restored *de facto* (RT 1991). After the disestablishment of the religious affairs' commissioner's office, there was a debate over what institution should take responsibility for the administration of relations between the state and religious communities. Religious affairs eventually became the responsibility of a new department with new personnel at the Ministry of Culture (Ringvee 2011: 38–39).

The processes that unfolded during the transition period in Estonia were similar to the ones in several countries of the former Communist bloc (Pollack 2002: 380–381; Tomka 2006: 39; Pollack & Müller 2006: 24). The years 1987–1992 in Estonia were characterised by religious revitalisation or a 'church boom,' a time of both enthusiasm and confusion. The numbers of baptisms and confirmations in the Estonian Evangelical Lutheran Church grew tenfold (Kiivit 1995: 111). Although this interest in organised religion and religious institutions soon waned, the attitude towards religion in its various forms remained positive. The idea of individual freedom was highly esteemed in the 1990s and this included freedom of religion; anti-cult movements did not take hold in Estonia. In the ensuing years, a variety of forms of religion and spirituality were popular. According to the 1990 World Values Survey, the 'church' was the third most trusted institution in Estonia, a position that has since been lost (Saar 2010: 113).

3   Legislating Religion in a Secular Society

The new Constitution was drafted by the Constitutional Assembly, a legislative body formed after the restitution of independence on 20 August 1991 on the basis of the Committee of Estonia and pro-independence members of the Supreme Council of the Republic of Estonia (Taagepera 2007). There was general agreement in the Assembly that religious freedom should be protected, but religion was not a subject of discussion (Kiviorg 2016: 29, 165). The new Constitution was adopted following a national referendum in 1992, and it enshrined the principle of freedom of religion or belief (RT 1992). In § 40 of the 1992 Constitution, freedom of conscience, freedom of religion and freedom of thought are guaranteed. The relations between the state and religious institutions are defined by the declaration that 'there is no state church in Estonia.' There is no reference to secularity or any religious tradition or institution.

The drafting of a new legislative act to regulate the status of religious associations began at the Ministry of Culture in 1990 and continued until 1992. The first parliamentary elections in 1992 gave power to political parties which had a firm belief in individual freedom, the principle of the free market, the urgent necessity for economic reforms establishing this free market and demolishing power structures inherited from the late Soviet period. Estonia saw rapid social and political changes and a wave of reform in the early 1990s. Neoliberal governance practices introduced the ideas of free markets to religion (Ringvee 2013).

The drafting of the new legislation took place in the midst of rapid religious change during the period of transition from Soviet rule to a fully functioning liberal democracy. As in other post-Communist countries this was also the period of rapid return to religion in individual and societal life. The number of baptisms and confirmations in the Estonian Evangelical Lutheran Church had grown tenfold since 1987; representatives of the Transcendental Meditation claimed to have 20,000 participants in their courses. The theological faculty at the University of Tartu was reopened, new charismatic and Pentecostal Christian groups opened new Bible schools and the 'church' was ranked among Estonia's most trustworthy institutions.

In 1993 Parliament adopted the Churches and Congregations Act (RT 1993). Although some Lutheran clergy argued that the Estonian Evangelical Lutheran Church, historically the majority church, deserved a special legal position and that there should be distinctions in legislation between 'old' and 'new' religions, such proposals did not gain wider support. The 1993 Churches and Congregations Act established a neoliberal governance practice concerning religion (Ringvee 2013). Under the law, all religious associations that were to be registered in accordance with this Act were equal. There were no distinctions between religious associations, either based on membership numbers or on their historical presence in Estonia. With the implementation of the 1993 Act, the responsibility for relations between the state and religious organisations was transferred from the Ministry of Culture to the Ministry of the Interior where a central register of churches and congregations was established.

In 1994 the first Non-profit Associations Act was adopted, defining religious associations as a special form of non-profit associations. The 1993 Churches and Congregations Act now became considered as a *lex specialis* for religious associations. In 1996 the Parliament adopted a new Non-Profit Associations Act that lifted the exemptions on religious associations. The President of the Republic, however, saw the Act as a violation of collective religious autonomy and refused to sign the law. The confrontation between the President and the Parliament ended with the Supreme Court decision in support of the President. As Parliament adopted a revised version of the Non-profit Associations Act, the Ministry of the Interior was ordered to draft a new Churches and Congregations Act that would take the changed legislation into account (Kiviorg 2016: 35–36). Parliament received the first draft of the new Act in 1998. The new Churches and Congregation Act was finally adopted in 2002 (RT 2002). The general principles regarding freedom of religion or belief remained intact. The changes in the 2002 Act were mainly technical; the most fundamental changes transferred the registration of religious associations as legal entities from the Ministry of the Interior to the Registrar's department of the court and replacing the Register of Churches and Congregation at the Ministry with the Register of Religious Association currently held by Tartu County Court.

During the drafting of the 2002 Churches and Congregations Act, representatives of the Estonian Evangelical Lutheran Church proposed an option for a religious association to become recognised under public law. This approach received criticism from other religious associations as legal experts alike (Kiviorg 2016: 37–38; Ringvee 2011: 93).

In 2004, Estonia joined the European Union. Although member states are free to define their own relations between governments and religious institutions, due to the diverse nature of these relations it could be argued that EU legislation has increased indirect regulation of religion in Estonia. The application of EU regulations on animal rights, as well as equal rights and gender equality caused conflicts of interest. Thus, in 2012 there were tense discussions between animal rights organisations and a Jewish community because the Ministry of Agriculture had drafted amendments to the Animal Protection Act that would have banned the slaughter of animals that had not been stunned. Protests from the Jewish community and from the Ministry of the Interior, which claimed that the ban violated religious freedom, led to a change in the draft. The exemption for religious slaughtering, introduced to Estonian legislation with the previous Animal Protection Act in 2001, also remained in place in the new Act. However, the new Act terminated the possibility of slaughtering on religious grounds outside of a registered slaughterhouse (Ringvee 2015c: 93–94). Interests of political decision makers and religious representatives have also clashed over other initiatives and legislation. The most publicised case concerns the debates over same-sex unions and the Registered Partnership Act that was adopted by the Parliament in 2014 (RT 2014). The reactions from religious communities and religious associations to the Registered Partnership Act have been largely negative; religious leaders have proposed that the

Constitution protect traditional marriage between one man and one woman (Viilma 2017).

4 The Legal Framework for Religious Freedom[1]

The 1992 Constitution of the Republic of Estonia lists freedom of religion as a fundamental right. The most important paragraph on freedom of religion is § 40, which ensures individual and collective freedom of religion or belief; enshrines the institutional separation of state and religion, and implicitly guarantees religious autonomy.

> Everyone has freedom of conscience, religion and thought. Everyone may freely belong to churches and religious societies. There is no state church. Everyone has the freedom to exercise his or her religion, both alone and in community with others, in public or in private, unless this is detrimental to public order, health or morals.

And § 41 adds:

> Everyone has the right to remain faithful to his or her opinions and beliefs. No one shall be compelled to change them. Beliefs shall not excuse a violation of the law. No one shall be held legally responsible because of his or her beliefs.

The rights of §§ 40 and 41 are protected in accordance with § 130 even in the case of emergency or in a state of war. Other rights and freedoms that are intrinsically connected to freedom of religion or belief and have Constitutional guarantees are equality (§ 12), freedom of expression (§ 45), the right to assemble (§ 47) and freedom of association (§ 48). According to § 9 (2) of the Constitution '[t]he rights, freedoms and duties set out in the Constitution shall extend to legal persons in so far as this is in accordance with the general aims of legal persons and with the nature of such rights, freedoms and duties.' Government agencies and local authorities are not allowed to gather or store information on person's religious convictions against her or his will (§ 42). Conscientious

---

[1] An updated free-access database containing Estonian legislation in both Estonian and English is available at the official website of *Riigi Teataja* (State Gazette) at www.riigiteataja.ee.

objection is protected in § 124 by guaranteeing the possibility for alternative service to service in the Defence Forces.

5 Churches and Congregations Act

In the Estonian legal framework, a 'religious association' is a legal entity with the status of a non-profit association, a person under private law, whose statute is registered in the Register of Religious Associations in accordance with the Churches and Congregations Act. The Churches and Congregations Act consists of seven chapters that set forth general provisions, principles for the protection of individual religious freedom; regulations for the foundation, registration, merger, division and dissolution of religious associations; procedures for the registration of religious associations, minister of religion, management boards, and assets of the association; procedures for the implementation of Act.

In Chapter 1 the purpose of the Act is set as protecting the Constitutional right to religious freedom. The Act sets forth a legal framework: requirements for foundation and, management, as well as membership procedures of religious associations as legal entities. The Churches and Congregations Act § 2 defines five types of religious associations: church, congregation, association of congregation, monastery, and church institution operating on the basis of an international agreement. The latter category was added to the Act in 2011. The only church in Estonia with an international agreement with the Estonian Government is the Roman Catholic Church (RT 1999a).

The Churches and Congregations Act defines a 'Church' (*kirik*) in § 2 (2) as an association of at least three voluntarily joined congregations that has an episcopal structure, and which is doctrinally related to three ecumenical creeds. In § 2 (3) of the Act, a 'congregation' (*kogudus*) is defined as a voluntary association of natural persons who profess the same faith. In § 2 (4) an 'association of congregations' (*koguduste liit*) is defined as a religious association of at least three congregations professing the same faith which have joined it voluntarily. According to § 2 (5) a 'monastery' (*klooster*) is a voluntary communal association of natural persons who profess the same faith, which operates on the basis of the statutes of the corresponding church or independent statutes, and is managed by an elected or appointed superior of the monastery.

In § 4 the Churches and Congregations Act defines a 'religious society' as a legal entity registered in accordance with the Non-profit Associations Act, which defined it as 'a voluntary association of natural or legal persons, the main activities of which include confessional or ecumenical activities.' Several religious communities in Estonia have acquired legal entity status as regular non-profit associations (not as 'religious societies'), which were registered in accordance with the Non-profit Associations Act (RT 1996). Some communities exist without any legal status.

Chapter 2 of the 2002 Churches and Congregations Act focuses on individual religious freedom. The minimum age to join or leave a religious association is 15. Religious associations may perform their rites in medical, educational, social welfare and custodial institutions and in the defence forces only with permission from the owner or the head of the institution. Besides the regular limits with regard to public order, health or morals, the limitations on religious freedom in these institutions include the rules and regulations of the institutions and the rights of others staying in or serving there.

Chapter 3 regulates the foundation, registration and dissolution of a religious association. According to § 13, a religious association must have at least 12 founding members over the age of 18 with active legal capacity. The association also needs a statute, the requirements for which are stipulated in § 12. The statute must include information on doctrine, obligatory rituals, the structure of management bodies and the principles of their formation. Additionally, the statute must contain information on the operation of a religious association, including rules concerning membership and procedures for terminating activities. The registrar shall not register the statute if the association's statute or other required documents are not in compliance with the requirements of the law, or if the activities of the religious association endanger the public order, health, morality or the rights and freedoms of others (§ 14 (2)). Chapter 4 of the Act regulates the maintenance of the Register of Religious Associations that is kept by the Tartu County Court.

In Chapter 5, the 2002 Churches and Congregations Act sets out requirements for a minister of religion as well as for the management board of a religious association. The only requirement for a minister of religion is to have the right to vote in local elections. The board of the religious association has the right to invite clergy from abroad and to apply for her or his residence permit in accordance with valid legislation.

Other requirements (including educational) for a minister of religion shall be set by the religious association. Guarantees for confessional secrecy are set in § 22: a minister of religion of a registered religious association 'shall not disclose information which has become known to him or her in the course of a private confession or pastoral conversation or the identity of a person who makes private confession to or has a pastoral conversation with the minister of religion.' Half of the members of a management board have to be residents in Estonia, another Member State of the European Economic Area, or

Switzerland. The Act does not set a requirement for the minimum or maximum number of board members, and exempts them from restrictions while in office.

In Chapter 6 the Churches and Congregations Act sets regulations for assets of religious association including the right to charge membership fees in accordance its association's statute as well as fees for religious rites, fundraising for specific purposes, accepting donations and lands and receiving income from its assets. Regulations for the implementation of the Act are set forth in Chapter 7.

6 Additional Legislation on Religion

Besides the Churches and Congregations Act, other legal acts directly or indirectly regulate individual and collective religion and religious activities. The Land Tax Act § 4 (1) exempts registered religious associations from land tax on land under places of worship (RT 1993b). According to the Income Tax Act § 11 religious associations are eligible for inclusion in the list of associations benefitting from income tax incentives (RT 1999b). In 2001, religious associations became eligible to apply for their clergy's right to officiate at civil marriages; this right is stipulated in the Family Law Act (RT 2009b). In § 6 this Act gives clergy the right to refuse to contract a marriage if the spouse(s) do not meet the requirements set by the religious association. Marriages contracted only on a religious basis have no legal validity or legal consequences in Estonia. The Vital Statistics Registration Act sets requirements for clergy eligible to perform the functions of vital statistics offices which respect to contracting a marriage. While every religious association is free to define who they consider as 'clergy,' the Act sets specific educational and other requirements for the applicant: a minimum age of 21, citizenship of Estonia, the European Union, a Member State of the European Economic Area or the Swiss Confederation, and proficiency in oral and written Estonian, the official language of Estonia (RT 2017). There are also certain exemptions for registered religious associations in Equal Treatment Act and Gender Equality Act with regard to work in a religious association (RT 2004).

Religious education is provided in Estonian public schools as a nondenominational voluntary subject. Approximately 10% of public schools offer religious education (Schihalejev & Ringvee 2017: 75). Religious associations are allowed to establish private schools under the Private School Act (RT 1998). While public schools can provide neutral religious education, private schools may provide denominational religious education. Governmental supervision of private schools does not differ from the general rules on private schools. The same principles for financing private schools from public funds apply to all private schools. In 2017 seven private primary schools were either directly owned by religious associations or by their affiliated legal entities. There are also three institutions of theological education owned by the Estonian Evangelical Lutheran Church, the Estonian Methodist Church and the Estonian Union of Evangelical Christian Baptist Churches.

Protection of the confessional secrecy by the Churches and Congregations Act is ensured in Code of Criminal Procedure § 72; clergy of registered religious organisations as well as their professional support staff are listed among those professionals who have the right to refuse testimony due to their profession (RT 2003). According to the Imprisonment Act §§ 26–27 prisoners have an unlimited right to uninterrupted meetings with their clergy and there may be visual, but no audio surveillance of these meetings (RT 2000). Imprisonment Act § 47 (3) states that prisoners have the right to have their religious dietary habits respected, and § 62 stipulates that the prison service should enable a prisoner to fulfil her or his religious obligations and needs.

In 2005 the right to wear religious headgear on document photos was granted by the decree of the Estonian Government; in 2009 this principle became part of the Identity Document Act (RT 2009a). Penal Code §§ 154 and 155 define violation of religious freedom as violation of a fundamental freedom and makes interference with either belonging or not-belonging to religion and interference with religious practices without legal grounds punishable. Freedom of religion or belief is protected by some laws (for example the Obligation to Leave and Prohibition of Entry Act) and the internal regulations of closed institutions. The Animal Protection Act has been regulated by the Minister of Agriculture since 2012 (RT 2012b). Chapter 41 of the Law Obligation Act regulates medical services and allows a patient, as much as possible, to choose medical treatment that is in accordance with her or his religious convictions (RT 2001b). The right to alternative service to military service, stipulated in § 124 of the 1992 Constitution, is regulated by the Military Service Act (RT 2012a).

7 Discussion

In Estonia the institutional separation of the state and religion, as stated in § 40 of the Constitution ('there is no state church') is a requirement for state neutrality (Maruste 2004: 522; Kiviorg 2016: 31). However, in Estonia state neutrality is not interpreted as excluding cooperation between the state and religious institutions. As Merilin Kiviorg (2012: 436–437) has noted, this (institutional) separation does not preclude the State from delegating certain public duties to religious associations. However, such delegation of duties may become a possible risk of preferential treatment of some religious associations (Maruste 2004: 522). There are few areas where the delegation of functions from the State to religious association has taken place.

There are, however, two positions in the chaplaincy service that require religious affiliation. The Military chaplaincy was re-established in Estonia in 1995, and as a reflection of that time, there is the requirement that the chief of chaplains in the Estonian Defence Forces must belong to the clergy of the Estonian Evangelical Lutheran Church. Since 1995, the job description of the adviser-chief of chaplains in the prison service at the Ministry of Justice requires the adviser-chief of chaplains to be ordained in a member church of the Estonian Council of Churches.

Regarding delegation of vital statistics office duties concerning contracting marriages with civil validity to clergy, preferential treatment is avoided. In October 2017, 115 ministers of religion from thirteen religious associations held this right (Ministry of the Interior 2018).

Although legislation has avoided preferential treatment of some religious associations, some religious institutions and organisations arguably have a more permanent dialogue with the state than others. Since the early 1990s, the two most active dialogue partners for the state have been the Estonian Evangelical Lutheran Church and the Estonian Council of Churches. While the Evangelical Lutheran Church has been the historical majority church, the Estonian Council of Churches is an ecumenical organisation established in 1989. The Estonian Council of Churches has always represented the majority of Estonia's Christian churches and congregational associations. Currently the member churches of the Council are the Estonian Evangelical Lutheran Church, the Estonian Apostolic Orthodox Church, the Estonian Orthodox Church of the Moscow Patriarchate, the Roman Catholic Church, the United Methodist Church in Estonia, the Estonian Christian Pentecostal Church, the Union of Evangelical Christian and Baptist Churches of Estonia, the Estonian Conference of the Seventh-day Adventist Church, the Charismatic Episcopal Church of Estonia, the Estonian Congregation St. Gregory of the Armenian Apostolic Church (Altnurme 2009).

In 1995 a joint commission was established between the Government of Estonia and the Estonian Evangelical Lutheran Church. The commission meets twice a year and is co-chaired by the Minister of the Interior and the Archbishop of the Evangelical Lutheran Church. In 2002, the Estonian government and the Estonian Council of Churches signed a protocol of concerns that marked areas of common interest, including social care, rehabilitation, education, and chaplaincy service (Protocol 2002). The delegation of the board of the Council of Churches meets once a year with the prime minister. In 2015 the Ministry of the Interior and the Estonian Council of Churches signed an agreement guaranteeing cooperation between the state and the Council (Agreement 2015). However, despite this relationship, neither dialogue partner for the state acquired any privileges or special treatment in legislation. Thus, for example, since 1992, the annual allocations from the state budget to the Estonian Council of Churches have become a tradition with no legal ground (Ringvee 2011: 53). It could be argued that financial allocations from the state or local government's budget to religious associations rely on political lobbying (Ringvee 2015a).

8   Conclusion

The idea of state neutrality on religion, articulated for the first time by the 1920 Estonian Constitution and the 1925 Religious Societies and their Associations Act was reintroduced after the reestablishment of Estonian independence. The 1992 Constitution guarantees the principles of freedom of religion and belief, and the Churches and Congregations Act from 1993 introduced legal egalitarianism among religious associations.

Current legislation on religion as well as relations between governmental and religious institutions in Estonia is the outcome of processes that started in the late 1980s and especially in the early 1990s, including rapid political, economic and social reforms. The ideas, ideals and ideologies of 1990s liberalism and neoliberalism were implemented in a secularised society.

Estonian legislation on religion and religious associations as legal entities reflects a situation in which most of the population is religiously unaffiliated, and religion is considered a private matter. The idea that state involvement in religion should be as minimal as possible, and that the free market of religions should regulate itself has been the norm since the early 1990s.

CHAPTER 6

The Influence of the European Union's Liberal Secularist Policy on Religion upon Religious Authority in Estonia Since 2004

Alar Kilp

1 Introduction

As a supranational institution, the European Union influences religious policy in its member states (Kilp 2017) and relations between religion and state in Eastern Europe (Berg, Kilp 2017). The question raised in this chapter is not whether the EU influences the politics of religion, but how the EU *wants* to influence the status of religious authorities in a country like Estonia, and what were the outcomes in the more than ten years that Estonia has been a member state.

The chapter consists of three sections. The first section presents the core arguments of the thesis of 'secularisation as the decline of religious authority' and presents four contextual conditions favouring either decline or changes in religious authority. The second section maps the politics of religion of the EU ('Eurosecularism') and identifies the tensions that are most likely to appear between the normative policies of the European Union and the authority that religious institutions enjoy in their national culture and politics. Finally, the chapter analyses the influence of the EU on religious authority in Estonia in the policy areas or ethnicity and sexuality. The conclusion is that the secularising impulse from the EU has been successful in the short-term, but in the longer perspective, this impulse has stirred up reactions, which have given new functions to religion and which have tended to revitalise religious authority.

2 Religious Authority

The decline of religious authority in society and politics is the main indicator of secularisation. However, decline of religious authority does not automatically mean that (functionally understood) religious needs cease to exist, disappear or remain unfulfilled. The theoretical approach taken in this chapter assumes that with the decline of religious authority, the existential, moral, social and political needs previously fulfilled by a religious institution remain unchanged; they will be fulfilled by other social authorities and political powers which operate with religious actors in the field of symbols, meanings, identities, norms and beliefs.

Religious authority declines for two reasons:

1. *De-institutionalisation and fragmentation of religion*. Like other types of organisational power, the power of a religious institution consists of the capability to define, guide and control ideas, moral norms, beliefs, values and behaviour of its members. The authority of an institution depends on the existence and strength of its institutional organisation.

2. *Differentiation of religion* (as defined and represented by an ecclesiastical organisation) *from non-religious spheres of social life*, leads to the emancipation of the latter from religion. As a result, religion loses its functions in non-religious fields.

In the historically Christian societies of Europe, traditional religious authority has been owned by a (single) religious institution (the church), which had specialised in religion vis-à-vis all other social institutions (Berger 1969: 123). The social and political authority of religion manifested in the church's ability 'to exercise authority over other institutional spheres' (Chaves 1994: 757) and to answers questions about the identity of humanity, societies, groups, families and individuals in a comprehensive way (Monsma 1993: 161; Wilson 1982: 34).

As religious authority manifested itself in the social status and political influence of the church, its foundation was laid by *connections* among a religious institution, social forces and political ideologies within a (European) social context (Therborn 1999: 35–36). Correspondingly, to the extent that religious institutions lose their functions in public life and for the political community, 'functionally religious needs' (Dobbelaere 2006: 143) will be handled in non-religious spheres which have emancipated themselves from religious authority. Besides politics and economy (Weber 1958), areas such as eroticism and aesthetics (Weber 1946: 323–359) are emancipated from religious authorities and sacralise their own values, such as the nation, race, state, class, work (Bell 1976: 156), or consumerism (Baudrillard 1998: 94).

The thesis of declining religious authority (and its corollary, the theory of secularisation) is an analytical and theoretical thesis, not a self-evident and universal empirical fact. The rise or decline of a religious authority depends on the following four conditions.

The authority of a religious institution is always contextual and particular. Each argument concerning a declining religious authority is a statement regarding the status of a particular institution in a given historic and contextual environment. There is no self-evident relationship between modernisation and the status of religious authority, because – depending on the socio-historical context, political regime and other variables – religious authority may both decline and rise during the processes of modernisation.

The *decline of the former type* of religious authority has often occurred simultaneously with the *rise* of a *new type* of religious authority. In early modern Europe, confessional Catholicism and Protestantism replaced universal Catholicism; new forms of political Christianity *obtained* authority and were sacralised at the time when the earlier religious authority of universal Catholicism was weakened (Kilp 2012: 16). In other instances, previous *religious* beliefs and institutions have been replaced by non-religious ideologies and institutions. Consequently, if secularisation is defined as the decline of religious authority and the need for religion is assumed to be constant, then each phase of secularisation ought to bring along a new (explicit or implicit, organisational or informal, ideological or religious) 'system of belief' (Tschannen 1991: 401, 408), which will be considered sacred by its followers just as traditional Christian beliefs were for Christians in a Christian society (Smith 1974: 8).

The thesis of the decline of religious authority is not about the decline (or rise) ingeneral religious quest and interest. Secularisation occurs when traditional religious authorities, 'institutionalized, hierarchical forms of religion, and established religious practices' are losing social support (Norris, Inglehart 2004: 4–5, 75). There is no self-evident relationship between religion and secularisation (as a decline of religious authority). Religion can be either negatively or positively related to secularisation (Smith 1974: 4, 7). In the 19th century, several European states were emancipated from the church in the realms of political legitimisation and cultural socialisation (education), while the degree of religious practice and affiliation was rising as confessional Christianity was being replaced by Christian nationalism. However, the autonomous authority and influence of the church over society and politics had declined (Kilp 2012: 11–12).

The explicitly religious authority of a religious institution depends on its ability to (monopolise) control the field of religious belief and practice. Additionally, for religion to be effective in the political sphere, religion should also have a positive function in society, culture and politics regarding what is considered sacred. The most likely functions fulfilled and retained by traditional religious institutions in the post-communist countries of Europe, are the social function of keeper of collective memory (Hervieu-Léger 1998: 23, 25); the cultural function of symbolic embodiment of the collective identity (Bruce 2002: 33); and the political function of marker of the national identity (Bruce 1999: 271).

3 The Politics of Religion of the European Union

The politics of religion of the European Union is characterised by a degree of moderate and practical, not ideological secularism (Modood 2010: 5). The states and cultures of Western Europe have been most in accordance with 'Eurosecularity' (Berger 2005: 112–119) which allows national variations in church-state relationships. In comparison with the United States, it is less committed to formal separation of church and state. The European Union's comprehensive and normative approach to religion in public life is characterised by the following principles:

1. Religious law and explicit references to the will of God are excluded from public debate aimed at taking binding decisions (Ferrari 2010: 761). As a result, the scope of authoritative religious content in electoral campaigns, party politics and political legitimisation is diminished (Habermas 2011: 17, 21, 24).
2. Religious actors in public politics have to express themselves in a secular 'language and through arguments that everyone can understand' (Ferrari 2010: 762).
3. The room for 'sacred values' in society and culture is narrow (Klausen 2009: 294), although the separation of church and state does not apply to all spheres of public life or to all religious traditions. Most European states collaborate with religious institutions that represent the historic religious traditions of the society. At the same time, religion and politics are expected to be separate 'for modern liberal democratic politics, for global peace and for the protection of individual privatized religious freedom' (Casanova 2008: 64, 67).

As far as religion is concerned, 'Eurosecularism' strives for the separation of religion and politics and for the protection of religion as a private matter. As is typical of ideological ideas, European secularism has acquired the status of a foundational myth of European identity (Casanova 2008: 64). Correspondingly, even in countries with established churches (such as Denmark or the U.K.), the ideal of the separation of religion and politics is still operative. As far as its sacred phenomena are concerned, Eurosecularism is committed to secular (and not religious) values (Foret 2015) such as democracy, citizenship, human rights, the rule of law, tolerance, peace, liberty, and anti-discrimination (Gearon 2012: 160; Larsen 2014: 426; Manners 2002: 242–243).

4 Eurosecularism in the Post-Soviet Context

In comparison with the West-European societies, religion in post-communist East-Central Europe has been far less privatised and individualised, because the involvement of Communist regimes in regulating the religion was greater, and the market for production and consumption of religion was less free. As a result, Communist regimes did not enhance religious modernisation, the development of religious individualisation and innovation, nor the de-traditionalising of religion (Kilp 2012: 18).

It may sound paradoxical, but traditional religion survived under Communist regimes better than it did in liberal Western European cultures. We tend to assume that socialist regimes 'ought to have caused or contributed to secularization', and to expect that post-Soviet societies are more secularised than those in Western Europe. Quite the contrary; when EU expansion to East-Central Europe began in 2004, Peter L. Berger argued that the latter, particularly Catholic Poland and Orthodox Romania, would receive 'Eurosecularism' with the rest of the package:

> Countries are pulled into secularity to the degree by which they are integrated into Europe. Integration into Europe means signing on to Eurosecularity (the legal norms, after all, are contained in the famous EU acquis) along with the rest of the 'Europe package'. This is already noticeable in Ireland and Poland. I doubt whether Eastern Orthodoxy will provide immunity against this cultural penetration.
> BERGER 2005: 113

As a result, the countries that wanted to become members of the European Union had to adapt their national legislation of church-state relations to comply with European human rights standards (Schanda 2003: 333). And when Turkey has wanted to join the European Union, the debate over its potential integration into the EU raised a discussion on whether Turkey's type of secularism is in accordance with the type of secularism that is normative in the EU (Hurd 2006).

Indeed, Catholic Poland and Orthodox Romania – one could also add Catholic Malta and predominantly Orthodox Cyprus, which acceded to the EU in the same wave (2004–2007), but did not share the previous experience of Communist regimes – are among most religious societies in Europe. The secularising effect of the EU may sound plausible, but what about Estonia, which has the least religiously affiliated society in Europe (where about one-quarter of the ethnic Estonian population is affiliated with a religion)? Can the EU contribute to secularisation (and to the decline of religious authority) even in Estonia?

Before analysing the interaction between the EU and religious authority in Estonia, it must be emphasised that the ideological attempt of Communist regimes to secularise 'from above' (Smith 1974: 8) was most successful in Protestant societies, where pre-Communist struggles between church and state had already weakened the organisational authority of traditional churches over their lay members and their authority vis-à-vis the secular state (Kilp 2012: 19).

In the post-communist space of Europe, Estonia is a special case, because until the mid-19th century it was exclusively Lutheran and lacked the considerable social presence of the Catholic Church. (For example, traditionally Lutheran Latvia has always had a sizable Catholic minority).

Even in Estonia, the secularising intentions of the EU have brought along desecularising reactions in the policy domains related to the rights and legal norms of ethnic and sexual minorities.

5 Civic Nationalism vs. Ethno-religious Cultural Nationalism

The European approach to political nationalism considers religious and national identities flexible but volatile sources of identity, which are now individualised, de-confessionalised and distanced from ethnonational context and history (Agadjanian 2015: 23). The transition from religious states to civic nationalism had taken place in 19th century Europe, when religions whose functions in public life no longer maintained them on the basis of dogmatic and confessional religion, but rather on the basis of civil religion (Rousseau 1950: 134–135; Ferrari 2010). However, in East-Central European countries, religion and political-national identity merge (Spohn 2003: 266, 271), and ethnic and religious identities as well as political and ethnic identities tend to overlap.

Consequently, we can imagine a situation in which a church which is not successful in purely religious terms (the number of adherents and regular participants in its services) may still maintain functions vis-à-vis what is considered sacred in (national) secular culture and therefore enjoy some religious authority. When religion functions as a symbol of national or ethnic community and identity, then this concerns all individuals who belong to these cultural communities, regardless of their religiosity and sense of religious belonging (Kilp 2012: 52).

If the European Union replaces ethno-nationalist political culture with civic nationalism, it weakens the status of the dominant ethnic identity and the authority of a religious institution that operates as the cultural representative of the national or ethnic religion.

In this dimension, the secularising influence of the EU was manifest in Estonia prior to its accession to the EU in 2004. Between 2001 and 2004 there was a period of integration of predominantly Russian-speaking ethnic minorities into the national community. In this period, the ethnic cleavage in party politics weakened; in 2003 the ethnic party of the Russian minority lost its seats in the national parliament; the attitude toward ethnic issues was multicultural and consensus-seeking due to the need to meet the norms of multiculturalism and political correctness required for accession to the EU (Ehala 2009: 152). In this period, it was considered a normal, self-evident and legitimate goal to integrate the Russian-speaking minority (about one-third of the Estonian population) into the civil society space of one common participatory democracy.

However, after Estonia's accession to the European Union, the main split in the presidential elections of 2006, and the parliamentary elections of 2007 and 2011 was along ethnic lines. In 2006, Toomas Hendrik Ilves was elected to the presidency after a campaign in which candidates from nationalist parties confronted the candidacy of the incumbent Arnold Rüütel who was supported by the People's Union and the Centre Party, the party system's 'internal others'. Earlier, Toomas Hendrik Ilves had written a preface to the Estonian translation of Samuel P. Huntington's *Clash of Civilizations and the Remaking of World Order* (1999), where he argued that Estonianness and Lutheranism were historically related and that this relation was manifested in the way Estonians behave (Ilves 1999: 18). Although his conceptualisation of the Lutheranism of Estonians was mostly instrumental with respect to the argument that Estonians are Europeans and thus naturally belong to the European Union, Ilves' conceptualisation of religion was essentially cultural. His approach focussed 'on affective and identity-oriented functions' (Williams 1996: 379) fulfilled by Lutheranism in Estonian culture. In contrast to President Rüütel, who had an amicable relationship with the Patriarch of Moscow Alexy II (Kilp 2013: 323), and was one of the main patrons of the inter-ethnic integration policy before the accession to the EU, Ilves' orientation was also pro-West, pro-EU and pro-NATO. Slowly but surely, the emerging political polarisation spilled over to the electorate and civil society.

The 2007 parliamentary elections were followed by riots at the end of April, related to the statue of the Bronze Soldier, when about two thousand Russian-speaking youth vandalised the Tallinn city center. The statue of the Bronze Soldier had been erected under the Soviet regime in memory of soldiers who had fallen in the Second World War. The cultural confrontation over the statue was framed in the form of two opposing understandings of history. For many Estonians, the Bronze Soldier symbolised the Soviet occupation of their country. For many Russian speakers it symbolized the liberation of Estonia from fascist occupation (Brüggemann, Kasekamp 2008: 429). It is not known exactly how many on either side understood history so uniformly and exclusively based on their cultural identity. Be this as it may, the perception of two monolithical cultural communities was consolidated in the months after the relocation of the Bronze Soldier by the Estonian government from the Tallinn city centre to the Defence Forces Cemetery of Tallinn. Such public discourses would have been counterproductive with respect to the accession to the EU between 2001 and 2004.

The ethnic confrontation over the Bronze Soldier politicised a secular symbol. Even though Estonia's Russian speakers are overwhelmingly Orthodox, and that for ethnic Estonians Lutheran Christianity is the national religious tradition, the parties clashing over the Bronze Soldier were neither supported by religious leaders, nor was the conflict reproduced in the field of religion.

On 27 April 2007 the Council of Estonian Churches, which unites the ten largest Christian churches including the Estonian Evangelical Lutheran Church and the Estonian Orthodox Church of the Moscow Patriarchate, called upon all parties to avoid hatred and chaos; to promote peace and dialogue and to live as 'one community' in a small Estonia despite their differences of opinion.

In the 2011 parliamentary elections, the main political division for interparty competition fell along ethnic lines, yet this time several churches had become symbols of ethnic identity that were used by political parties. On 20 February 2011, two weeks before the election, the opponents of the Centre Party (the largest opposition party) celebrated the reopening of St John's (Lutheran) church in St Petersburg with a religious service, where the Estonian president, the foreign minister and the minister of culture argued that this church symbolised Estonianness, the Estonian national movement, and the Estonian culture. In March 1917, when Estonia was still part of tsarist Russia, a rally for autonomy for Estonia was held at the doors of this church.

One day earlier, on 19 February 2011, the mayor of Tallinn and Edgar Savisaar, leader of the Center Party participated in the consecration of the cross of the Orthodox Church of the Icon of the Mother of God 'Quick to Hearken' of the Estonian Orthodox Church of the Moscow Patriarchate (EOCMP) in Tallinn's Lasnamäe district. Savisaar had admitted in a press conference that he planned the Lasnamäe religious service to make a positive impression on the district's 115,000 Russian-speaking inhabitants, and that in scheduling the event, he was using the same tactic used by parties that had scheduled the reopening of St John's Church in St Petersburg in the final phase of the electoral campaign (Kilp 2013: 315). Consequently, the Orthodox Church in Tallinn's Lasnamäe district became an ethnic and cultural symbol of the Russian-speaking minority in Estonia just as St John's church was a symbol of Lutheran Estonianness in St Petersburg. The religious services at these sites served 'the function of exclusion by drawing symbolic boundaries between the national government and the opposition; between the Estonian cultural mainstream and the Russophone minority culture' (Pankhurst, Kilp 2013: 236).

From the perspectives of secularisation and religious authority, both sides of the confrontation involve the religion into which one is born, not the religion to which one belongs by his or her own choice or through religious participation. This sense of belonging can be called ethnic Christianity (Storm 2011), collectivist religion (Jakelić 2010) or cultural Christianity (Demerath 2000). When such a religious-symbolic connection between the nation and a church becomes stronger (either in their self-perception or the cultural other) that connection can continue to be strengthened with or without the sense of belonging to the church. Among ethnic Estonians there was no identifiable rise in church affiliation from 2000 until 2011. As described in the chapter on the Orthodox Church, the 2011 national census showed the forthcoming of Orthodoxy. Fifty percent of the Russian-speaking population in Estonia identified with religion (overwhelmingly with Orthodoxy), while only 19 percent of Estonian speakers identified with a religion. Thus, the identification of Estonian speakers with religion (and with Lutheranism) has slightly decreased, while Russian speakers in Estonia increasingly identify with Orthodoxy.

In general, Estonian political *culture* is and remains secularised: in electoral campaigns, appeals are not made to religious arguments; churches do not make distinctions among political parties; the parliament does not include any explicitly religious party or even or even a single party committed to Christian democracy. Additionally, the politicisation of cultural religious identities has been pursued by political actors (Pankhurst, Kilp 2013: 236), not religious ones. However, the religious symbolism that is represented by churches and that defines the cultural identity and the national community, again became important – or more important after the accession of Estonia to the EU.

How should we interpret this finding in the light of secularisation, defined as the decline of religious authority? For ethnic Estonians, identification with Lutheranism seems to have taken place for cultural and political reasons, and not for reasons directly related to church or religion. Religious symbols in the form of church buildings and ceremonial religious rituals have been important politically (particularly during electoral campaigns), but their essence and meaning remains secular:

> To the extent that the religio-political symbiosis is not accompanied by a predominant membership in a related religious tradition, the religion that is functional in this symbiosis is represented singularly by a *political community,* the sense of affiliation is singularly *political.* The sacralized political community retains its connections to religious symbols, but has become autonomous from a religious institution.
>
> KILP 2011: 173

At the same time, religious symbols of culture carry power or are signs of authority. By means of religious buildings, which attain politically relevant symbolic status, boundaries can be drawn between cultural communities, which cannot be drawn physically, visibly and legally (Kilp 2013: 322). The religious substance and autonomous influence of religious institutions remains minimal, while their political function remains highly relevant.

6   The Liberalisation of Legal Norms Regulating Sexuality

In the policy area of 'moral issues', the European Union is strongly committed to individual autonomy (McCrea 2010: 10), which tends to consistent with the laws on sexuality in the largest West-European EU member states, where clerical control over individual choices has been significantly weakened since the 1960s (Klausen 2009: 292; Thomas 2005: 110). Since then, religious institutions in Western Europe have lost much of their authority over the social definition of marriage in three dimensions: *legally,* due to the liberalisation of laws on sexuality and marriage (Kilp 2009: 70–71); *socially,* as people's preferences and ways of life have changed (Ben Porat 2013: 24) and *religiously,* as *internal* secularisation took place in religious associations (Casanova 1994: 22), whereby members of religious associations accommodated liberal social values.

It is particularly important to notice that a situation emerged where moral norms, which had previously regulated sexual behaviour and gender relations among church members, no longer overlapped with the norms of behaviour that operated in society or with the newly adopted legal norms. As a result, churches lost their moral authority 'to define what people should believe, practice and accept as moral principles guiding their lives' (Dobbelaere 2006: 142). Churches did not necessarily lose authority over church members, but more importantly they lost authority over those members of society who were 'not churchgoing', 'not believing', and 'did not believe in belonging' (Christoffersen 2006: 118).

During the 1990s, the European Union became a supranational actor instrumental in bringing about the globalisation of normative conflicts, those that centred on public morality and social identity (Berger 1998: 352). The EU had become one of the main supranational actors promoting the decriminalisation of homosexuality in Europe (Hildebrandt 2014: 230). More recently, within the EU there has emerged 'a new establishment', which in Julian Rivers' assessment has elevated respect for the choice of the individual to determine his or her sexual identity and replaced the heterosexist patriarchy with an ethic of gender equality (Rivers 2007: 24, 33, 38, 41). At present, the protection of the LGBT rights has become one of the pillars of 'a model of European citizenship based on the continent's unique role as guarantor of human rights' (Ammaturo 2015: 1152).

The EU's commitment to a principle whereby all human rights apply to homosexuals as they apply to heterosexuals is explicitly articulated in the 2013 'Guidelines to Promote and Protect the Enjoyment of All Human Rights by Lesbian, Gay, Bisexual, Transgender and Intersex (LGBTI) Persons' which states:

> LGBTI persons have the same rights as all other individuals – no new human rights are created for them and none should be denied to them. The EU is committed to the principle of the universality of human rights and reaffirms that cultural, traditional or religious values cannot be invoked to justify any form of discrimination, including discrimination against LGBTI persons.
> THE COUNCIL OF THE EUROPEAN UNION 2013

Since the shaping of members' behaviour and attitudes according to certain ethical standards and norms has traditionally been a core role of religion (Monsma 1993: 161), churches in East-Central Europe tend to participate in public debates, when the possibility of legal recognition of same-sex partnerships or cohabitations as forms of family becomes realistic. To avoid the veto power of religious institutions, EU guidelines for the protection of the rights of LGBTI persons emphasise that 'cultural, traditional or religious values cannot be invoked to justify any form of discrimination, including discrimination against LGBTI persons' (The Council of the European Union 2013). The EU appreciates national patterns of church-state relations and the preferential treatment of culturally traditional religions by states and governments, but for the EU, traditional religions cannot control or limit the protection of human rights of the LGBTI.

Outside of the European Union (for example in Latin American countries such as Argentina or Uruguay), high levels of social approval of homosexuality have been present at the moment of adoption of laws recognising same-sex unions, while among members of the European Union (e.g., Malta, where same-sex unions were legally recognised in 2014) such laws can be passed without significant social support and without 'a demand from below' (Kilp 2015: 117).

Thus, the EU can undermine the authority of religious institutions when religious institutions have the social authority to define the family and the norms that should govern sexual relations in ways that the EU does not.

What social authority do Estonian churches have regarding policies related to the legal recognition of same-sex couples? Indeed, they do have a degree of authority, but there is certainly also opposition to the legal recognition of same-sex couples which is secular in origin. In a country where the percentage of people who disapprove of homosexuality is significantly higher than the percentage of the people claiming to belong to a religious tradition, attitudes on homosexuality must also have a non-religious and secular basis.

In Estonia, homosexuality was decriminalised in 1992. In the Soviet Union, homosexuality had been criminalised since 1933/1934 (Zorgdrager 2013: 219). Thus, the policy legacy of the Soviet Union can partially explain the rather high disapproval of homosexuality in Estonia. However, in contrast to the Soviet Union, where the ban on homosexuality represented the social authority of the anticlerical Communist party and Communist ideology and where the cleavage between liberals and conservatives was between secular parties, *after* the dissolution of the Soviet Union, conservative value orientations were linked to the adherence to religious authority (Kniss 2003: 335).

Public discussion of the legal recognition of same-sex families began in 2009, when a draft of the Cohabitation Act was included in the Estonian Parliament's and the Government's agenda. At that time, there was no significant social demand for the adoption of this law and according to World Values Survey, social disapproval of homosexuality had declined from about 60% in 1996 to 41.4% by 2011. Like many other countries of the European Union, in Estonia it was first and foremost the state – the parliament or the government – which was willing to accommodate the norms of the EU and which, in its attempts to reconcile national legislation with European law, came into conflict with the religious elite and with social attitudes.

Until 2014, the legal initiative lacked government support, which had included a national-minded conservative union Pro Patria (Isamaa) and the Res Publica parties. On 26 March 2014, the situation changed, when the liberal-right Reform Party and the Social Democrats formed a new parliamentary coalition. In the summer of 2014, there was heated public discussion over the draft law. On 9 October 2014, the Estonian Parliament passed the gender-neutral Cohabitation Act, which recognised the lifestyle choices of unmarried same-sex and opposite-sex couples. The Act went into effect on 1 January 2016 without the Parliament having passed the provisions required for its full implementation. Given that implementation requires the support of an absolute parliamentary majority (51 of 101 members), as of March 2021, the law lacked sufficient support.

In August 2014, Estonian Public Broadcasting had ordered a national poll, which demonstrated that only 40% of Estonians supported the gender-neutral Cohabitation Act (in 2012 the support rate had been 51%). Among non-ethnically Estonian respondents, the support rate was even lower at 17%. This indicates that the adoption of this law was not the result of social demand and that support for such a law even decreased during its adoption.

The religious elite (either leaders of the dominant religious organisations individually or together in the form of public addresses by the Council of Estonian Churches) unanimously condemned the Cohabitation Act. To assert their moral authority, the Christian churches of Estonia have adopted a united ecumenical conservative Christian moral position. In their public statements they have rejected the Cohabitation Act, and expressed concerns about the autonomy of religious associations to maintain heteronormative positions on sexuality and marriage without risking legal consequences. On 28 September 2012, the Estonian Council of Churches (ECC) published its Position on the Concept of the Cohabitation Act, arguing that when religious ministers take public positions stemming from their church doctrine on the homosexual lifestyle, it cannot be determined whether people with different viewpoints may not consider this as a systematic incitement to hatred or discrimination. On 30 April 2014, the Estonian Council of Churches published an address to the Estonian Parliament where they argued that the adoption of the Cohabitation bill might pose a serious security threat, because it polarises Estonian society and forces non-Estonians, who do not agree with the abandonment of traditional European values, to seek support from the Orthodox culture area and the Russian state, where traditional marriage and family are sacrosanct.

By redefining the legitimate forms of family, the Cohabitation Act can be seen as an act of the state that transforms the Estonian population's common-sense understandings of what a family is. The Cohabitation Act has attempted to undermine the social and cultural authority of Christian churches, because it has empowered the state against the dominant churches of Estonia by establishing a new set of legally recognised forms of family that do not correspond to the norms, will and practice of the Christian churches.

With the exception of the Cohabitation Act, there have been no significant conflicts in the between Estonia's religious and political elites in the past decade. The Estonian party system lacks the Christian parties that exist in Scandinavian parliaments and the Christian Democratic parties, which are the major conservative pro-church parties in continental Western Europe. In Estonia, religious rhetoric is absent from daily politics or, when it is used, it is assumed that Christian values operating in Estonian politics are defined by the political elite and are represented by the ideological positions of all parliamentary parties (Kilp 2009: 70–71).

Paradoxically, while the traditional religion of Estonians, Lutheranism, is losing adherents, it retains a degree of social authority in the policy area of the rights of homosexuals, when supported by other religious confessions, by socially prevalent traditionalist value orientations and also by the Conservative People's Party, which entered the Parliament in March 2015. It is quite likely that without the secularising impulse stemming from the EU and the reaction of Estonian civil society, the social authority of the Lutheran Church could be weaker than it is at the present.

7 Conclusion: What Can Be Generalised?

The perceived threat to norms and value systems is rising virtually everywhere in Europe along with a demand for greater cultural and religious homogeneity (Ben-Nun Bloom, Arikan, Sommer 2014: 274). What seems to be at stake is cultural homogeneity and cultural unity, in a situation where societies are seeking unity among the diversity of nations, ethnicities, nationalities, sub-national and immigrant minorities, religious traditions, languages, social, cultural and ideological attitudes (McCormick 2010: 6).

When religion is part of these processes, it is less about religious practice, belief or doctrine, than it is about identity (Segato 2008: 210) or religion as a way of expressing an identity, status or claim (Schlesinger, Foret 2006: 61).

In this regard, Western and Eastern European countries are quite similar: the religion at stake is the one which in one form or another is publicly perceived to have a connection to history, memory, tradition, ways of life, beliefs and identities. This chapter has discussed the processes, where 'who we as Estonians are' and 'what types of relationships are included into the concept of family among us' are similar to 'the politics of nativism' (Casanova 2012) in Western Europe, where 'Christian natives' are distinguished from 'Muslim immigrants' (Carol, Helbling, Michalowski 2015: 647–671). In both, religion is conceived culturally. In both, the sacred is defined by secular society and culture. In both, we may be witnessing the rise of a new form of *religion-as-culture*.

CHAPTER 7

The Religious Turn in Estonia
Modern Self-understanding in a Flood of Esotericism

Lea Altnurme

1   Introduction

1.1   *Christianity: Secularisation*

The drastic decrease in the importance of Christianity among ethnic Estonians is undisputable. If 160 years ago Christianity was still highly influential as a central unifying ideology, its position today has become marginal (Altnurme 2013a: 36–55). Estonians have accepted this state of affairs and redirected it toward a self-image based on nationalist, modern values, 'one of the European nations farthest from religion', an attitude that accompanies an imagination of success-mindedness. In view of various sociological questionnaires, approximately one-fifth of ethnic Estonians define themselves as Christian.

The spread of secular worldviews in Estonia gained momentum at the beginning of the 20th century. In the course of their education, students were increasingly exposed to a scientific-materialist worldview. In the growing cities and industrial regions, leftist worldviews and ideologies found resonance. For historical reasons, Estonia was characterised by a hostility to Christianity due to socialist influences in national ideology that stressed modern values; this hostility was amplified under Soviet rule. Under an atheism campaign (1958–1964), extensive secularisation took place (Altnurme, 2013: 36–45).

Modern values such as belief in progress, science, technology, education and culture have driven Estonian development in a liberal market economy since 1991, after the restoration of independence. Estonians are proud of their rapid economic growth, the success of the digital society, their love of education and innovation; their children's high scores on the international Program for International Student Assessment (PISA) tests; the fact that they have the longest bookshelves in the world, their higher than average consumption of culture (Lauristin, Vihalemm 2017: 223–250) and their world-class cultural life. Estonians also connect religion with culture less than average Europeans (Lauristin, Vihalemm 2017: 224). Even animated films convey modern values, such as the popular *Lotte of Invention Village*, manufactured in Estonia.

Modernity is characterised by belief in human reason, capabilities and creativity. In 2014, 83% of Estonians placed their belief only in themselves and their capabilities (RTE 2014). It should be added that since the restoration of independence, the number of Estonians, particularly young ones, who have been looking beyond national borders has continued to grow; young people consider themselves carriers of a unified culture based on European liberal values in which religion is marginal. On this basis, the image of Estonia as a religion-free nation has spread across Estonia. The reference point for self-designations such as 'atheist', 'non-religious', 'indifferent to religion' is Christianity. Due to its cultural self-evidence, sociological surveys often state this imprecisely. An estimated one-third of Estonians designate themselves as atheist, non-religious or indifferent to religion.

1.2 *New Spirituality*

In other countries, New Age or new spirituality has emerged since the 1970s. The New Age movement arose during the cultural turn of the 1960s as a part of the counterculture; its structure of ideas reflects an intensified individualisation with respect to society. The new phenomena have been defined and designated in the scholarly literature of religion: *new spirituality movements and culture* (Shimazono, 1999); *occulture* (Partridge, 2004); *alternative spirituality* (Sutcliffe, 2004); *holistic milieu* (Heelas, Woodhead, 2005); *New Age religion* (Hammer, 2010); *new spirituality* or *new spiritualities* (Berghuijs, Pieper, Bakker, 2013); *New Age religiosity* (Andersen, Gundelach, Lüchau, 2013); *New Age culture* (Huss, 2014).

In this chapter the concepts of New Age and new spirituality are used in parallel, marking the production of an environment and a globally disseminated religious culture. The teaching and practices of new spirituality have spread through books and magazines, and through internet portals, forums, films, television and radio shows. In such contexts people create and spread their cultural tastes and values as expressed by modalities such as music, dance, and the visual arts. Cults are organised in the form of groups, training groups, lectures, seminars, discussion groups, camps, festivals. In this environment there are spiritual leaders, teachers, facilitators of groups and practices and organisers of all kinds of activities, that is to say a great number of activists. We should also mention those active in creating art, participants in activities and practices (long-term or need-based), lifestyle practitioners, who constitute communes, communities and relationship networks whose influence extends beyond the borders of the culture.

New Age discourse emphasises spiritual self-development. Its teachings and practices are directed toward the fulfillment of individual needs, even in the case of group activities. As opposed to prescribed teachings, personal experience is regarded as most important, following the principle 'find what is right for you, what works for you'. To find what is right it is suggested to use one's intuition and to avoid rational deliberations. Through repeated calls to 'walk your own path', 'become aware that you are the creator of your world', and emphasis on personal experience as the final authority, participants' thinking of themselves as creators of their own, original spirituality is facilitated. There is a rich variety of sources in New Age culture that inspires and facilitates such self-creation; most of it derives from five sources: psychology and alternative medicine; esotericism and occultism; Eastern religions, primarily Buddhism, Hinduism and Taoism; natural sciences and science fiction; tribal cultures and eco-movements. Such rich material permits the creation of individual syncretic mixes based on a discourse of self-development. The concept of endless spiritual quest and self-realisation is set in opposition to religion, which New Age culture regards as dogmatic and restrictive of human development. Terms such as self-spirituality (Heelas 1996: 18), me-spirituality (Stoltz et al., 2016: 102) or me-centredness (Stolz et al 2016: 101) have been used in the scholarly literature to mark the discourse of an individual walking the path of spiritual development.

The discourse of self-spirituality and syncretic mixes may lead one to imagine that people are themselves creators of their own religion, and that such creations are entirely different from one another. Such a view applies not only to participants in the new spirituality, but also to those who stand outside organised forms of religion, people with individual religiosity, who claim that their religion is their own. However, neither version of this view finds support. Indeed, it is easy to recognise participants in New Age culture by their persistent self-oriented spirituality and repetitious beliefs, practices, attitudes and value judgements. If everyone had their own thoroughly subjective religion, this concordance would not be possible. Self-oriented spirituality is not created by each person, but is acquired through the influence of New Age culture (Hammer 2010: 49–67; Versteeg, Roeland 2014: 102–105). The same obtains for individual religiosity. The content of individual religiosity (at least as assessed by scholarly research) is primarily drawn from the surrounding cultural space, and its variability is quite limited (Altnurme 2012: 193–212).

The ideas and practices of new spirituality arrived in Estonia during the 1960s and 1970s, but were limited to the hippie movement and a circle of young artists and educated people searching for alternative ways of thinking and living. In the 1980s the influence of new spirituality broadened through the circulation of illegal manuscripts. People practiced on their own or in circles of acquaintances; they gathered around local leaders. Around the same time, the first half-public yoga and meditation groups were organised, and meetings were arranged with spiritual teachers and the most popular spiritual healers.

The mass dissemination of global New Age culture and the emergence of its local version took place during the Singing Revolution of 1987–1991. By the end of the 1990s, Estonians had begun to distance themselves from the New Age self-designation. Though it began as a movement of alternative spirituality, the New Age movement has become a part of the mainstream (Uibu 2016: 262). On a social level, attitudes toward New Age culture have generally been tolerant, because it is not considered a religion. Nevertheless, there are signs of skepticism (Uibu 2012: 337–357). According to sociological surveys, at least a third of Estonians designate themselves as 'spiritual but not religious'.

1.3 Native Faith

Around the time new spirituality arrived in Estonia in the 1970s, a movement was gaining ground among educated Estonians. It was a second wave of Finno-Ugric brotherhood, intended to strengthen national identity in opposition to Soviet ideology. These circles stressed Finno-Ugric peoples' (including Estonians') closeness to nature (Kuutma 2005: 56). This was by no means a new idea: it had been articulated almost a half century earlier by Oskar Loorits, who idealised ancient Estonians as a people who lived in harmony with nature (Loorits 1990: 44–47). Under the influence of theologian and mystic Uku Masing, the myth of ancient borealic culture began to spread. According to this myth, Estonians belonged to a unified culture of northern peoples with an ancient feeling for nature. This was not a new idea; it existed in 19th-century Baltic German colonial discourse (Plath 2008: 56), but 100 years later it had been appropriated.

The belief in Estonians' special sensitivity to nature became a component of national self-determination, which stressed modern values, and the simultaneous process of building an industrial society. The latter coincided with the destruction of peasant culture, urbanisation, pollution, waste and the squandering of natural resources. Indeed, conservation became a national question, and thus one can hardly be astonished that the Singing Revolution was triggered by the Soviet Union's centralised plan for extensive phosphorite mining in 1987. In such an atmosphere, native faith (in Estonian *maausk*, literally meaning faith in the land/earth) evolved, entailing belief in a living and animated nature. From a scholarly perspective, this is equivalent to the new paganism, but practitioners of native faith would disagree, emphasising the role of authentic folk heritage and customs (Västrik 2015: 130). Nevertheless, the influences of Finno-Ugric kinship, borealism and nationalism can clearly be seen, though native faith has ceased to emphasise its connection with nationalism as foreign and imported ideology, choosing to speak of the 'people of the land' (*maarahvas*) or the 'indigenous people' (*põlisrahvas*) instead of Estonians. At the same time, the nationalist historical narrative which is opposed to Christianity can be regarded as the basis of native faith, and native faith itself can be seen as a kind of fundamentalism (in the literal sense of returning to one's roots), in reaction to modernity. Native faith (*maausk*) was registered as a religious community in 1995 (in Estonian, *Maavalla Koda*). Attitudes to native faith in Estonian society remain predominantly positive.

In 2002, 60% of Estonians considered nature to be animated and holy, and 55% believed that Estonians possessed a special love of nature (Raudsepp 2005: 399, 404). Against the background of such understandings, the environmental movement 'Let's Do It!' met with broad-based and strong response; as a result of this initiative, approximately 50,000 out of 1 million Estonians participated in cleaning up the country's trash in only five hours. The initiative drew international attention and expanded into the global campaign 'Let's Do It! World'.

In 2016 opposition to the building of Rail Baltic infrastructure emerged, based on expected environmental damage. In 2016 the citizens' movement 'Help Estonian Forests' was born, protesting clear-cutting of Estonian forests. In 2017, the struggle to oppose the construction of a cellulose factory in Tartu began, and culminated in a clash between developers and Tartu residents. The Estonian government abandoned the plan. Nationally minded love of nature and native faith are not the same thing, however, though they are tied together at the level of individual self-designation. The number of Estonians who consider themselves adherents to native faith has grown every year, though most of them are not members of the native faith community (*Maavalla Koda*). In 2017, 8% of Estonians identified themselves as adhering to native faith (Religio 2 2017).

Estonians seem to believe in modern 'progress' and 'nature religion' in either an antimodern or a postmodern way. Although these two directions conflict when economic interests clash with environmental conservation, and especially in the case of native faith when economic interests threaten the protection of sacred places, these are not grounds to claim that Estonians have been divided into two warring parties. Their 'belief in progress' and 'belief in nature' exist in symbiosis. Nevertheless, there is a value-based split in Estonian society along the conservative-liberal vector, one wing of which is made up of supporters of conservative, closed-minded nationalism; the other of proponents of open-minded nationalism, who adhere to a unified culture based on transnational, liberal European values.

1.4 The Religious Turn

Christianity, new spirituality and native faith with a provisional 'nature religion' are the three cultural sources among which Estonians make their individual choices, indicating their preference for one option or several. According to the results of the 2011 census, 33 more formulations were mentioned (which belong neither to Christianity, new spirituality or nature religion). Among these were world religions such as Judaism, Islam, Hinduism and Buddhism. However, the total number of members of these religions amounted to less than 1% of the population. Still, the influence of Buddhism and Hinduism on changes in Estonians' religiosity has been noteworthy, though this has not been direct, but mediated by the new spirituality, particularly after the restoration of Estonian independence.

How can we understand this situation? It is definitely a change, but religion, like other facets of culture has changed throughout history. What is unusual is the emergence of new spirituality as an influential religious paradigm alongside Christianity. In Estonia one must also note the growth of native faith. The religious landscape of the West has become differentiated; a homogeneous Christian culture has been replaced by a multireligious one. Organised forms of religious life are giving way to individual forms. In view of all of these observations and in connection with the emergence of new spirituality, can we talk about a religious turn? The debate over such a turn began with Paul Heelas and Linda Woodhead's 2005 study, 'Spiritual Revolution. Why Religion is Giving Way to Spirituality': one side of the debate claims that non-Christian spirituality has gained or is gaining a majority (e.g., Houtman & Aupers 2007: 305–320), while the other side argues against this view (e.g., Andersen, Gundelach, Lüchau 2013: 385–400; Popp-Baier 202: 34–67).

Attempts to demonstrate that a turn has occurred cite the broadening of the individual self-designations 'spiritual' or 'spiritual but not religious', assuming that 'spiritual' signifies both individual and non-Christian religiosity, which have been influenced by new spirituality. Research has shown that such an association might exist, but not necessarily in certain countries. For example, the association applies to Europe rather than the United States, where the self-designation 'spiritual' has spread among Christians (Ammerman 2013: 258–278). In addition to the argument from individual self-designations, attempts have been made to prove the existence of a religious turn based on other indicators, such as beliefs, practices, experiences, and the religious preferences of different age groups (Heelas 2013: 169–171).

Sociological research aside, it can be claimed on the basis of historical facts alone that the centuries-long hegemony of Christianity has diminished or disappeared in many European countries, Estonia included. Although there are culturally self-evident factors that derive from Christianity and a considerable number of residents continue to select Christianity as their religion, this decline shows no signs of coming to an end, at least in Estonia. Callum Brown has used the term 'discursive Christianity' (Brown 2005: 175), to mean Christianity's ability to give sense to life. Brown used this concept to analyse gender roles, particularly the change in the basis for rethinking women's roles in the 1960s, when Christianity lost its discursive power over secular worldviews. The shrinking of Christianity's discursive power has not only affected gender roles, but various other areas of life and everyday life in general. For centuries areas such as politics, economy, education, medicine, science, and art have moved away from Christianity's sphere of influence, and have come to be regarded as purely secular fields.

However, today one can see a reversal of this process, even though it is in connection with new spirituality instead of Christianity. New spirituality is not limited to the bounds of religion, but it has found a place in other fields, such as economy, art, sports, medicine, education, media, science, and as a provider of supplements or alternatives to the cultural periphery. The discursive power of new spirituality is considerable. Over a short period of time New Age discourses have found their way into people's everyday lives, including their health behaviours, eating habits, entertainment, self-education, physical culture, home decoration, interpersonal relationships, and articulation of gender roles. For example, courses are offered in learning to listen to one's body, introducing feng shui principles for planning a room, for the improvement of intergenerational relations, and to articulate what it means to be a woman or a man. One can also notice the use of New Age discourses in people who do not participate in new spirituality, and who are probably not even aware of it. Until now, new spirituality has been on the upswing, at least in Estonia.

After accounting for the discursive aspect, we can repose the question: are we dealing with a religious turn? Keeping in mind that new spirituality has replaced Christianity in providing religious viewpoints in life and everyday activities, the turn is certainly there. The relation of new spirituality to secular worldviews is a separate question: to what extent has new spirituality supplemented or replaced them? Since New Age has common ground with some principles of Western culture (evolution, individual development) and worldviews (the scientific-materialist worldview that fits well with modernity), it is not difficult to switch among them, and it is not always possible to distinguish among them.

The research question of this chapter is therefore whether and, if so, how one can speak of the current situation as a religious turn among ethnic Estonians.

How can the existence or extent of a religious be proved and measured? I now answer these questions based on sociological data and scholarly studies.

2   Method

No research has yet sought answers to the questions raised in the previous section. However, in the last 20 years, many qualitative and quantitative studies have examined changes in the individual, his/her religious self-designation, beliefs, participation in various practices, and religious attitudes. Individual choices reflect and shape social trends, and thus conclusions can be drawn from individually-oriented research which apply to the sociocultural context.

Before introducing the investigations, it should be explained that in this chapter, in keeping with the disciplines that study religion, no distinction is made either between religion and spirituality, or between the religious and the spiritual. Spirituality and the spiritual are regarded as religious according to the following definition: images, understandings, ideas, discourses, narratives, practices which presume or contain belief in the real existence of a spiritual realm and which consider it possible to make contact with, relate to, influence, make use of, or create such entities (beings, things, forces, relations, events, processes). This definition takes into account belief in a spiritual realm, either dependent on or independent of human activity. An example of a spiritual realm dependent on human activity is the belief, pervasive in New Age culture, that through their thoughts, words, and deeds each person is the creator of a spiritual realm that can influence the real, material world. An example of a spiritual world independent of human activities is theistic religion, in which all creative activity attributed to God.

Since 1995, the Estonian Council of Churches has periodically sponsored surveys with the designation 'Life, faith, and religious life' (LFRL), with Christianity as the focus. The last two of these surveys conducted in 2010 and 2015 were carried out by the social and market research firm Saar Poll. The respondents were people from all over Estonia between the ages of 15 and 74, selected on the basis of proportionate random sampling and interviewed in their homes face-to-face using written questionnaires. In 2010 the sample size was 1009 people; in 2015, 1002. Based on the data from both surveys, numerous research studies were carried out covering range of topics; the resulting articles were collected in two volumes: *Step Down among the People. Articles and Discussions on the Spiritual Inclinations of the Estonian Populace* (2012) and *Where are you going, Mary's Land? Quo vadis Terra Mariana?* (2016). The 'The New Spirituality 2010' survey (NS 2010) was carried out by Saar Poll using the same sample but with different questions. The questionnaire was drawn up by the author of this chapter. The goal of the study was to measure the participation of Estonian residents in New Age culture.

In 2014 the 'Religious trends in Estonia 2014' survey (RTE 2014) was conducted by the market research agency TNS Emor. Respondents were questioned over the telephone, half on mobile phones and half on standard desk phones according to the CATI-bus method (Computer Assisted Telephone Interviewing). The sample consisted of 1100 residents of Estonia 15 years of age or older, and the proportional model of the whole was used to constitute the sample. The interview questionnaire was drawn up by the author of this chapter in consultation with a research expert at TNS Emor. The goal of RTE 2014 was to compare the dissemination among the population of Christianity and the new spirituality. Additional goals were measured attitudes toward religion, the extent of native faith, and the dissemination of religious self-designations among the people. The backbone of the results section was factor analysis of the data of RTE 2014.

In 2017 the market research agency Kantar Emor administered the survey 'Religio 2 2017'. The author of this chapter designed the questionnaire. The study took place via telephone interviews on the CATI-bus method on the basis of the proportional model of the whole. The sample size was 1100; the age range 15–74 years. The goal of the survey was to investigate the extent of the dissemination of vicarious religion in Estonia.

Numerous graduate dissertations have been defended at the University of Tartu based on qualitative studies of religious changes in Estonia. Significant for this chapter is Lea Altnurme's doctoral dissertation, *From Christianity to Personal Religion* (2006), in which changes in the religiosity of Estonians over the last half-century are analysed, primarily based on 77 life stories gathered through interviews. In addition, Marko Uibu's doctoral dissertation, *Religiosity as Cultural Toolbox: A Study of Estonian New Spirituality* (2016) certainly deserves mention, as it brings together eight separate studies new spirituality in Estonia. Liina Eek's dissertation, *On the Catechesis and Beliefs of Estonian-speaking Orthodox Believers* (2017), focuses on the question of how Estonians came to be adherents to the Orthodox faith in a secular society with a mainly Lutheran history. Eek's study stands out in relation to the context of changes: the 2011 census showed that the largest Christian confession was now Russian Orthodoxy (as discussed in the chapter on the Orthodox church). The main justification for these results was the gradual passing of an older generation that had remained faithful to Lutheranism.

In addition to the doctoral dissertations, numerous master's theses have been defended on topics dealing with religious change, some of which have been published in the series *Multireligious Estonia* I-IV. The first of these collections (ed. Altnurme 2004) gives an overview of Estonian residents' attitudes toward religion, conversion to a new spirituality worldview in the context of healing, and the spread of Islam, Buddhism and Hinduism in Estonia. The second collection (ed. Altnurme 2007) is composed of research on changes within Christianity and among its various contemporary forms. Topics include Christianity and nationalism; sister congregations of the Estonian Evangelical Lutheran Church and their mutual aid; the history and organisation of Taize pilgrimages; university students' religious quests in a Christian milieu; changes in Christian spirituality; the Rastafari and their dissemination in Estonia. The third volume (ed. Uibu 2013) focuses on the arrival and dissemination of new spirituality in Estonia from historical and sociological points of view. Topics include the phenomenon of new spirituality; the history of its precursors in Estonia, such as theosophy and anthroposophy; dissemination of new spirituality via literature and journalism; syncretic forms of new spirituality and Christianity and their relations to healing. The fourth collection (ed. Eek 2015) is an overview of the history of different forms of the Orthodox faith in education and art. The history of atheism in Estonia has been examined by Atko Remmel, who defended his doctoral dissertation, *Anti-religious Struggle in Estonian SSR in 1957–1990. Main Institutions and their Activities* in 2011. Remmel has continued his research on atheists and the religiously indifferent in the disciplinary framework of the sociology of religion.

This chapter will not discuss these studies one by one, but according to their relevance and in relation to subthemes. Comparisons, analyses and syntheses of the results of various studies are presented here according to the following categories: Christianity and Christians; atheists, the religiously indifferent, anti-religious attitudes; the spiritual, new spirituality; practitioners of native faith, native faith; individual religiosity. Results will focus on changes and the current situation.

Before turning to the results, we should comment on a special characteristic of Estonians that Paul Heelas has named 'ratherism', since Estonians prefer to answer multiple-choice questions intended to measure religiosity by choosing answers that include the restrictive word 'rather'. Heelas interpreted this to mean that sacred vs. secular opposition was unimportant to Estonians, who in Heelas' view ascribe to themselves a certain kind of spiritual humanism (Heelas 2013: 175–177).

Until further research explains why Estonians prefer answers containing 'rather', several explanations could be offered based on their sociocultural context. To date, three generations in Estonia have not received religious education in school (although they could have received it elsewhere). Of course this does not mean that all Estonians are non-religious, but rather that some respondents think their knowledge of religious views is insufficient, and thus feel less than confident in their answers. Another group of respondents finds it difficult to agree with simplistic religious claims with a single meaning, because their understandings are more complex and conditional; inevitably, social surveys couch such concepts in simplistic, single interpretations. In addition, some Estonians are suspicious of solid ideological identities and claims, which may extend to distrust of the the interviewer; therefore, they prefer ambiguous answers.

There is a historical basis for such distrust, as literary scholar Jaan Undusk has pointed out (Undusk 2003; 2016). Indeed, from the viewpoint of rulers who have deemed themselves 'bringers of culture', Estonians have continued to be bearers of the wrong identity. Concerning the more recent past, one may recall that the 19th century Estonian peasant, who spoke the local dialect, identified himself by the village or region where he lived, and considered himself a Christian. The peasants were the 'people of the land' who were later to become Estonians, as well as Europeans, as they followed the leadership of the national elite, which had been influenced by modernism. At that time Christianity was conceptualised as an ideology that had accompanied the process of violent christianisation, and which Estonians never fully adopted. Indeed they needed to break free from this ideology, which was a relic that obstructed progress. With the help of nationalist ideology, peasants were shaped into Estonians. This was regarded as false in the eyes of the new, Soviet regime. A struggle ensued against bourgeois nationalism, and a new Soviet person was created. Since the restoration of Estonian independence (1991), the struggle has been against relics of the Soviet era and *homo soveticus,* with the goal of becoming citizens of the European Union. Thus one can hardly be amazed that people are loath to express their views openly and to align themselves personally, both due to their distrust of ruling ideologies and worldviews and the fear of stigmatisation.

3 Results

3.1 *Christians: Christianity*

This chapter addresses only the religiosity of ethnic Estonians. The reason is that there are two cultural spaces in Estonian society – Estonian speakers and Russian speakers. With respect to religion, particularly Christianity, these two spaces are dissimilar. As distinct from Estonians, Russians are much more friendly to Christianity, regardless of a common Soviet past. Russian Orthodoxy is a part of Russian national identity, but Estonians cannot say the same of Lutheranism.

An estimated one-fifth of Estonians designate themselves as Christians (RTE 2014 21%; LFRL 2015 26%; Religio 2 2017 16%). One-fifth to one-quarter of Estonians support Christian claims such as 'Jesus holds an important place in my faith'; 'I have felt God's guidance in my life', or ascribe to such Christian beliefs as 'a personal God exists', 'Heaven exists'; 'Hell exists'; 'Jesus saved humanity from their sins on the cross'; 'Jesus rose from the dead'. Nevertheless, not all those who designate themselves as Christians support such beliefs. One-quarter of Estonians reads Christian literature, including the Bible. Seventy percent of them claim to have found truth there, that is, truth that they adhere to in everyday life (RTE 2014). Five percent of them read the Bible regularly every week (LFRL 2015).

Though almost half of Estonians have been baptised, only 17% of those claim to belong to a Christian congregation (LFRL 2015). Twenty-seven percent of Estonians pray and 43% attend religious services (LFRL 2015). Most of these go to church once a year on Christmas Eve, a practice connected to old family traditions (LFRL 2015). Christianity is most widespread among women of the older generation.

In order to better understand the religiosity of the respondents, connections and patterns among their choices, the study RTE 2014 employed factor analysis (principal components method, varimax rotation, eigenvalues greater than 1). Factor coefficients starting from 0.35 are presented in the table. Based on agreement with claims that measured the spread of Christianity, three factors emerged as significant: Christianity, Lutheranism, and those interested in religion.

The first factor sums up almost all the Christian claims of the RTE 2014 study. This shows that those who have faith in specific Christian beliefs consider themselves to be Christian and practice Christian religion. It is noteworthy that belonging to a Lutheran congregation is not located within this factor, but constitutes a second one together with the characteristic of Christian identity (which is also observable in the first factor). The explanation for this might be that belonging to a Lutheran congregation is not associated exclusively with a Christian worldview, but also with choices among other worldviews including new spirituality. (The syncretism of Lutherans will be discussed further below.) The third factor indicates awareness of and interest in religion. Approbation of a Christian past as the basis of modern society and culture is not self-evident in Estonia, as it is elsewhere in Europe. Forty percent of those surveyed agreed with the statement 'The roots of today's Estonian culture lie in Christianity'. In comparison, 61% of those surveyed agreed with the statement, 'The true

TABLE 7.1 Christian factors based on factor analysis RTE 2014

	F1	F2	F3
F1 Christianity			
In faith the person of Jesus Christ holds an important place	0.74		
Jesus Christ saved humanity on the cross	0.66		
I am interested in participating in religious services in the future	0.64		
I like Christian principles	0.63		
I consider myself a Christian	0.63		
Christian teaching is the basis for becoming a moral person	0.62		
I read the Bible or other Christian literature	0.62		
I have felt that there exists a higher power which directs my life and gives protection in times of danger	0.55		
I have prayed or taken part in religious services within the last five years	0.46		
I have faith only in myself and my own abilities	-0.37		
F2 Lutheranism			
Belongs to a Lutheran congregation		0.90	
Considers themselves a Christian		0.48	
F3 Those with religious interests			
The roots of today's Estonian culture lie in Christianity			0.52
Don't consider themselves religious, but have a strong interest in various religions and spiritual teachings			0.36

religion of the Estonian people is native faith' (RTE 2014). The explanation is that the latter is implicitly accompanied by the understanding of native faith as the continuation of pre-Christian ancient religion which, based on the national narrative is considered more authentic than Christianity.

In a previous section, there was a discussion of growth in new spirituality's discursive power. The same obtains with respect to religion as an area of life. The influence of the new spirituality is most clearly observable in the traditional churches – the membership of Lutheran, Orthodox, and Catholic churches – and far less in the case of free congregations. A good example is the Lutheran church, which continues to be the most numerous Christian confession among Estonians. (According to census data from 2011, 14% of Estonians considered themselves Lutheran.) People seek confirmation in the Lutheran church for pragmatic rather than religious reasons (e.g., following family traditions they wish either to be baptised or to baptise their children; they plan to be married in a church). As a rule the bond with the congregation is weak, and thus there are plenty of those who do not consider themselves religious despite regarding religion as holding an important role in their lives. For members of the Lutheran church, God is less and less the Biblical personal ruler of the world, but instead a more abstract power aligned with goodness or a higher power.

Almost half of these respondents believe in reincarnation, a bit over half of them in horoscopes, while the majority of them (88%) believe in the power of faith healers to heal the sick. Though only a small number of members of the Lutheran church engage in practices of the new spirituality such as yoga or meditation, they are receptive to them. There are those who believe in possibilities of integrating Christianity and the new spirituality. Although not many Lutherans engage in the practices of new spirituality, almost half indicate interest in other religions, spiritual quests, or meditation (Pärkson 2007: 150–200; Pekko & Koppel 2013: 139–152).

The decline of Christianity has been gradual. Lack of participation in or direct contact with Christian culture does not yet mean the complete cessation of the influence of Christianity, which may continue to exist in hidden forms. Study of individual religiosity showed that people who claimed not to be religious, who did not consider themselves Christian, who were even opposed to institutional religion, and who did not use Christian language, still articulated the view that 'though I do not believe in God, there is nevertheless someone or something that watches over me, protects me, gives order to my life, rewards the good and punishes the bad'. The cultural source of such a belief is still Christianity, regardless of whether people understand it as such. Similarly, there is widespread belief in predetermination, cosmic justice and the like, and once again one should presuppose Christian origins, even though today other religious systems may offer support and content to such beliefs (Altnurme 2012: 199–200, 202): horoscopes and the idea of karma, which derives from Eastern religion. In 2014 60% of Estonians agreed with the statement that there exists some kind of higher power that directs their lives and protects them in times of danger (this statement also belonged to the Christian factor), and 52% believed that important life events do not happen by chance, but are predetermined (RTE 2014). Ninety percent thought that everything that a person does, good or bad, will have repercussions during their lives (LFRL 2015). Such veiled Christianity could be termed 'hidden Christianity'.

In such belief Christianity is not only veiled or hidden, but in some self-evident beliefs one can see the disappearance or doubt thereof, which might reveal the phenomenon of vicarious religion. This term, vicarious religion, derives from Grace Davie, who stated: 'the notion of religion performed by an active minority but on behalf of a much larger number, who (implicitly at least) not only understand, but, quite clearly, approve of what the minority is doing' (Davie 2007: 22). The expectation that the church should preserve traditional practices and moral norms has spread beyond the 17% who consider themselves members of a congregation and the 26% of Estonians who consider themselves Christian. However, not all members of congregations are in favour of things continuing as they have; on the contrary, they support the updating of the church to reflect contemporary reality. Nevertheless, in 2015 66% of Estonians thought that the church should be included in the marking of significant national holidays or events. Similarly, 69% of respondents thought that the church should continue in its traditional observances and make little effort to render them 'contemporary'; the same percentage believed that the church remain solid in its teaching and moral norms and not respond to all social changes (LFRL 2015). By 'Christian principles', people mainly mean moral standards; in 2014, 55% of Estonians thought that Christian teachings were the foundation for growing up to be a moral person (RTE 2014).

A separate study of vicarious religion in Estonia showed that Estonians' expectations were primarily directed toward others, especially as concerns morality – other people could or should be better, according to the requirements of Christianity; some institution, the state or the church might or should support and guarantee that they fulfill these requirements. As far as the respondents themselves were concerned, Christianity was not suitable, and on the individual level self-designations tended instead to be non-religious or mediated by a practice of new spirituality. The results of this study also clarified that after the social discussions around the cohabitation law, whereby homosexual partnership was made equivalent to heterosexual partnership, and after the refugee crisis that hit Europe in 2015, the demand for Christianity grew as a provider of public services. These events and the discussions that accompanied them put many important assumptions into question. People began seeing Christianity as a support for traditional gender roles and the defence of the family: indeed, conservative Christians had been public critics of the cohabitation law. Christianity was also regarded as a bulwark against the spread of

Islam. In 2017, 62% of Estonians agreed with the statement, 'European culture should remain Christian first and foremost' (Religio 2 2017).

In sum, the decline of Christianity has by no means been linear. It continues to have a veiled sociocultural influence, markedly greater than the percentages of participants in Christian religious life.

3.2   *Atheists, the Religiously Indifferent, anti-religious Attitudes*

Estonians who designate themselves either as atheists, non-religious, or indifferent to religion constitute approximately one-third of the population (RTE 2914 29%, LFRL 2015 31%, Religio 2 2017 38%). These figures do not include the 'spiritual but not religious', which will be discussed later.

As mentioned, on an everyday level, 'religion' usually denotes Christianity. Based on the LFRL 2015 data it can be said that this one-third either oppose Christianity, distinguish themselves from it, are indifferent to it, or lack any contact with it whatsoever. However this study gives us no information about alternatives, because it mainly measures the influence and spread of traditional Christianity (Remmel 2016: 145–150). Among those designated as non-Christians, there may be representatives of various secular and religious worldviews.

Likewise, the designation 'atheist' or 'non-religious' does not necessarily exclude those who are characterised by religious beliefs or even practices. Indeed, as would be expected, there is less support, but it is not entirely missing, and there is little difference in the beliefs and practices of new spirituality (Remmel 2016: 138–141). The composite model of the 'secular Estonian' signifies the 32% for whom faith and church are unimportant; who does not belong to any congregation, does not believe in God; never attends church, never prays, considers themselves indifferent to religion, and leans toward atheism (Remmel 2016: 141). One-third of Estonians have no contact with Christianity.

Among the non-religious there are no noteworthy differences in gender, age, or education, except for the fact that 75% of convinced atheists were men (Remmel 2016: 144).

In addition to indifference and opposition, some Estonians have negative stereotypes about Christianity, and even fear it. Stereotypes and fear have not been studied separately, but they have repeatedly emerged in interviews conducted for other qualitative studies. During Soviet times, and as a result of atheist propaganda, religious people were be regarded as abnormal, misled, or betrayed (Altnurme 2013a: 47; Altnurme 2006: 158–160, 221). These images have not disappeared. One can fear religion as if it were an infectious disease, with which it is best to avoid contact. There are three deeply rooted negative stereotypes about religion and faith among Estonians: they make one stupid; they make one weak, or are for the people who need spiritual or psychological support; and that they make one aggressive. With respect to the first stereotype, some Estonians believe that a religious worldview restricts the ability to think beyond the bounds of the faith canon. When a person becomes a believer, their capacity for independent thinking disappears, and they become a zombie who simply parrots religious claims.

According to the second stereotype, faith makes one weak or is for the weak. It is thought that religious people are passive, that they believe that they do not have to do anything in their lives; that everything comes from the heavenly powers, and all they have to do is to sit and wait for God's direction. They do not engage in sports. Likewise it is thought that faith is for the weak, for people who have been struck by harsh fate, and who can manage their difficulties only with the support of faith. In some cases, faith is held out as a last resort, 'I'll go to church only when nothing else can help' (cf examples Mõtte 2007: 140). The third stereotype includes imaginations that faith makes one violent. This is connected to the first stereotype, that faith makes one stupid. It is believed that once faith has turned a person into a zombie, it will lead to them acting in ways that non-religious people wouldn't, for example, forcing them to participate in street missions where they have to confront and proselytise other people (cf examples from Kilemit, Nõmmik 2004: 19). From this perspective, one can hardly be amazed that Estonians are not eager to describe themselves as religious people or Christians, even if they are.

One part of the secular modern myth of progress is the belief in the unbridled growth of human reason and achievements, the belief in the human being himself. This becomes set in the process of individualisation, and in the development of a welfare society that offers general security; people have considerably more freedom to shape their destiny, making their own choices about education, career, life partner, religion, lifestyle, sexual orientation, etc. 'Belief only in oneself and one's abilities' is very widespread among Estonians: in 2014, 83% agreed with this statement. However, this does not prevent some of them also from believing in 'a higher power which directs their life and protects them in times of danger'. It should be added that those whose claims were brought together to constitute the Christian factor agreed less than the average with the statement 'believing only in oneself and one's abilities' (Table 7.1). This corresponds to expectations, for according to Christian teaching, the fate of the world and of each person depends, in the final analysis, on God, not the person.

In summary, non-religious Estonians are first and foremost the indifferent, those who lack both contact with and interest in Christianity. Mass distantiation from the church was already taking place in the middle of the 20th century, and most of today's non-religious are non-religious not because of an individual choice, but as a result of family traditions and a secular cultural environment. Negative stereotypes about Christianity are widespread, and these make it more difficult to choose Christianity as a religious quest.

With respect to the religious turn, it should be noted that during its sharpest decline, Christianity was not replaced by other, competing religious worldviews but rather by secular ones. Quite soon thereafter the new spirituality began gathering strength, which does not have noteworthy common ground with Christianity, but with secular, modern, and postmodern ideas and liberal values. Common beliefs include an optimistic outlook on human development and the advance of humankind towards a better future. In New Age culture this is called 'self-spirituality'. It should also be pointed out that the content of new spirituality also derives from secular sources, such as science, education, medicine, and psychology. Such material is turned into religion by basic mythological patterns and beliefs, and the related practices also begin functioning as religious ones.

3.3   The Spiritual: New Spirituality

Those Estonians who think of themselves as 'spiritual but not religious' constitute approximately one-fourth to one-third of the population (RTE 2014 34%; LFRL 2015 28%; Religio 2 2017 28%). However, in Estonia no research has been done on the meaning of the word 'spiritual'. Also, for the time being we do not have an answer to the question: is the individual identity 'spiritual but not religious' connected with New Age culture? Before proceeding with analysis based on this question, we need to to see how the term 'spiritual' (*vaimne*) is used in Estonian cultural space.

In general, this term connotes psychological or intellectual activity (e.g., reading books, seeing films and theatre performances, listening to music), and it is used for both secular and religious culture. If we ask a respondent how important 'spirituality and self-development' are to them, we do not actually know whether they mean this in a secular, New Age, or Christian culture context. Spirituality and self-development were designated as 'especially important' by 25% of Estonians, 'important' by 58% (for a total of 83%). As a comparison, faith was regarded as very important or important by 26% of respondents (LFRL 2015).

The situation is made more complicated by the fact that although in new spirituality the word 'spiritual' is used to designate oneself and one's teachings and practices, there is no collective designation. The concept 'new spirituality' is of etic rather than emic origin. The term 'New Age', which was common parlance in the 1990s, has long since been discarded. In 2014, Marko Uibu investigated the attitudes of participants in new spirituality toward the consideration of their spiritual practices as 'new spirituality' or as 'religion'. It turned out that the term 'new spirituality' was surprisingly well accepted, as 56% of respondents agreed with it. There were, however, two criticisms. First there was sensitivity to attaching labels; and second, there were objections to the adjective 'new', because it was believed that the practices were old, if not ancient. The content of 'spiritual' was discussed by the respondents in the framework of self-spirituality, which is characteristic of New Age culture. Opposition to the term 'religion' was strong. Religion, particularly in its institutional form, was regarded as a constraint on human development.

In order to draw a distinction between the self-realisation that takes place in secular and in New Age culture, the RTE 2014 questionnaire asked two consecutive questions. The first was, 'My spiritual self-realisation takes place through literature, music, films, art, and theatre' (87% of Estonian respondents agreed). The second was, 'I believe in spiritual self-development in the sense that with the help of consciously internalised affirmations and spiritual practices such as meditation it is possible to change oneself, one's life, and the surrounding world' (33% were completely agreed, 36% rather agreed, a total of 69% of Estonians). These statements are not equivalent, because one measures the extent of self-realisation through cultural consumption; the other – the faith that through spiritual practices it is possible to evoke desired changes and thereby develop spiritually – instead signifies the spread of the idea of spiritual self-development. Real participation in the practices of new spirituality is smaller than the belief in their life-changing impact. We will discuss this below.

While investigating the life stories of religious people of different generations, it emerged that the need for meaning was especially intense when one had been struck by misfortune or illness. As expected, older Christians interpreted adversity in a Christian framework, signifying the testing of one's faith, standing firm in one's faith, a battle of faith or God's punishment. Secular worldviews treat suffering mainly as bad luck. With the influence of New Age ideas, the interpretation of such misfortunes as lessons necessary for spiritual development has begun to spread (Altnurme 2006: 126–152; 250–268; 287–289). In the RTE 2014 survey, 74% of Estonians agreed with the statement 'Mishaps and sufferings are lessons on the path of spiritual development'.

In 2014, 32% of Estonians read literature of the new spirituality. Sixty-eight percent of these claimed that this literature offered them teachings that they followed in everyday life (RTE 2014). Within the last five years, 22% of Estonian respondents claimed to have engaged in practices such as yoga, meditation, breathwork, or Reiki, while only 5% were members of spiritual groups (RTE

2014). How is it possible to explain such a great difference between those who practice and those who are members of a group? The largest proportion of practitioners was in their 20s, and those who belonged to groups were mostly in their 30s or 40s. One can suggest that perhaps the latter group has more money and time to leave home to practice, while the practitioners engaged in their chosen activities on their own. Attitudes toward the practices of new spirituality are generally positive, as indicated by the level of interest in them. Indeed, 42% of Estonians agreed with the statement that they would be interested to try something like yoga, meditation, breathwork, or Reiki, in the future. One's contact with New Age culture – just as with any kind of subculture, ideology or worldview – is facilitated by the involvement of one's closest friends in this. Thirty-seven percent of respondents claimed that they had a close friend or family member had read about or practiced spiritual self-development (RTE 2014).

With respect to agreeing with statements concerning the spread of the new spirituality, one factor stands out (Table 7.2). People who are engaged in these practices are also interested in doing so in the future. Such respondents have friends or family members with similar interests who agree with the conception of self-spirituality.

On the basis of this factor, we can claim that the new spirituality is a real phenomenon, at least in Estonia (Table 7.2). Doubts have been expressed on this score using yoga as an example, since practicing yoga does not necessarily mean being influenced by other aspects of New Age culture. Although yoga gymnastics, which is extracted from its related spiritual teachings, does indeed exist, such a practice is more inclined to go hand in hand with other characteristics of new spirituality than be separate from them. In addition, we can state that despite the individuality emphasised by the rhetoric of self-spirituality, the new spirituality is based on an integrated network of like-minded people, meaning that practitioners have close friends or family members who are also active in New Age culture. This has also been confirmed by other research (Stolz et al., 2016: 86). However, contrary to expectations, this factor lacks the self-designation 'spiritual but not religious'.

Thus it is apposite to return here to the question, are those who chose the self-designation 'spiritual but not religious' connected with New Age culture? Are these respondents 'non-religious' or less influenced by Christianity than average Estonians? Indeed, the data shows that this is true. If one-fifth of Estonians espouse Christian beliefs, then only one-tenth of the 'spiritual but not religious' attend church; 92% of them are not members of any congregation. Among those who self-designate as 'spiritual but not religious', more than the average believe that the church is meant for manipulating with the masses

TABLE 7.2   Factor of the new spirituality based on factor analysis from RTE 2014

The new spirituality

Within the last five years I have engaged in practices such as yoga, meditation, breathwork, or Reiki	0.80
In the future I am interested in trying something like yoga, meditation, breathwork, or Reiki	0.74
I read literature about spiritual self-development, yoga, abundance, etc	0.66
I participate in a spiritual group	0.61
One of my close friends or family members is involved with spiritual self-development, reads spiritual literature or is engaged with a spiritual practice	0.46
I believe in spiritual self-development in the sense that with the help of consciously internalised affirmations and spiritual practices such as meditation it is possible to change oneself, one's life, and the surrounding world	0.38

and keeping them under control (42%) (RTE 2014). As for New Age culture, the data show that those who self-designate 'spiritual but not religious' are indeed more influenced by it than Estonians on the average. One-third (31%) has been involved with spiritual practices and half (54%) are interested in trying them in the future. Forty-four percent read spiritual literature and 8% participate in a group; 80% believe in the conception of spiritual self-development (statement 'I believe in spiritual self-development in the sense that with the help of consciously internalized affirmations and spiritual practices such as meditation, it is possible to change oneself, one's life, and the surrounding world'). The designation 'spiritual but not religious' was most popular among those aged 15–24 (RTE 2014).

New Age culture contains many esoteric and magical components. Such beliefs are very popular among Estonians: signs and omens can predict turning points in life (54%); some people have the ability to predict future events (81%); by means of certain magical transactions or rituals it is possible to influence the course of events and other people (40%); some sensitive people have the ability to heal the sick (74%); a person's character and destiny are influenced by the position of the stars and planets at the moment of birth (50%). One-quarter of Estonians owns a talisman or other meaningful piece of jewellery that they believe protects them (LFRL 2015). In addition, 41% believe in the idea of reincarnation in Eastern religions, as in the statement 'it is likely that a person's soul will be born into this world again as someone else' (LFRL 2015).

What are we to think about this? Are we really dealing with a flood of esotericism? Estonian journalists have been astonished by this, and there has also been shaming. Such phenomena have been regarded as the flourishing of superstition, which can be explained either by lack of education, lack of religious education, or the manifestation of spiritual emptiness that is a side effect of secular worldviews. How can we explain the great popularity of esotericism and magic among Estonians who, according to their national self-image are rational and progressive? Most of those active in these areas do not think of new spirituality or esotericism as religion, and even less as superstition. Such respondents tend not to consider themselves religious. For many the teaching and practices being disseminated express self-evident claims, understandings confirmed by experience, even truth, which is sometimes supported by scientific authority. To express such claims, respondents often use non-religious language, terminology borrowed from fields like science, education, or medicine. The ideas of new spirituality are merged with scientific ideas. For example, the belief in healers is easily reconcilable with the progressive idea of the ongoing development of human abilities. Modern thinking suggests that such persons have special talents and abilities which they are been born with, or that they have cultivated.

As a counterweight or supplement to the modern explanation, one can encounter postmodern beliefs about the 'sensitives': they have retained ancient abilities despite modern society and education. In Estonia, most new spirituality events take the form of seminars, lectures or courses. Sometimes these are held in schools, kindergartens and libraries, thus allowing them to be classified as educational, which speaks favourably to their credibility. Self-development and study as the practical implementation thereof are values both according to the modern and the new spirituality worldviews.

Andrew Dawson has argued that the belief in the mind-body duality in New Age culture ended because the two ceased to be considered as in opposition. The material world has been sacralised, and the spiritual has materialised. The spiritual sphere is now understood as something immanent, basic to material processes; therefore, the material world is highly valued as a possible site for spiritual fulfillment (Dawson 2011: 311). Such an understanding of the world actually lays a foundation for magical thinking, which is found at every step of the way in the new spirituality. Thus there need not be so much of an opposition as first appears between popular inclinations toward the magical and modern self-images.

On the basis of the RTE 2014 survey, we can conclude that younger and more educated groups have been more influenced by the new spirituality than others, and that their participation has been more active. Women also outnumber men (RTE 2014). The same cannot be said of the magical thinking and esotericism; these are spread across all age groups and levels of education. Here again, women remain in the majority (LFRL 2015).

In sum, it is more difficult to understand the breadth of the dissemination of new spirituality is than that of Christianity. New Age culture has fuzzier boundaries than institutional Christianity; New Age culture has neither creed nor a signifier of collective identity. In the best possible case, participants in New Age spirituality self-designate as 'spiritual', though this is certainly not always the case. Many of those who adhere to the worldview of new spirituality are not conscious of this. In view of these facts, we have grounds to maintain that at least one-third of Estonians have been somehow influenced by New Age culture.

3.4 Follower of Native Faith: Native Faith

Beginning in 1995 when native faith was officially registered, the number of its practitioners has continued to increase. For example, in 2014, 4% of Estonians designated themselves as practitioners of native faith (RTE 2014), and in 2017, 8% did (Religio 2 2017).

Though we have Jenni Rinne's study of the members of the Maavalla Koda (official community of native faith) (Rinne 2016), we know very little about those who consider themselves followers of native faith but do not belong to the community; this is true of the majority of those who self-designate as followers of native faith. Because there are no qualitative studies on native faith as understood by this majority, it has been difficult to measure it in quantitative surveys, and there is little data. In 2010 37% of Estonians were receptive to native faith, and 20% considered it the religion of their ancestors (LFRL 2010). The statement 'The Estonian people's true religion is native faith' in the survey RTE 2014 was supported by 61% of Estonians. Twenty percent responded affirmatively to the question: 'Do you have a close friend or family member who could be considered a follower of native faith?' As stated earlier, in 2014, 4% of Estonians considered themselves followers of native faith (RTE 2014).

On the basis of agreement with statements on the dissemination of native faith, one factor could be constituted. This shows that those who have close friends or family members who follow native faith are more likely to consider themselves believers as well. They believe that native faith is Estonians'

TABLE 7.3 Factor of the native faith based on factor analysis from RTE 2014

The native faith

Someone among my close friends or family members can be considered a follower of native faith	0.66
Considers themselves a follower of native faith	0.65
Native faith is the true religion of Estonians	0.51
There is a place, a tree, a stone, or a spring that is especially important to me	0.35

true religion and they have a place in nature, a place that they consider holy (Table 7.3).

Having a natural place with special meaning is not only characteristic of followers of native faith, but also of people with any other religious or secular identity. Thirty-eight percent of Estonians claimed to have such a place, usually a tree (RTE 2014). A natural place with special meaning occurred also in another factor; on the basis of content, this could be deemed the factor of secular intellectuals who appreciate nature (Table 7.4).

If we examine native faith according to gender, age, and education, we find that most of those who think native faith is the true religion of Estonians tend to be less educated. The same is true of those who have close friends or family members who are followers of native faith. The statement 'The true religion of Estonians is native faith' has the greatest number of supporters in the youngest age group (15–24). However, the largest number of those who claim a place in

TABLE 7.4 Factor of the secular intellectuals who appreciate nature based on factor analysis from RTE 2014

The secular intellectuals who appreciate nature

Spiritual self-development comes about through literature, music, film, art, and theatre	0.67
There is a place, tree, stone, or spring that is especially important to me	0.42
Believes only in themselves and their own abilities	0.40

nature with special significance belongs to the oldest age bracket (50–74), with women outnumbering men. No other noteworthy differences emerged.

In sum, we can conclude that though native faith is not widespread, adherence to it has been growing continuously. Future growth might be facilitated by other developments: strengthening nationalism on the one hand and acute problems of natural conservation on the other. The common ground between these two developments may find its expression in native faith, where both the national narrative and nature mysticism are equally strongly represented. In any case, native faith deserves more thorough attention than it has received to date.

3.5   *Individual Religiosity and Personal Religion*

The concept of 'religiosity' designates the extent of religious adherence of peoples, groups, or individuals. It can also be used to describe the differences among religious teachings, activities and commitments. Individual religiosity has always taken the form of popular versions of official religion, and that may have contained elements of unofficial faith; for example in the Lutheran era, folk religious customs of pagan or Catholic origin. Since the time of Christianisation, popular religion has been linked to church religion, which has pushed it to the periphery (Altnurme 2012: 193). The influence of the church on individual religiosity is now less recognisable than ever.

Here we use 'individual religiosity' to signify an individual religious version of different beliefs, values and practices which is more or less independent of social institutions (e.g., the church, school, or clinic) or the forms of organised religion. Independence refers to the lack of institutional power, prescriptions, and control. However, this does not mean a total loss of the importance of cultural sources of religion (such as Christianity, new spirituality, native faith, nationalism, psychology), because they still shape individual religiosity.

We have already noted a tendency to equate individual religiosity both with new spirituality and with a person's own creativity. In both cases the reason is that the self-spirituality that is dominant in New Age culture, where the main teaching is 'find your own spiritual path that is distinct from that of others', has tacitly been transferred to a scientific, analytical level and assumed to be factual as concerns individuals. This is not correct. When we speak of individual religiosity, we do not mean the individual's original creativity; nor can it be deduced that new spirituality is an environment in which participants really cultivate the religion or spirituality that they have created themselves. There can also be individual religiosity quite apart from the influence of new spirituality, though today it is quite difficult to find such a person in Estonia.

To refer to individual religion, the popular expression 'one's own religion' has spread among Estonians. For example, people say, 'I don't go to church, I have my own religion' or 'I don't believe what they say in church, I have my own religion'. In quantitative surveys, 'one's own religion' has become the most popular religious self-designation among Estonians, but it has not been measured in the framework of a question with other self-designations to choose from, such as Christian, atheist, or spiritual. It has been considered a separate statement in the version, 'I don't support any religion or church; I have my own religion' (LFRL 2010, 2015) or the version, 'You have your own religion which is independent of distinct churches or religions' (RTE 2014). In 2014, 55% of Estonians who supported the statement about 'one's own religion' (RTE 2014) and in 2015, 48% did (LFRL 2015).

The statement 'my relationship with God is very personal and my religion does not need the support of a church' can also be considered an expression of individual religiosity. This statement was affirmed by 42% of Estonians (LFRL 2015). More than half (52%) wished 'to enter a church sometimes, but not during services' (LFRL), indicating that church buildings continued to be attractive places, but for most without the Christian content.

If one looks at the way the 'one's own religion' group answered the self-designation question when they were given multiple-choice answers – Christian, follower of native faith, atheist – they did not differ from the general sample. For example, 20% of them considered themselves Christian (the average was 21%); 35% saw themselves as spiritual but not religious (average 34%); 6% as followers of native faith (average 4%); 9% as atheists (average 11%) (RTE 2014).

There is one qualitative study of the content of individual religiosity, based on 76 interviews collected in 2002–2010. The sample consisted of subjects in the 18–76 age range (57% were 18–29 years of age); had completed secondary and higher education, and residing in the country or the city. Sixty-two percent of the subjects were women. The main question was, what do people who do not think of themselves as representing any specific religious worldview actually believe? The results fell into three groups: 1) syncretic dominated by Christian language; 2) syncretic mixes with no dominant religious language; and 3) syncretic mixes dominated by the language of new spirituality.

For those in the first group (as it did for all the others), believing stood for general trust, hope, conviction, and certainty. Most believed in God, but as distinct from believers in traditional Christianity, they also believed in themselves, fate or destiny, or believed that nothing in this life happens by chance. When describing the meaning of believing and their own faith, these subjects combined Christian vocabulary with the beliefs of new spirituality, such as reincarnation and a monistic image of God. There were also visible traces of esoteric teachings.

Those in the second group reported belief in God, but they preferred as ambiguous a wording as possible. They lacked a recognisably Christian language, and generally were not members of a congregation. Most prominent was belief in themselves, their abilities, their capacity to cope on their own. Some reported belief in the effectiveness of a principle of justice, destiny or fate, supernatural forces, nature, the sacredness of life and love. There were lengthy discussions of the non-randomness of life: there had to be something or someone who directs people and gives order to their life circumstances. In addition, despite a belief in fate, people believed that one could influence the course of one's life in a positive direction by moral behaviour and good deeds. In some cases a position was taken through contradiction, mostly in opposition to the church, its power and teaching, but also religion in general. Some opined that religion is for the weak. Like the first group, this one was characterised by ideas deriving from New Age culture.

Members of the third group could be regarded as carriers of the new spirituality. They were distinguished from the two previous groups by the topic of spiritual self-development, and their frequent, self-confident use of concepts such as chakras, mandalas, previous lives, reincarnation, meditation, energy, karma, though such concepts were also mentioned in other two groups. Members of the third group participated in New Age culture, read the literature, and engaged in its practices. They expressed belief in a higher power, themselves, their own experiences, self-healing, spiritual self-development, and all kinds of energies.

One can observe a tendency among the individual religion groups: the appearance of the new spirituality and its steadily increasing influence (in the case of Christians) on individual religiosity. However, Christian ideas have been preserved in a very general sense, for example, the idea of a higher power or being that influences the individual life course and metes out justice. Concepts specific to Christianity have disappeared; subjects even avoided the word 'god' (Altnurme 2012: 197–202). We term this 'hidden Christianity'. With respect to the third group, it remains a question whether its members could at all be thought of as people having individual religiosity, since the syncretic mixtures that should characterise them are also characteristic of New Age culture, from which they are derived, as if they had been premixed in the thought-worlds of the subjects. Thus the members of these three groups could not be considered as creators of their own religion, but rather as people who express general combinations of popular beliefs.

TABLE 7.5   Factor of anti-Christian attitudes + 'one's own religion' based on factor analysis RTE 2014

Anti-Christian attitudes + 'one's own religion'	
The church is intended to manipulate the masses and keep them under control	0.67
Christianity has never been characteristic of Estonians	0.62
Religion prevents a person's freedom of spiritual development	0.60
I have my own faith, apart from of various churches and religions	0.38

Agreement with the statement 'You have your own faith which is independent of various churches and religions' in the RTE 2014 survey resulted in two factors, one which is parallel to anti-Christian attitudes (Table 7.5) and the other that is related to the beliefs of new spirituality (Table 7.6).

One-third of Estonians hold anti-Christian attitudes which originate from several sources, including left-wing ideologies, nationalism influenced by modernity, and the new spirituality. However these do not constitute a factor along with self-designations such as 'atheist' or 'non-religious'; rather, they are aligned with the claim 'I have my own faith apart from various churches and religions' (Table 7.5). Thus, in the Estonian cultural space, those who oppose Christianity – particularly its institutional forms – still regard themselves as religious in some sense. This group includes people who espouse all kinds of religious self-designations and beliefs.

In Table 7.6 we see that those who selected statements expressing the beliefs of the new spirituality tended to agree that they had their own faith, apart from various churches and religions.

From this data one can conclude that although New Age culture is not a religious environment, and its practitioners do not consider themselves religious, there are those for whom the beliefs of new spirituality do constitute a religion, which is then understood as 'one's own religion' (Table 7.6).

Andrus Saar, who analysed people with 'their own religion' based on the data of LFRL 2010 came to similar conclusions. He emphasised the following tendencies: such people are more frequently seekers who are less satisfied with what the church offers; they agree less often with Christian beliefs, and they

TABLE 7.6   Factor of the beliefs of new spirituality and 'one's own religion' based on factor analysis RTE 2014

Beliefs of new spirituality + 'one's own religion'	
Mishaps and sufferings are lessons on the path of spiritual development	0.65
I believe in spiritual self-development in the sense that with the help of consciously internalised affirmations and spiritual practices such as meditation it is possible to change oneself, one's life, and the surrounding world	0.49
I have my own faith, apart from various churches and religions	0.35

are influenced more than the average person by the literature and practices of the new spirituality (Saar 2012: 60–62).

If we analyse 'one's own religion' on the basis of gender, age and education, we can see that the more highly educated more frequently agree with the statement expressing individual religiosity. Other than the correlation with educational level, there are no other noteworthy differences.

In sum, although most Estonians have distanced themselves from or been in opposition to institutional Christianity, and though beliefs articulated in specific Christian terminology have little support, Estonians are not as far removed from religion as they think. 'One's own religion' combines popular beliefs (possibly also practices that have not been sufficiently studied), that constitute folk religion rather than the fruit of original creativity. Such folk religion contains material from several religious sources, primarily new spirituality, associated esoteric beliefs, but also beliefs drawn from Christianity – if we consider the belief in a higher power who directs and protects a person during their life course and metes out justice. In addition, there is most likely the influence of the national narrative and the provisional 'nature religion' and a popular version of native faith arising from this, which certainly merits further research.

To conclude the results section, we might pause to recognise one other topic, the importance and intensity of religion in the personal life. For New Age culture, participation is based more on the need to solve problems than on continuous commitment (cf e.g., Stolz et al. 2016: 116; Uibu 2016: 35, 62). The same could also be said about Christianity, which dominated for centuries.

Those believers who led an intense religious life have always been few; for most believers, religion became relevant according to life situations (worries, problems, and routine religious customs such as saying grace and attending religious services). The study of religious life stories showed that religion became relevant either at turning points in life or complicated periods, such as the search for identity during puberty or in crisis situations (Altnurme 2006). The same applies to new spirituality: there are not many committed participants in the total population. As has already been noted, it becomes a serious issue for people who are seeking solutions to problems, particularly connected to health, relationships, and finances, but also in identity crises and the search for the meaning and purpose of life (cf Altnurme &Lyra 2004: 117–139; Saluste 2011: 39–61). In view of the topic of the religious turn it is thus important to find out what part of the population regards Christianity and the role of the new spirituality as a credible resource in coming to terms with the problems of life. The statistics presented in this chapter support the hypothesis that fewer Estonians than ever see Christianity in this role, and more Estonians than ever have accepted the new spirituality.

4 Conclusions and Discussion

A noteworthy competitor for a declining Christianity is the new spirituality, which has been steadily growing for the last 40 years. Can we speak in this connection of a religious turn among ethnic Estonians? How and in what conditions has this term taken place? In 1934, 99% of Estonians were aligned with Christianity, and those who had learned of it in school catechism classes were familiar with its tenets. Despite the rapid dissemination of the new spirituality, we do not have a basis to claim that the same percentage of Estonians have accepted it. If the turn can be accepted as having taken place only if the majority of the population has converted to it, then such a turn has not happened. However, if we look closely at what is happening in the religious landscape, then we have reason to think that such a turn is, in fact, taking place.

One-fifth to one-third of Estonians can be regarded as Christians, most of whom belong to the older generation. However, one-third of Estonians lack any contact with Christianity. Negative stereotypes of Christians and Christianity are widespread. Another third of Estonians hold anti-Christian attitudes, and these are not so much connected to indifference or atheism as to individual religiosity, where some veiled Christian beliefs may persist, supplemented by the new spirituality. The membership of the Lutheran church, the largest Christian confession among Estonian-speaking people has been notably influenced by the new spirituality. Institutional Christianity continues to lose ground on the individual level. On the social level, the demand for Christianity has been consistent, and in the last few years it has actually grown. Here we are referring to vicarious religion, which has not helped raise interest in Christianity among individuals.

One-quarter to one-third of Estonians are participants in New Age culture to some extent, but there are even more people in its sphere of influence. The appeal of new spirituality is greatest among the young and the educated. It had begun as an alternative movement in the 1970s, and entered the mainstream in the 1990s. Despite a growing skepticism, the general attitude to the new spirituality has been positive; for example, almost half of Estonians who were asked stated that they were interested in trying some New Age practice in the future.

In relation to a religious turn, therefore, the deciding factor is which religious worldview and practice will be called for when the need arises, by those who are not active practitioners of either Christianity or the new spirituality. Deepening individualism and subjectivism tilts choices toward the self-spirituality of New Age. However, unlike Christianity, the environment of the new spirituality does not offer a clearly articulated group identity, particularly in Estonia, where participants believe that everyone 'is walking their own spiritual path' with no understanding that self-spirituality is collective, acquired from its cultural space, and operates with the support of social media. Therefore, on the social level Christianity continues to maintain a significant position whenever questions are raised about religious norms, values, and customs.

Native faith has also seen a resurgence, and it should not be disregarded when considering a religious turn. However, compared to Christianity and the new spirituality, the dissemination of native faith has been smaller. Native faith is connected to the collective narrative of the nation, which strengthens it, increases its trustworthiness, and turns it into an viable social competitor with Christianity. There is common ground between native faith and the new spirituality in beliefs and values, especially with regard to nature.

To arrive at a better understanding of the changes that have taken place and of ongoing developments, it is not enough to measure the extent to which different religious worldviews and practices have been disseminated on the individual level, though such work is important and should continue. Indeed, there is still much to learn, such as agreement with religious statements by people who self-designate as atheists or non-religious, or the disagreement with Christian statements by people who self-designate as Christians. Additional studies of social agents should certainly be conducted, as their activities and goals depend on the spread of one religious worldview or another. We should also think about how it would be possible to compare such paradigmatically different religions as Christianity and the new spirituality. What might be a more satisfactory model for discussing and clarifying the changes that have taken place?

To date, the topic of the religious turn has been little researched, and when it has been, the discussion has been one-sided; deeper cultural layers have remained hidden. Clearly more attention should be paid to connections among secular and religious worldviews, and their reciprocal influence. For example, how are secular ideas and practices taken over by the new spirituality and rendered religious? What are the dynamics of change in the area of religion, and how do these dynamics influence other areas of life, such as education, medicine, science, culture, media, and sports? These and similar questions are worthy of further research.

CHAPTER 8

The Spiritual Milieu in Estonia
Challenges and Opportunities for Studying Contemporary Forms of Religion

Marko Uibu

For historical and cultural reasons, the forms of religiosity in Estonia are fluid and concealed.[1] The limited belief in God and the minor role of institutional religion do not mean that people's life-worlds lack a supernatural or transcendent dimension. Religiosity has just become more disguised, emerging instead in the guise of forms of contemporary spirituality that do not use explicitly religious language.

Instead of religious commitments and obligations, participation in spirituality is grounded in the 'demand-based' and 'situational' model. People turn to spiritual-esoteric teachings with a specific need and in certain moments: for example, if they feel 'off track' in their lives or cannot handle crises using only non-religious and materialistic frames. Despite the prevalence of (mostly latent) beliefs and a general interest in spiritual ideas, the number of permanent, active practitioners of spiritual techniques in Estonia remains small (Altnurme 2013b). However, it is difficult to measure levels of involvement, because most spiritual practices and ideas are not clearly classified or even seen by practitioners as religious or spiritual.

New spirituality is not a coherent and institutionalised phenomenon, but instead consists of a wide variety of ideas and techniques such as westernised versions of Reiki healing, Tantra, or body-mind-spirit self-help. Such New Age-based syncretic teachings are a form of contemporary religiosity where boundaries between diverse traditions and between secular and sacred are either fluid or entirely lacking. As it would be difficult to define 'new spirituality' based on the content of the teachings and ideas, it is more accurate to describe this 'nebulous social phenomenon' as a 'milieu', 'sphere', or 'marketplace' where training centers, courses, books, teachers, and healers contribute to the circulation of diverse ideas and practices (Van Hove 1999: 161).

Due to its differences from conventional understandings of religion, the spiritual milieu challenges scholars to find new ways to describe religious participation and the religious phenomenon. Because of the difficulties in

---

[1] This chapter is based on the author's PhD thesis, defended at the University of Tartu on 7 November 2016.

studying the 'fuzzy' characteristics of new spirituality and similar forms of contemporary religiosity, less attention has been paid to these phenomena. As Linda Woodhead states:

> Even today, vast areas of religious, sacred and ritual experience are routinely ignored or dismissed as 'fuzzy', insubstantial, and lacking in salience because they do not conform to the lineaments of what a dominant consensus considers 'real' religion.
> WOODHEAD 2013: 4

Therefore, quantitative studies tend fall short of indicating the real range and importance of religious and spiritual ideas and practices. However, in a secular society like Estonia, where several indicators of the importance of non-institutional religiosities have emerged, the role of new spirituality cannot be ignored. This calls for new instruments and conceptualisations for religious studies (Heelas 2013).

This chapter explores several of the key characteristics of Estonian new spirituality – for example, the mainstreaming process and situational participation – that make it a fascinating but complicated research topic. I will discuss some of the scholarly challenges posed by the inconstant and disguised religious belonging and new forms of mediated distribution of spirituality.

1   Estonian New Spirituality

Several comparative studies have described Estonia as a 'highly secular' and 'dominantly un-churched' country (Berger et al 2008; Borowik et al 2013). Estonia seems to be an example of 'widespread indifference' to institutional religions as an endpoint of secularisation (Bruce 2002: 42). However, this 'indifference' might be misleading: there has probably not been much of a decrease in people's seeking of meaningful and effective religious and cultural tools. Estonians believe in non-theistic phenomena, and the scientific-materialist worldview is not as dominant as one would expect. For example, in 2010 only 10.9% of respondents completely rejected the premise of astrology – that the position of the stars and planets influences people at the moment of their birth (Jõks 2012: 294). The percentage of believers in 'some spirit or life force' has been recorded as the highest in Europe: 54% in 2004 (Eurobarometer 225 2005: 9) and 50% in 2010 (TNS Opinion & Social 2010: 204).

In a secular context deprived of a dominant religious tradition, syncretic forms of religion tend to emerge (Pollack and Müller 2006). 'Fuzzy fidelity' could tip the balance in the direction of one or another religious-spiritual tradition: in Europe the major influences come from Christianity and New Age (Voas 2009). In Estonia, individual religiosity is mostly based on New Age (Altnurme 2012).

Over the last 10 years, spiritual and esoteric topics have appeared in mainstream media that has legitimised their public presence. Alternative treatments, lifestyles, and other spiritual topics are no longer covered only in thematic journals with amateurish layouts and poorly written stories (as in the 1990s). Now these topics almost invariably have their own sections in women's or lifestyle magazines (Luik 2012). This has accompanied the pluralisation and fragmentation of the media landscape, especially with the emergence of new internet portals and forums. The pluralisation is ideologically related to the value of the independent citizen and consumer – the legitimacy of alternative views is based on individuals' inherent freedom to choose among many sources of knowledge (see Uibu 2016). In the process of 'spiritual seeking', everybody is free to create their own syncretic beliefs and practices.

However, topics related to spirituality are considered controversial and problematic in mainstream and intellectual channels. Despite its popularity, spirituality is still considered a personal, socially a rather marginal phenomenon, described as 'alternative' or 'esoteric' (Uibu 2016). As the editor of the Estonian cultural newspaper *Müürileht* confessed:

> I have been afraid of the esoteric world like fire. This fear is related neither to the Big Unknown Somebody nor to the (imaginary?) threats coming from the esoteric world; on the contrary, this is the fear that maybe I will start believing something myself as well; maybe I could become someone like them!
> TAMMJÄRV 2016

This text was published in an editorial for a special issue dedicated to the analyses of spiritual, alternative and esoteric topics. Although this theme was chosen because of the undeniable popularity of spiritual, esoteric and alternative teachings in Estonia, this comment clearly echoes the social stigmatisation of the religious and the spiritual that is also visible in the narratives of spiritual practitioners (Uibu 2012).

2   Indicators of Growing Popularity and 'Mainstreaming'

Estimating the popularity of spirituality is difficult, as spirituality does not have clearly defined core characteristics and boundaries. Based on my interviews with Estonians from 2011 to 2015, there seems to be a shared understanding among the practitioners of spirituality that the popularity of spiritual-alternative practices is growing, which is a potential indicator of spirituality's higher visibility (Uibu 2016). Questionnaire results also indicate some increase in the popularity of spiritual ideas and practices: for example, the proportion of people who reported reading literature about 'spiritual self-development, yoga, or something similar' rose 8% from 2010 to 2014.

Spiritual-esoteric ideas have emerged to a greater extent in mainstream channels such as public broadcasting and popular magazines. The tendency of spirituality to outgrow its common niche could be seen as a cultural mainstreaming of spirituality. Mainstreaming brings religious and spiritual elements into the public domain. Therefore, such trends in the Estonian religious sphere cannot be interpreted as secularisation or disenchantment (in Weberian terms), but rather signify the opposite – the processes called sacralisation, spiritual revolution, or re-enchantment (Heelas 2013, Partridge 2004). However, mainstreaming also means that the spiritual becomes more blended with the secular, becoming even more hidden and less identifiable as clearly religious phenomena. Thus it becomes even more challenging to decide what elements could be classified as religious and/or placed under the label of new spirituality.

For some scholars of religion, the blurring of boundaries between the spiritual milieu and mainstream culture seems to weaken spirituality, as 'many elements of the New Age are vulnerable to being co-opted by the cultural mainstream and trivialised by the mass media' transforming spirituality into a 'cheap, lightweight product' (Bruce 2000: 234). At the same time, the cultural appropriation of these ideas (and the spiritual milieu's mingling with mainstream culture) intensifies their cultural significance. I argue that a high degree of adaptability of spiritual values and understandings to popular culture is one of the key factors for the cultural significance of the spiritual milieu. Of course, there is a danger that it might become too diluted to be considered a distinctive phenomenon. However, this seems to concern more the scholarly research tradition than the impact of the phenomenon itself.

3 Weak Inclinations instead of Stable Beliefs, Practices and Belonging

The complications in the conceptualisation of the spiritual milieu become clearer when we look at the commonly analysed central elements of religions with an aim to apply them in the studies of contemporary spiritualities. Conventionally used indicators in the study of religions – the big 'Bs' of religion: belonging, belief, and behaviour (Day 2013) – have simply lost much of their functionality in describing the modes of religiosity in highly secularised societies (Wuthnow 2001; Woodhead 2010). The big Bs are difficult to apply to people who participate in the spiritual milieu: one can exist without the other(s); all three are simultaneously fulfilled by very few people. In Estonia, several factors, such as low visibility and little knowledge of religions, probably make the situation even more complicated.

Although surveys demonstrate a high level of beliefs in special extrasensory power or the higher spiritual order of the universe, these remain abstract and do not have necessarily any real-life implications. As I have argued based on interview data, such beliefs are commonly not activated, and even dedicated practitioners admit that they are not constantly practicing anything spiritual at all (Uibu 2016). Without strong commitments and official institutions, spiritual practices are situational and necessity-based. It must be noted that situational participation and the use of spiritual techniques at certain moments are still more than just instrumental consumption of a 'product'. New Age has a 'strongly transpersonal character together with an additional mystico-transcendent or sacred content', requiring belief in a 'form of connection with an all-pervading 'Force' or 'Energy'' (Rose 1998: 13). Situational contact and participation – even for utilitarian/practical concerns – require some willingness to use this type of teachings, while participation tends to bring about some further changes in values, lifestyle, or understandings of the world.

With situational and unstable connections, people with an interest in spirituality cannot be described accurately through any specific identity labels (as they do not feel strong commitment). According to my estimation, such people have become the main supporters of the social and cultural significance of new spirituality. People with a *weak inclination* to spirituality could be simply readers of some books or internet news portals, or members of communities on social media, like Facebook communities. Weakly inclined people could belong to the category of 'nones' and are especially relevant in the Estonian context because they, most probably, make up the majority of the population. For instance, the network of members of Facebook communities has risen steadily. People follow certain teachers and pages but do not become active participants – they have an abstract interest in the potential of these topics to be interesting or useful.

The latent possibility of turning to the spiritual milieu is similarly visible, for example, in the surprisingly popularity of belief in spiritual self-development or the efficacy of spiritual solutions (the belief in healers with extrasensory power is as high as 80% among Estonians). Situationality is also expressed in the common discourse of seeking: people tend to see themselves in a constant search and development that fits well with weak inclinations and situational participation in the spiritual milieu.

There are several other indications of inclination-type of connections. In the survey data, 'inclinations rather than believing and belonging' are visible not only in the confusion over identity labels, but also in the widespread occurrence of 'ratherism' – where respondents tend to avoid unequivocal answers and prefer to choose 'rather believe/not believe' options (Heelas 2013; Remmel & Uibu 2015).

Inclination-based weak commitment is not considered a truly valid form of religious participation by some scholars of religious studies. Similarly, there is a tendency to underestimate the social resonance/importance of the phenomenon because of its inability to create a cohesive group with values, practices, norms, and social relations. When evaluating the significance of a religious phenomenon, New Age spirituality has great 'range' but little 'depth':

> For the vast majority of people interested in the New Age milieu, participation is shallow. They read a book or two and attend a few meetings. They do not become committed adherents to particular cults; they do not regularly engage in time-consuming rituals or therapies; they do not radically alter their lives.
> BRUCE 2000: 233

It is argued that individual participation in the spiritual milieu diminishes the latter's influence and social significance as 'the individualism of the New Age acts as a major constraint on its influence' (Bruce 2000). Indeed, the new spirituality has a different kind of influence which seems elusive from the vantage point of the conventional sociology of religion. The spirituality relies on new types of institutions and the 'depth' of its cultural importance is more disguised.

4 Virtual Networks and Media as the New Dominant Institutions

Situational membership in New Age spiritualities does not fit well into the classification of religious organisations – church, sect, cult. 'Spiritual people' prefer fluid networks to settled collectivities (Possamaï 2005). As Colin Campbell has pointed out, spirituality as a cultic milieu is believed to be unstable, and if does not evolve into a sect-type organisation, it would 'fade away in the face of societal opposition or the absence of a charismatic leader' (2002 [1972]: 13). From this point of view, the perseverance and even growth of the spiritual milieu in the absence of strong central institutions raises the question of what keeps spiritual inclinations alive.

The lack of conventional institutions does not mean the lack of institutions. New spirituality has specific institutions and forms of distribution that are not visible to scholars of religious studies when they look for conventional traits. One important factor that supports weaker commitments is the availability of virtual networks and media to share information and experiences. New information technologies appear to be a key factor in enabling the spiritual milieu to operate. Instead, in the absence of traditional belonging or participation but with the inclination-type of relatedness, several indirect channels link like-minded individuals to each other and to the specialists. It is, therefore, suggested that the spiritual milieu is a kind of 'network' (Van Hove 1999). Adam Possamai (2000, 2007) has found several useful theoretical approaches to describe this type of belonging such as situationalistic networks or the German term *Bund* used by Herman Schmalenbach in the 1920s and later by Kevin Hetherington (1994). Based on his qualitative study of Australian spiritual practitioners, Possamai (2000) writes:

> My participants move to one group and leave it after a while. Afterwards, they might visit one or many other groups or simply stop 'seeking' for a while. 'Alternation' involves constant mobility: there is never a radical change but a constant 'flip flopping' among, or back and forth 'visits in and out' of, many *Bünde*.
>
> POSSAMAI 2000: 372

This description accurately summarises the type of involvement most widespread in the Estonian spiritual milieu; it could very well be a common pattern for different contemporary religions and spiritualities that lie outside the 'life-as-religion' type of belonging.[2] These trajectories and 'flip floppings' are fruitful to study, especially in a pluralistic society lacking primary socialisation

---
2 Conversion to Christianity could similarly have different intensities. However, because of institutional regulation and support, the process is still more standardised, with explicit and

into religion(s), and where scientific-materialistic understandings are widely perceived as the norm (Uibu 2011).

Media and communication channels build the networks and create the *bünde*. Especially relevant for the dissemination of spiritual ideas are books,[3] internet portals, and thematic web-sites. Dissemination of spiritual ideas and solutions by books already has a long history (Puttick 2005), but the internet has become an increasingly important resource for discussion and information sharing. Fitting well with new networks and virtual structures and institutions, the spiritual milieu harnesses the potential of new media. Virtual networks, internet forums and media channels might be individually unstable but surprisingly solid when taken together. Even if one stream dries up, several others are ready to take its place. Dependence on user-generated content is not a problem if there are enough willing contributors.

There are some mechanisms by which virtual communities function as efficient carriers and platforms for spiritual teachings and values. For example, the Estonian internet forum 'Nest of Angels' has become a channel for 'cultural tools' to produce the enchanted meanings, values and techniques that have found their place in people's lives. The angel forum provides emotional support either directly by fellow users, or by confirmations that angels will definitely help the person in need. The web forum also allows people to acquire knowledge on both spiritual and practical issues. Most people seek feedback and reassurance about their spiritual or extraordinary experiences and get confirmation that many other people have had similar visions and perceptions. The angels' divine nature supports people directly, but more importantly, it speaks a language of goodness and guarantees that fellow users of the internet forum, although not real angels, are at least trying to be angelic. Angels embody power, softness and benevolence, making them the perfect

---

often ritualistic-symbolic dimensions. The 'spiritual marketplace' model is more chaotic and fluid.

3 As an 'inner' and 'hidden' phenomenon, spirituality is well served by books which are excellent cultural symbols: a book is seen as a source of wisdom and reading as an individual ritual of acquiring this wisdom (Uibu & Saluste 2013). Therefore, some authors – for instance, Danièle Hervieu-Léger (2001) – call spirituality a book-centred network of individual readers. The lack of clear-cut boundaries and universally accepted labels makes it difficult to give estimations of print run and circulation; nonetheless, there are several indications in the form of best-selling books, the highest-ranked TV or radio shows with spiritual-esoteric content, yearly horoscopes that tend to nearly double the print run of newspapers. Despite this popularity, spirituality is seen as 'alternative' and considered inappropriate and even contemptible by Estonian mainstream media. Therefore, spiritual topics have found an outlet in more targeted channels such as women's and lifestyle magazines and internet news portals (Uibu & Saluste 2013).

symbols for legitimating values and epistemological positions of the spiritual milieu, which is one major reason why they have become so popular in Estonia. Therefore, this virtual platform and communication among anonymous users provides strong emotional and practical support for the functioning of the spiritual milieu (Uibu 2012).

For people who have 'weak inclination' to spirituality (see more Uibu 2016), the internet offers many comfortable options for being in informal contact without making any commitments. In Estonia, spiritual and esoteric Facebook groups and internet forums are popular: tens of thousands of members receive constant updates in their newsfeeds. Therefore, in a world where Facebook and other virtual platforms (with a great proportion of user-generated content) take the central position in information distribution, it would be shortsighted to describe the spiritual milieu as non-institutional. Institutions have changed, and channels hitherto considered private have a wide and significant social impact (see discussion in Knoblauch 2008). The process of increasing media-centredness (including social media), together with individualisation are transforming religion: as 'media democratize access to the sacred, the quest for religious fulfilment and salvation or whatever 'rewards' expected from encounters with transcendent realities' is less structured by institutions (Asamoah-Gyadu 2008: 59). People use their perceived natural autonomy to create their own 'religious projects'.

Technological and social changes have challenged the role of dominant institutions: some authors have even pointed out 'the end of Big' – a decreasing dominance of big and traditional authorities, especially in certain spheres like the media, where the internet is making David the new Goliath (Mele 2013). Obviously, this claim has many limitations, but the functioning of the spiritual milieu illustrates similar tendencies related to the religious sphere: more channels that support a vernacular dimension.

5 Vernacular Narratives as 'Model of' and 'Model For'

Despite the common individualistic idea of 'finding your own personal path', participation in and experiencing of something spiritual have a powerful social dimension. The trajectories and destinations reached by individual 'spiritual seekers' are remarkably similar. As Hammer (2010: 52) points out: 'rarely is the gap separating the ideal of subjective experimentation with spiritual alternatives and the reality of a fairly homogenous discourse as striking' as in the spiritual milieu. Therefore, cultural norms obviously direct individual decisions.

The typical reader of books and and the occasional participant in seminars and trainings do not have a sense of belonging to a community. However, this does not mean that readers and participants lack guiding models or make decisions based only on their 'inner self'. Despite the allegedly private nature of experience, the spiritual milieu provides supportive structures, institutional frames for experience, and narratives indicating certain patterns of experience. A qualitative study of the readers of spiritual books in Estonia pointed out some characteristic and shared elements that are distributed in this network of readers. Readers tend to describe themselves as seekers who are walking on the path of 'self-development', avoiding explicitly religious commitments. Among their motivations, some post-materialistic and counter-cultural elements were visible – for instance, they were searching for something meaningful that was missing in their lives. The study demonstrated that readers have adopted a vocabulary and reading practices as cultural tools (Uibu & Saluste 2013).

Stories about finding a spiritual path or getting confirmations that teachings really work follow common patterns. According to Geertz, narratives are both 'models of' and 'models for': a story about something that has happened becomes a template for people to interpret and remember their future experiences (Geertz 1973). 'Models for' are important elements in the spiritual milieu that are shared extensively. Narratives and stories 'structure experience' and 'define and illuminate inner experiences' (Bruner 1986: 6) – this is an important factor of the inner coherence of spirituality.

The New Age discourse places special emphasis on direct experience: 'something as seemingly personal as a first-hand experience becomes a privileged way of transmitting socially constructed explanations' (Hammer 2010: 62). This could be seen as a characteristic tendency for the distribution of knowledge and norms in a network society, and a key factor in the process of the vernacular gaining more and more prominence compared to institutions. A critical factor for the broader social effect of this type of narrative construction is the 'amplification of narratives' by the media (Mitchell 2008). Social networks and conventional forms of media – such as women's magazines (Utriainen et al. 2012) – distribute the models. Virtual communities like the Nest of Angels are good illustrations of a 'soft' institution: narrative structures are shared and they serve as powerful interpretive guides.

6 Conclusions and Discussion

Given the low rate of belief in God and marginal church attendance in Estonia, it could be assumed that Estonia's Soviet past has caused scientific materialism to become the prevailing worldview. However, survey results indicate that 'fuzzy spirituality' is an increasingly influential source of knowledge and ways of relating to the world. The meanings and methods that spirituality offers fit well with people's expectations, and are growing in popularity. The spiritual milieu has become an important carrier of socially shared values, indicated, for example, by the growing popularity of the claim about the importance of personal spiritual growth. It is difficult to assess the popularity or the social position of spirituality and the spiritual milieu, but there are diverse indicators of mainstreaming, which point to the increasing visibility of religious and spiritual elements in the public domain.

From the practitioners' position, spiritual teachings and techniques are commonly used in case of need and are seldom considered as distinctively religious, nor perceived as a source of longer-term or stable obligation. The Estonian example – with its low level of 'classical' and theistic religious belief or belonging – makes it obvious that scholars should focus on those people who are not 'members', 'followers', or 'committed believers' but have only some 'inclination' to use spiritual solutions in certain situations. People with only a *weak inclination to spirituality* have mostly latent beliefs in spiritual principles like vital life energies or karma; they may have experienced something of the spiritual milieu but are not consistent practitioners of any spiritual techniques or dedicated followers of principles. This type of involvement has often been omitted (or excluded) from the religious studies perspective.

In the absence of strong church-type institutions, several other factors contribute to the proliferation of spirituality. Free-market competition functions rather well in the spiritual milieu: professional practitioners are 'stimulating demand' by meeting the needs of individuals, by sharing innovation and a constant supply of new teachings. With technological and social transformation, the required forms of institutional support have changed. Different types of media (books, online media) and information dissemination platforms (like event databases and internet forums for sharing experiences) offer better opportunities to keep inclinations alive than those of traditional institutional structures such as churches.

The key to the success of the dissemination of spirituality are narratives which function as both 'model of' and 'model for'. Stories of personal spiritual experiences (models 'of'), also work as 'models for': they establish templates for structuring people's experiences (e.g., what to feel or see during breathing sessions). Such stories and arguments are shared in the media and/or in lectures/seminars as guidelines for individualistic experiencing.

The public-private distinction has lost its relevance as virtual and informal channels for vernacular content have become stronger and broader in scope and influence than religious institutions (churches, for instance). Instead of explicit power structures implemented by institutions, ideologies and norms are being shared in subtler ways. In these new 'institutions' – such as Facebook groups and communities – the lines between 'soft' and 'hard' or 'alternative' and 'dominant' are blurred. For example, we might ask, can a Facebook group even be considered an institution? How are the power relations and normative frames played out?

Conventional distinctions between *hard* (institutions, explicit power) and *soft* (values, stories, cultural tools) might be misleading, since institutionalised *soft* means have a stronger impact on people's beliefs and behaviours than dominant institutions. Participants themselves are producing and strengthening the tools (e.g., by sharing the stories of their experiences and suggestions). As vernacular networks continue to play a key role, the categories of 'dominant' and 'vernacular' are losing their relevance. Like the media, for example, religion has developed new types of institutions, which are network-based and less centrally organised, although they are still clearly structured by internal rules, normativity and power relations.

Considering the low level of belonging to traditional religious institutions and a high level of New Age-based individual religiosity, conventional sociological methods used to study religion in Western societies simply do not work in Estonia (or perhaps in Europe as a whole). Predominantly weak commitments should receive their place in religious studies, broadening their perspective, as there is no reason to limit participation to its stable forms. A broader approach is necessary not only because of the large proportion of weakly inclined people, but because of the fluid and layered modes of participation.

Therefore, religious studies should move closer to media or cultural studies and anthropology or folkloristics to observe stories, memorates and new distribution channels that are the backbone of the new spirituality. There is much to learn from ethnographic approaches that study micro-level phenomena, like the lived experiences of spiritual people (Sutcliff & Bowman 2000). However, it is also important – although difficult – to describe macro-level societal processes in light of religious fragmentation and fluidity.

The growing importance of new spirituality has several implications the discipline of religious studies. I agree with Paul Heelas' claim that the Estonian example indeed endorses the idea that 'traditional disciplinary boundaries – specifically those which revolve around 'religion' – should be relegated to history' (2013: 195). While it is allegedly one of the least religious countries in the world, the case of Estonia clearly shows the need to reject a narrow understanding of religion in order to detect and understand the full range and depth of contemporary religions, including 'situational' or 'low-intensity' religiosities.

There is still a strong need to find better concepts to describe the involvement and functioning of the spiritual milieu. Considering the disciplinary background of religious studies or sociology and anthropology of religion, this is a complicated question closely related to the identity of the scholarly field itself.

CHAPTER 9

Similarities and Differences between Estonia and the Other 'Most Secular' Countries

Riho Altnurme

1 Secularisation, Modernity and Special-case Estonia

The previous chapters have shown that Estonia has historical and contemporary reasons for its evolution into a society in which secularisation has had notable success. Therefore, before comparing seemingly similar countries, it is worth exploring how Estonia has positioned itself in the theoretical understandings of secularisation. According to Max Weber's understanding of *Entzauberung* (disenchantment) of the world, one could speak of secularisation in sociology, although the theory itself was developed later. In the 1960s and 1970s, the support for a theory of secularisation as the historical process in which religion loses social and cultural significance thanks to the modernisation of society was shared among prominent sociologists, such as Peter L. Berger who wrote the seminal *The Sacred Canopy* (Berger 1969 [1967]).

> In 1997 Berger expressed regret about the use of the simplistic theory of secularisation:
> I think what I and most other sociologists of religion wrote in the 1960s about secularization was a mistake. Our underlying argument was that secularization and modernity go hand in hand. With more modernization comes more secularization. It wasn't a crazy theory. There was some evidence for it. But I think it's basically wrong. Most of the world today is certainly not secular. It's very religious.
> BERGER 1997: 974

He later added: 'This, however, does not mean that there is no such thing as secularisation; it only means that this phenomenon is by no means the direct and inevitable result of modernity' (Berger 2001: 445). Berger and his colleagues even started to use term 'de-secularization' (Berger 1999). It was certainly the influence of historical events that disproved the theory– at least in its simplest form – claiming the linear connection of modernity and secularisation. The Islamic revolution in Iran and rise of Islam in general, the rise of

Pentecostalism, a different kind of fundamentalism – and last but not least – the collapse of an atheist empire Soviet Union in 1991 and desecularisation. In some countries it was just the temporary reflow.

It is a similar development as with Harvey Cox, one of the key theorists of secularisation in the 1960s with *The Secular City* (first published in 1965), who later claimed that the theory of secularisation has proved to be incomplete and saw the future of religion in certain grassroots movements in *Religion in the Secular City* (1984). Along the same line, but seeing the prominence of religion in society, Jose Casanova's main claim has been that religion may still become important in public life (a rebuttal to Thomas Luckmann (1963) who claimed that the religion may stay in modern society, but as privatised), speaking about 'deprivatization' of religion, at the same time not denying the differentiation and the loss of societal functions of religion. It was an empirical conclusion of what happened (mostly in the Western) world in the 1980s, based mostly on comparative case studies of the Roman Catholic church.

Around the end of the millennium there were many discussions of secularisation theory. One of the most impassioned opponents of the theory was Rodney Stark, who insisted that secularisation theory is based on faith. William H. Swatos and Kevin J. Christiano (1999: 225) wrote that the theory itself competes with different religious traditions. The collapse of Soviet Union and the resurgence of religion proved that the desecularisation is indeed possible.

> Everyone 'knows' that once upon a time the world was pious – that in olden days most people exhibited levels of religious practice and concern that today linger only in isolated social subcultures such as the Amish, ultra-orthodox Jews, or Muslim fundamentalists. But, like so many once-upon-a-time tales, this conception of a pious past is mere nostalgia; most prominent historians of medieval religion now agree that there never was an 'Age of Faith'.
> STARK 1999: 255

Speaking of the decline of religion is therefore unjustified, as there was no time when religion was doing better than it is now. Stark also cites Northern and Western Europe as areas where participation in religious services has been low for the past several centuries, but at the same time, subjective religiosity has remained noteworthy (Stark 1999: 253, 254). This historical argument is used to confirm the developments in different areas, quite often neglected in studies of the contemporary situation. Still, the discussion brought out Steve Bruce's (2001) strong counterargument that at least in Britain one can see a steady decline in church attendance and membership since 1851. Bruce goes so far as to claim that 'unless trends are reversed, major British denominations will cease to exist by 2030' (Bruce 2001: 191).

Historical changes of 1989–1990, and the rise of Islamic terrorism were the starting point for Jürgen Habermas' (2006) famous essay, 'Religion in the Public Sphere'. The meaning of religions used for political purposes created interest in the connection mentioned in the title of the essay. 'The normal model for the future of all other cultures suddenly becomes a special-case scenario' (2006: 2) as Habermas reflects from the point of view of Europeans who had been leading the wave of secularisation, is somewhat unhappy conclusion for a secularist. This was also the conclusion for a common effort by Peter L. Berger, Grace Davie and Effie Fokas (2008), who compared Europe and America, finding several historical and other reasons that explain why the development of two leaders of modernisation followed different paths of secularisation. One conclusion that they reach is that there are secular and religious versions or modernity (2008: 16) depending on the historical circumstances of development.

One should agree with José Casanova that the mythical understanding of secularisation which sees the progressive decline of religious belief in the modern world has to be replaced by 'comparative sociological analyses of historical processes of secularisation, if and when they take place' (Casanova 1994: 17). Karel Dobbelaere has proposed the use of the term 'secularization' as a descriptive, not paradigmatic term, particularly pertaining to the religious situation in Europe (Dobbelaere 1999). His approach stresses the decline of religious authority – as Alar Kilp has discussed. In one of his later works, Dobbelaere has seen the connection of his approach to secularisation to 'rational choice theory', developed by Stark, Roger Finke and Laurence R. Iannaccone, as this theory presupposes secularisation on the level of the state and studies the effect of competition among religious firms (Dobbelaere 2014: 223). Therefore it fits well with the three macro (society), meso (religious organisations) and micro (individual) levels of secularisation observed by Dobbelaere.

Several factors affect religion; the dominant confessions also have their role in shaping the religious situation. David Martin's *A General Theory of Secularization* (1978) traced the paths of secularisation in several countries using the influential variables and Protestantism. The Protestant Reformation was an important factor for secularisation, according to Charles Taylor in *A Secular Age* (2007) and Steve Bruce in *Secularization* (2011), both following the early example of Max Weber. We will keep this in mind when comparing Estonia to the other most secular countries in Europe.

In one of his last works, Berger (2014) claims that as secularisation theory has been disproven – modernity has not necessarily brought the decline of religion – one has to look for a new paradigm such as pluralism: the co-existence of religions and the co-existence of religious and secular discourses. According to Berger, 'Modernity necessarily leads to pluralism' (Berger 2014: 20). Here Berger confirms that religion may have lost some of its social functions to the state, economy and education (*differentiation*), but people still remain religious. To use the terminology of Dobbelaere, secularisation may happen at the macro level (society), but remain less influential at the micro level (individual).[1] This raises Habermas' question about pluralist society: how can secular and religious citizens coexist and behave in the political public sphere (Habermas 2006: 20)?[2] Berger concludes, 'Therefore, if a differentiation has occurred between religious institutions in society, this differentiation must also be manifested in the consciousness of individuals' (Berger 2014: x). We can be secular and religious at the same time, but in different areas. This is how we can see Estonia's situation where 'a flood of esotericism' and 'spiritual milieu' (as observed by Lea Altnurme and Marko Uibu) exist in the society where religion does not have that much of a public function.

Modernity and modernisation still have a role in secularisation (Martinelli 2005). The possibility of choice is one of the main influences. 'After all, in existential and religious matters, generalised choice, real or imagined, is what modernity is all about' (Mouzelis 2012: 220). In the European context the secularising impact of modernisation was strengthened by elements of European culture that had their own secularising potential (Davie 2002). The Estonian case showed that a national movement can promote secularisation through its detachment from (or even hostility to) religious movements. At the same time, sociologists speak about the 'modernization of religious consciousness' as a response to the challenge religious traditions have been facing from pluralism, the emergence of modern science, and the spread of positive law and profane morality (Habermas 2006: 13).

---

1 Dobbelaere has been seen as one of the followers (or at least one of the users) of Berger's understanding of secularisation, his theory being built on *The Sacred Canopy* (Hjelm 2018: 165).
2 Habermas has discussed the topic with Cardinal Joseph Ratzinger (who later became Pope Benedict XVI) in early 2004, proposing the ideal of unfettered communication as a solution (Habermas & Ratzinger 2006). The secular state must be truly neutral, without favoring any of religious and non-religious positions in society.

2 Latest Discussion on Secularisation

The theme of secularisation is still on the table, as new comparative studies have tried to show (Pollack, Rosta 2017). In this case the focus is still on the Western world and Christian denominations. Moreover, the continuation of the debate on secularisation theory and research, initiated by Jörg Stolz (2020a) shows the ongoing interest in the topic. This section summarises this discussion and reflects on the place of Estonia in this framework.

Stolz mentions seven proposed explanations for secularisation: insecurity, education, socialisation, secular transition, secular competition, pluralism and regulation. His conclusions are based on the mostly quantitative research on secularisation in the last decades.

The connection between insecurity and religion was most famously described by Pippa Norris and Ronald Inglehart (2004). In his recent book, Inglehart (2021) shows that since 2007 the decline in belief is strongest in high-income countries but that it is also evident across most of the world. Franz Höllinger and Johanna Muckenhuber (2019) have shown that among individuals this connection is much less developed. According to Stolz, 'there is ample evidence that individuals in countries with high existential insecurity are more religious than individuals in countries with low existential insecurity' (Stolz 2020a: 285). He does not seem to include countries like Estonia that have not had such high living standards but still had less of a connection to religion earlier than countries that were ranked higher in the Human Development Index.

Speaking of education, he reports that studies have clearly shown the negative effect of education on religion (Stolz 2020a: 286). Here Estonia's high standing in PISA rankings (PISA 2018), second only to China in reading, mathematics and science come to mind, although these tests are certainly not the absolute measure of education.

Stolz (2020a: 288) notes that parental socialisation is the single most important predictor of adult religiosity. This factor is strongly influenced by society; people are much more likely to become religious in highly religious countries than in predominantly secular ones, regardless of the religiosity of their parents. Other researchers have shown that declining religiosity in Western countries mainly occurs through the replacement of cohorts. Therefore the individual loss of faith is not the central factor. Similar research has been done on Estonia (Altnurme, L 2006). Of course, one still has to understand the secularising effect on parents and children, as Stolz (2020a: 289) rightly points out.

David Voas' (2008) contention that all countries are in the same 'secular transition', only at different points in time, means that Estonia is ahead of the curve. Stolz has found that although West Germany fits the model very well,

East Germany does not (Stolz, Pollack, De Graaf 2020). His argument is that 'the secular transition can be strongly influenced by external shocks' (Stolz 2020a: 291). It can therefore be debated whether Germany should be treated as a single country at all – given the different Eastern and Western historical paths. At the same time this theory is in trouble with new spirituality, perhaps being relegated to Voas' (2009) 'fuzzy fidelity'. East Germany and its comparable features with Estonia are relevant to the discussion about regulation. Also important is the influence of the (missing) connection between national identity and religion comes in eastern Germany (Stolz, Pollack, De Graaf 2020: 640).

Religions may enter into secular competition in fields associated with society and the secular world: in providing social capital, social welfare, counselling and support (Stolz 2020a: 293). The influence of religious organisations may decline when the more innovative secular state takes over those fields. In the Soviet bloc, Soviet authorities assumed most of the functions of the churches when there was little competition. After the end of Soviet era, some functions were taken back by churches, but not always successfully.

Pluralism has been a matter of debate, as Berger noted in his definitive *The Sacred Canopy*. Did it depress religious vitality or strengthen it? Recent studies have shown the negative effect of religious pluralism on church adherence. Yet the way in which pluralism actually influences religiosity remains unclear (Stolz 2020a: 295).

For former Soviet countries, the debate over the influence of state regulation seems to be important, particularly the ways in which the state may suppress religiosity by restricting religions or even banning certain religious groups and practices (Stolz 2020a: 296). The relationship between state regulation and religiosity is statistically significant for attendance at religious services and whether people consider themselves religious, but rarely for belief. The consensus is that religiosity is lower in former Communist states. Indeed, East Germany is the example that Stolz (2020a: 297) uses.

In conclusion, Stolz identifies the synthesis of different factors, as the processes of modernisation and secularisation may have many variables. 'Modernization is a process that leads to more existential security, more education, more pluralism, and more secular competition' (Stolz 2020a: 299). He claims to follow the neoclassical version of secularisation theory (like Peter Berger (1969 [1967]), and David Martin (1978)), but with better empirical grounding.

Opponents can be quite critical. According to François Gauthier (2020), the 'main acceptable claim [of Stolz] is the apparently inexorable decline of churched religion in the West', but not much else. Gauthier adds, 'Churched religion can no longer be the standard for 'religion'" (Gauthier 2020: 314).

Moreover, the comparison between Western and eastern Germany does not seem appropriate:

> the idea that the difference between the strong secular pathway of East Germany compared with West Germany's supposedly "normal" curve is due to "an external shock"— communism. Portraying the communist pathway in Eastern Europe as an 'external shock' (an expression also borrowed from economists) is flawed, as is the implicit assumption that liberal, capitalist democracies represent some kind of normal or natural trend. Religion is a part of society and culture, and it cannot be simply isolated from wider society.
>
> GAUTHIER 2020: 311

He is certainly right in saying that 'the formerly stable institutionalizations of the 20th century are being subjected to a radical critique, almost everywhere. Religious institutions are thus not the only modern institutions subject to disaffiliation and critique, far from it' (Gauthier 2020: 313).

'In a post-9/11 world, many hold religion to be the key challenge to what Jürgen Habermas calls the normative *Selbstverwiesenheit*, self-referentiality, of the project of modernity itself', according to Tobias Müller (2020: 316). His main concerns are (1) unresolved conceptual quandaries about religion and the secular, (2) the call to decolonise secularisation theory, and (3) the importance of gender and the role of religious minorities in Europe (Müller 2020: 317). The mode of secularity that was brought out by Charles Taylor in *A Secular Age* (2007); the ontological awareness that my view of the world is necessarily only one option among others, is excluded from empirical studies – also the rise of very strongly committed or strictly observant religion. Müller confirms that we are living in a world 'in which data, theoretical models, and scholars of secularisation predominantly come from Europe and the United States. The 'majority world' is often only loosely included as anecdote, context, or extrapolation' (Müller 2020: 318). And indeed, Eastern Europe may easily be left out of this strict view. He is also critical of the 'secular transition' theory that sees some countries as historically 'lagging behind' and therefore perpetuates the colonial discourse. The differentiated understanding of which groups are experiencing what kind of religious transformation might result from greater attention to gender (Müller 2020: 319–320).

David Voas describes the research on secularisation as a 'research programme' rather than mere 'theory', using Imre Lakatos' terminology. As a programme, its premise is that modernisation creates problems for religion; the key questions are how and why. He sees it as successful, comparing to the market model, which 'appears to have had its day; it led to some interesting work, but it always seemed designed for the United States' (Voas 2020: 326). The negative assessment – degenerate research programme (also Lakatos' term) – goes about religious transformation (instead of secularisation). To Voas, too many ad hoc hypotheses are needed to maintain the approach. At the same time, secularisation as a research programme keeps formulating hypotheses that lead to new predictions – a condition for a progressive research programme according to Lakatos. Nevertheless, when studing how the secularisation happens, some anomalies (like eastern Germany) appear, according to both Stolz and Voas (Voas 2020: 327). When regulation is concerned, it seems for Voas that 'the impact of official regulation seems fairly marginal except in extreme cases (e.g., East Germany, Iran)' (Voas 2020: 328). For him, 'secular transition' (connected with socialisation) seems to be the best (not surprisingly), but the research programme of secularisation seems to have weak points.

Sarah Wilkins-Laflamme's (2020) questions pertain to (1) the continued search for the causes of secularisation in the West; (2) individualisation theories' critique of secularisation as a concept; (3) the substantive content of non-religion; and (4) the risks of limiting ourselves to grand theories. She cites additional possible causes of secularisation mentioned in the literature, including 'heightened values of individualism, choice and antiauthoritarianism, as well as processes of de-traditionalization and global mobility'. In discussion the causes of secularisation, the connection with living standards is important, but does not explain everything. Wilkins-Laflamme notes that the research by Höllinger and Muckenhuber (2019) points to the connection between the elevated position in HDI and the decline of religion, but operates with a limited number of countries. Czechia, for instance, is not included: it has one of the lowest levels of religiosity in the world, but ranked only 27th for HDI (2017). Estonia is 29th in this table, it is included in the research – but is obviously less well known. The precise cause of secularisation remains the unanswered question, according to Wilkins-Laflamme. For example, 'there is an association between HDI and lower religiosity at the country level, but it is not necessarily the most materially secure individuals within a given society who are the least religious' (Wilkins-Laflamme 2020: 333).

Individualisation theories argue that religion and spirituality are changing, not declining; this is another issue that Wilkins-Laflamme finds conspicuously missing from Stolz's address. The problem is that very little quantitative research has tested the secularisation and individualisation frameworks against one another. It includes the secular transition hypothesis. In addition, the research on non-religion as a replacement for traditional religion is missing in Stolz's account (Wilkins-Laflamme 2020: 334).

The importance of context in the process of religious decline, as proposed by David Martin (1978), is used also in the religious transition model. Still the temptations of 'grand theory' have discredited secularisation theory. 'What drives important exceptions to the secular transition trend, such as in France and East Germany (that Stolz points to in his address) as well as in Russia?' remains the question for Wilkins-Laflamme (2020: 335).

In response to critics, Stolz admits that 'Many questions in the social sciences need qualitative or historical methods' (Stolz, 2020b: 340). He adds that 'finding an all-encompassing definition of religion is a quite difficult (according to Talal Asad: impossible) task when looked at epistemologically'. Still he knows that quantitative researchers have to solve this problem, 'and hence the importance of qualitative and historical research as a precondition of good quantitative studies' (Stolz, 2020b: 341).

In the debate between 'individualisation or secularisation', Stolz finds 'that the emerging consensus is that individualisation is not an alternative to secularisation, but actually accompanies it'. 'We know that fundamentalist movements have not been able to stop secularization – if they had, this would have shown up in our data' (Stolz 2020b: 341). He is quite confident that 'there is accumulating evidence that modernisation indeed leads to secularization all over the world, in Western as well as in non-Western and in Christian as well as in non-Christian societies, and that some societies have moved farther along this process than others' (Stolz 2020b: 342). Alternative religiosity is still a fringe phenomenon for him.

> Thus, there has indeed been an important individualisation of Western societies, and it has had an effect on religion. But it goes hand in hand with secularisation, and in no way stands in opposition to it. In our mixed-methods study on religion and spirituality in Switzerland (Stolz et al., 2016), for example, we found exactly this: religious individualisation (an importance given to the 'I' and its needs) was very strong across the entire religious field; alternative spirituality had appeared, but remained a rather minor phenomenon; and all this was embedded in a very strong intergenerational process of secularization overall.
> STOLZ 2020b: 343

One should agree with this in Estonia's case – this is why we have paid so much attention to individualisation and alternative spirituality.

Making conclusions before reaching the comparison – what is left from secularisation theory for Estonia? Modernisation does not bring secularisation; the 'grand theory' has failed. Even desecularisation can be temporary. Estonia can be treated as a special case, not as a model – and not in 'secular transition'. Rather the historical circumstances are important that in Estonian case have helped to go for modernisation in its secular version, most importantly thanks to the special (negative) connection of national movement to religion. One should not forget the long-term historical processes, like the influence of Protestantism. The society itself may become secular, but for its members to stay religious, we have to see secularisation as a multilevel process. In this way we can also see individualisation as the accompaniment (not alternative) to secularisation. To look at different explanations of secularisation, it seems that credibility is left in the Estonian case for education and socialisation, and also for secular competition, but only in tight connection and under the influence of either state regulation or pluralism. We still should not forget that we are speaking of society, not of the individual who can also have different identities (and approaches) in different situations. Let's see if similar conditions apply to other countries that belong to the group of 'least religious' ones.

3 Comparison with Some European Countries

In terms of religiosity, the European countries and regions that are most similar to Estonia seem to be Sweden, Czechia and eastern Germany (Schildermann 2014: 37). Sweden is sometimes left off this list, but only because it was omitted from the original list of countries researched (Pickel 2014: 55). Another difference is that Sweden is not a former Soviet-bloc country.

The identity of Estonians is often connected to the idea that Estonia is a Nordic country, not a Baltic one. At the very least, Estonia is the Baltic country that most resembles the Nordic countries. Estonia is geographically the northernmost of the Baltic countries, and the one with the closest relation to Nordic countries, particularly Finland, but also Sweden.

Therefore it is a good idea to compare Estonia with Nordic countries – where both Sweden and Denmark have been visible examples of secularisation in recent decades (Zuckerman 2008). Sweden has been among the group of countries competing for the designation of 'most secularised' country in the world. The project 'The role of religion in the public sphere. A comparative study of the five Nordic countries' (NOREL, 2009–2014, led by Inger Furseth, Norway) has created some good opportunities to make comparisons (Furseth 2018: 5–8).

4 Sweden

Several features of Sweden's secularisation are described in comparison with developments in Estonia, including cases from other Scandinavian countries. Declining membership in majority churches is certainly a common feature (Furseth et al. 2018: 42–43), especially in Sweden. Disaffiliations from the majority churches are particularly high in both Sweden and Finland. Although one can say that this is a feature also held in common with Estonia, in Sweden and Finland there is no connection between church membership and tax payments in those countries as there is in Estonia.

Although there is no data about 'nones' (people who claim no religious affiliation) in Sweden in this book, this is a feature in several European and Scandinavian countries. Attendance at church rituals is low in Scandinavian countries in general; 78% of all funerals in Sweden were connected to church (the smallest proportion in Scandinavia). Indeed, this is a large number compared with Estonia, where in 2015 only 18% of funerals were conducted by a Lutheran minister (EELC 2019). Individual secularisation, seen as the decline in religious practices (as described by Casanova 1994: 19) is most pronounced in Sweden, followed by Norway, then Denmark, though it is also evident in Finland and Iceland.

There is a large number of Christian minority churches in Sweden – their membership has been in decline since the late 1980s. The number of Roman Catholics in Sweden fell by half after the dual membership option was abolished in 2000. The rise in the numbers of Roman Catholic church members in Scandinavian countries is due to the immigration of people with a Roman Catholic background. No such immigration has affected Estonia – if one ignores Orthodox immigration during the Soviet period. In Scandinavia, there has been a sharp increase in the number of Muslim communities – 797% in Norway and 92% in Sweden between 1988 and 2014, accounting for 2.6% of Norway's population and 1.1% of Sweden's. The actual numbers may even be greater than the official statistics (Furseth et al. 2018: 51). If we look for comparable figures for Estonia, we can see that the percentage of Muslims in the population in 2000 was 0.12% and 0.14% in 2011. Thus Muslims do not seem to have exerted a remarkable influence on the community. The same has been claimed for Scandinavia (Bruce 2011: 203–205).

Although holistic spirituality is widespread, one still cannot claim that there has been a 'spiritual revolution' as described by Heelas and Woodhead (2005). Belief in reincarnation is shared by 17% of Sweden's population (Furseth et al. 2018: 54); in Estonia the comparable figure is 41% (see Lea Altnurme's chapter, 'The Religious Turn in Estonia'). Nevertheless, young people approach religion in a completely different manner; their holistic values may be more widespread than can be measured by this question about reincarnation (Furseth et al. 2018: 55).

On a fundamental question such as belief in God, Sweden has the lowest proportion of believers in Scandinavia: 37% in 2008–2010 (Furseth et al. 2018: 56). Yet in an earlier Eurobarometer study the number was lower at 23% and in Estonia at 16%. At the same time, more than half of the population in those countries believed in some sort of spirit or life force: 54% in Estonia, 53% in Sweden and 50% in Czechia (Eurobarometer 225 2005: 9).

In terms of practice, one can look at attendance at religious services. Sweden has the largest percentage of the Scandinavian population that never attends religious services. Between 2008 and 2010 (Furseth et al. 2018: 56), only 8% of its population attended once a month. The percentage of regular churchgoers is even lower in Estonia: 4% in 2004 compared to 5% in Sweden (Manchin 2004). The two countries are very similar in this respect.

In Scandinavia, the observation 'The data show religious complexity in the sense that there are several religious trends at different levels toward more secularity, a shift in religion itself, and greater religious diversity' (Furseth et al. 2018: 60) also applies to Estonia.

Why are Nordic countries so secular? Is Estonia secular for the same reason? According to one theory, 'religion was killed by welfare utopianism' (Dinham & Jackson 2012, Woodhead 2012). Religion was forced out by an aggressive, secular state (Furseth et al. 2018: 61). Such a description is similar to what has been said about Estonia or other territories formerly under Soviet rule, although in this context 'welfare' is a relative term. Still, the Nordic welfare states did not force religion out, as Furseth argues (61, 62). Furseth also refutes the theory by Norris and Inglehart (2004: 4) that religion is weaker in countries whose people feel 'existentially secure'. The history of Nordic countries (with some recent fluctuations) does not seem to support this, and in Estonia it is more accurate to speak of quite a high level of insecurity.

The reason for the secularisation of the Nordic countries may be connected to the social changes of the 1960s. Furseth (63) cites the expansion of the middle class, large groups of women entering full-time employment, and changing family patterns. These changes have influenced women's religiosity. It is similar to what Callum Brown has called 'the sixties discourse revolution' in Britain (Brown 2005: 175). This revolution changed women's self-understanding through the 'second wave of feminism and the recrafting of femininity' (176). This process is indeed universal enough to be influential in Estonia. Even if it was a Soviet-style society, such processes were similar to Western society of the time (Vahtre 2002). Still the reason for secularisation for Estonian was further back in history.

When compared with historical arguments for secularisation, the fates of Sweden and Estonia (and also those of other Nordic countries) are connected by their histories as Protestant countries. We cannot speak of similar 19th-century national movements in Sweden and Estonia. The historical highlights for Nordic countries in secularisation lie either in earlier (Reformation) or later (1960s) history. Indeed, education and (weak) socialisation, also secular competition are present in both countries, leaving a similar space for individualisation.

5   Czechia

According to the Pew Research Center, in 2012 there were six countries in which more than half of population claimed to be non-religious: China, Hong Kong, North Korea, Japan, Czechia, and Estonia (Pew Research Center 2012). When we look at a European country like Czechia, we will find several similarities with Estonia, but also differences.

Dana Hamplová and Zdeněk R. Nešpor (2009) analysed the secularisation of Czechia. Most of their empirical data came from the 2006 national survey 'Detraditionalization and Individualization of Religion in the Czech Republic' by the Institute of Sociology (Academy of Sciences of the Czech Republic). Their idea has been that for historical reasons, attitudes to Catholicism do influence Czech attitudes on religion. Here we can see some historical similarities – as Estonia's history suggests foreign domination and alienation from a Lutheran church that was too close to the ruling Baltic Germans.

Czechia's out-of-church movement was established early in the country's history and reinforced by Communist anticlericalism, resulting in today's prevalence of 'non-believers' (Hamplová & Nešpor 2009). The latter is certainly true of Estonia, although one cannot trace its organised out-of-church movement. There were still remarkably high numbers of people during Estonia's interwar independence period who simply did not pay the church membership tax, also under the influence of the prevailing social democratic mood.

The effectiveness of religious socialisation also seems to have been a problem in Czechia – particularly for the Catholic Church and the Czechoslovak Hussite Church (Hamplová & Nešpor 2009). The stronger traditional religiosity of older Czech people can be explained in terms of socialisation and the fact that they attended church when they were young (Hamplová & Nešpor 2009: 587). Under Soviet rule, opportunities for religious education were prohibited in Estonia; homes and families did not take over responsibility for religious education (Altnurme 2011). The re-creation of tradition of religious education has not been successful in independent Estonia (Valk 2009). The comparison of Estonia's 2000 and 2011 censuses proved that the younger generation was almost completely out of the reach of the Lutheran church, as shown earlier in this book.

The connection between modernisation and secularisation may seem similar in the histories of Estonia and Czechia. For Czechia there is stronger evidence that secularisation goes hand in hand with modernisation (Hamplová & Nešpor 2009). In the International Social Survey Programme (ISSP) of 2005, Estonia is not mentioned, but Latvia is. Non-affiliation is very high in Czechia – 61% in 2005, but only 34% in Latvia. According to the 2001 census 59% of the people in Czechia were 'Atheists'. Whether this is an accurate description of non-affiliated people is another question, but if the people questioned dared to describe themselves as atheists, then this would show a strong anticlerical attitude. In the 2000 Estonian census the comparable number of those who chose the category 'no religion' is 40.16%. One has to take into account that in Estonia 30.61% of respondents did not declare a religious affiliation. In any case, the number of non-affiliated persons is already high in Estonia and Czechia while elsewhere in Europe the rapid spread of non-affiliation seems to be a more recent phenomenon. Of course, the censuses may not be absolutely reliable, but they show some indication of people's identity.

The high number of 'nones' is certainly a similarity between Estonia and Czechia. However, one has to look behind the numbers to see the content of religious beliefs. In Czechia the lack of church affiliation and low church attendance go together with the belief in the existence of supernatural phenomena and/or in some form of transcendence. Belief in reincarnation was also found to be high not only among people with no church affiliation but also among a large number of regular churchgoers. For example, in 2006 more than half of the respondents in Czechia agreed that some fortunetellers can foresee the future or that there is some form of supernatural power (Hamplová & Nešpor 2009: 586). These phenomena are also found in the Estonian population.

One can agree with the conclusions of Hamplová and Nešpor (2009: 594):

> If we understand secularization as pluralization and the decomposition of church affiliation, it has definitely occurred in the Czech lands, but as a result of the impact of elites imposing secularist thought on the people rather than as an 'automatic' result of structural changes in society itself. Although such secularization predominantly affected church religion,

de-traditionalized spirituality is still common in this outwardly non-religious country.

In addition, it does seem that both the current situation and the historical roots of its development are quite similar in both Estonia and Czechia. When Czech authors argue that 'the rise of Czech "atheism" is associated with Czech nationalism and the secularistic attitudes of the elites in the 19th and the beginning of the 20th centuries rather than with the impact of the Communist regime' (Hamplová & Nešpor 2009: 595), then one has to make only a few replacements in terms in order to arrive at a reliable picture of a similar development in Estonia. If in Czechia 'the nationalist movement rejected the Roman Catholic Church due to its connection with the Austro-Hungarian Empire and portrayed Catholicism as a religion imposed by the Austrians or Germans and alien to the nation's more "natural" "Hussite past"' (ibid), then in Estonia one could speak of the Lutheran church and the Moravian church (or nature religion) as 'counter-religions'. The anti-church movement attacked either Roman Catholicism or the Lutheran church (the Orthodox church to a lesser extent). I agree with the claim:

> The sum of irreligious/anti-religious attitudes which had arisen before the Communist takeover, and which were strengthened by it, affected the nation's attitudes towards religion more strongly than modernization processes such as industrialization, urbanization and the growth of popular education.
> HAMPLOVÁ & NEŠPOR 2009: 595

If to leave out the fact that Czechia is not a dominantly Protestant country (but rather divided in conflict rooted in early Hussite Reformation and Catholic church), combination of factors influencing Czech secularisation seem to be most similar to Estonian, also having the high level of individualisation.

6 Eastern Germany

The former German Democratic Republic or East Germany is composed of the states (*Länder*) of Mecklenburg-Vorpommern, Brandenburg, Berlin, Saxony, Saxony-Anhalt, and Thuringia. As a part of united Germany it still holds a different set of characteristics in many areas, including religion. When one studies irreligiosity or secular countries in Europe from the perspective of East Germany, then the countries that are most often points of comparison are Czechia and Estonia – not Sweden or any other Nordic country that was outside of the Soviet bloc. Esther Peperkamp and Malgorzata Rajtar (2010: 1) claim that those countries have always posed a problem for scholars of religion, because traditional theories and models of explaining secularisation do not give completely satisfactory answers. 'The most common explanations view either the socialist past or large scale processes of modernization to be the cause of eastern German secularization' (Peperkamp & Rajtar 2010: 2).

Religiosity in eastern Germany is described as rooted in small active communities; religion plays an important and visible role in the public sphere through charity organisations and social assistance – even when the society is secular.

'Forced secularisation', a popular term in the research on eastern Germany (Wohlrab-Sahr et al. 2009) was used first by Heiner Meulemann in 1996, with the meaning that 'secularization has been the result of the communist dictatorship' (Meulemann 2003). Of course, one cannot ignore the fact that the decrease in official church membership coincides with repression and discrimination against Christians. Still it is remarkable that in some countries the return to the churches was much easier when the political situation changed than it was in others. The comparison with Poland is appropriate here. In post-1989 East Germany, no religious revival, as measured by sociological indicators such as church attendance, a trust in the church, and a belief in God was found (Pollack 2000). The same is true of Estonia, although there was certainly a temporary rise in the performance of church rites, but this did not bring a stable rise in church membership, which instead continued to fall (EELC 2019). Religion should have been weak due to 'internal modernisation' (especially with regard to Protestantism).

Here we encounter the historical argument that the weakening of church structures had begun as early as the Nazi era (Nowak 1996). Secularising tendencies in Protestant churches have been traced to the 19th century (Nowak 1996: 24; Pollack 1999). Detlef Pollack has claimed that

> in the nineteenth century ties with the church were already extremely weak in large parts of central Germany. Segments of the working classes and even quite a number of country people had developed a "let-us-be-Christians-without-going-to-church" approach, a kind of inner secularization while remaining church members and continuing to rely on christening, wedding, and burial rituals.
> POLLACK 1999: 166

In some regions, for instance in Saxony, a decline in religiosity began in the 18th century (Nowak 1996: 25). The East-West religious divide could be observed in 1910 – as Lucian Hölscher (2001: 7) claims, based on church statistics. States in western Germany had a higher degree of modernisation, but secularisation was more successful in the east (Pollack 1999: 164). Monika Wohlrab-Sahr has admitted that secularisation in the GDR 'was neither a simple process of repression nor a simple process of modernization' (Wohlrab-Sahr et al. 2008: 136). This is additional confirmation of how different the link between modernisation and secularisation can be and at the same time how important the long-term historical influences are, and observable also regionally, not just by country.

In East Germany, the former GDR, some scholars blamed the failed recovery of religious organisations after the political turn on the Protestant church and on the complete alienation of the East German people from religion (Peperkamp & Rajtar 2010: 10). Belonging to a church may have been some 'indirect protest' under Soviet rule (Pollack 2000: 42–43). The churches lost this extraordinary position after the unification of Germany. The established churches in East Germany received the state privileges enjoyed by churches in West Germany. Churches became a part of the system and therefore less attractive (Peperkamp & Rajtar 2010: 11). This is indeed true, but it is commonplace in the Soviet bloc – and therefore perhaps not the best explanation of the differences among some countries of this area.

The second idea involves the structural weaknesses of Protestantism, combined with the educational and discriminatory policies of GDR which created a 'culture of churchlessness' (*Kultur der Konfessionslosigkeit*) in eastern Germany (Pickel 2000: 207) or 'irreligious culture' (Pickel 2012: 145). One could claim that the 'default' decision for somebody in eastern Germany is not to belong to church, whereas the opposite is true in western Germany (also Schmidt and Wohlrab-Sahr 2003: 90). The same can be said about Estonia, although it is not taken as a symbol of some identity connected with the Soviet past as it may have been in eastern Germany, according to Gert Pickel (2000: 215, 227–228).

The point of convergence in Estonia and eastern Germany is also the neglect of the possibility of connecting religion with education: in 2006, most the Estonian and eastern German populations agreed, 'education at school should be free from religion'. This was a much larger section of society than in other European countries (Pickel 2012: 139). Here the study 'Church and Religion in an Enlarged Europe 2006' was used, comprising nine countries, including East and West Germany and Estonia. Both Estonia and eastern Germany had the lowest percentages of agreement when responding to the statement about 'religion as an important part of my life' (Pickel 2012: 140). In addition, religious socialisation is very low both in eastern Germany and Estonia according to the European comparison in 2006 (Pickel 2012: 145). The importance of religious socialisation for the vitality of religion is developed in this case by Pickel (2014: 61).

Wohlrab-Sahr concludes that the GDR population had three convictions that survived the socialist system – gender equality at work, secularism and scientism (Wohlrab-Sahr 2010: 210). Indeed, Estonia seems to have the highest wage disparity between men and woman – and scientism as such is not so popular. In this sense, Estonia has more in common with Czechia. East German citizens 'have decisively distanced themselves from transcendental matters in general', 'they differ from the Estonians who have displayed the same distance to denominational matters so far' (Pickel 2012: 143). As Pickel concludes, the low religious vitality in eastern Germany 'simply reflects the unfavorable social conditions' that 'similarly exist in Estonia, the other European country with such low religious vitality' (2012: 148). These social conditions are modernisation, socialist repression and the Protestant heritage (2012: 147). As Anja Frank (2010) has shown, the younger generation in eastern Germany believes in the afterlife and in occultism. This change has turned eastern Germany into a country similar to Estonia and Czechia.

Again, the similarities for Estonia and eastern Germany are remarkable, perhaps the only factor that stands out – the individualisation of religion – seems to appear in new generation.

7   Conclusion

What can be seen in light of the recent developments in secularisation theory and empirical research in Europe's 'least religious' countries? The comparison of Sweden, Czechia, eastern Germany and Estonia brings out some interesting results. The differences between Sweden and other countries in this group, shown by the high score of users of church rituals in Sweden, seem to confirm the influence of Soviet system, even though religiosity itself is not much different from other countries. Two factors influencing secularisation are shared by Estonia, Czechia and eastern Germany. Although they share a Soviet past, this does not seem to be the most important common denominator. The importance of the more distant historical past (in Estonia and Czechia particularly, the missing or weak connection with the local national movement during modernisation) and the weakness of socialisation of the dominant church (Roman Catholic in Czechia, Evangelical in eastern Germany and Lutheran in Estonia) seem to be the two most important. State regulation combined with secular competition and pluralism have had their role in each of those countries in its own way, with Protestantism and Reformation as a historical event. Education may not be the most important factor, although in all the countries observed the results of PISA tests were above the OECD average. Estonia was in a particularly high position (PISA 2018). Individualisation accompanies secularisation, leaving a possibility of survival and change of religion in an overly secularised society.

Conclusion

Riho Altnurme

Estonia belongs to a group of highly secularised countries, comparable to Sweden, Czechia and eastern Germany. Attendance at church rituals is low in Scandinavian countries such as Sweden, but in countries with a Soviet past like Estonia, Czechia and eastern Germany, the numbers are even lower, because of Soviet policies against religion. The importance of the historical past (missing or weak connection to national movement) and the weak socialisation of the dominant church seem to be important common factors in Estonia, Czechia and eastern Germany.

The historical heritage of Estonia, a mainly Protestant country, has shaped its contemporary religious situation. This is the connection between Estonia and other predominantly Protestant countries like in Scandinavia (and eastern Germany). The decisive factor in the diminished importance of Christianity in Estonia was the overlap between social class and ethnicity. Since the national narrative was created in both social and cultural opposition to the Germans, the Marxist myth of class struggle and the ideological hostility of Marxism to Christianity were included, and in these terms Christianity began to be regarded as a part of the German ruling classes' strategy of subjugating the Estonian lower classes. As most pastors were German until the early 20th century and belonged to the landowning class, Estonians tended to see them as foreigners. In this sense Estonia differs from Finland where Lutheran ministers were ethnic Finns – and the church became an important factor in Finnish nationalism.

The Estonian national identity became disconnected from religion. Although religion and the churches remained a vital part of the society, by the end of the 1930s the society was already secularised to the point at which religion and the church were challenged, and a transformation of religious values and institutions toward nonreligious and secular institutions had begun.

Soviet ideology regarded religion as obsolete, something to be expunged from the minds and daily routines of modern people. Believers and churches in Eastern Europe suffered from this attitude. There were a few periods of persecution of religion and religious organisations, and a general disdain for faith and churches was cultivated, using the old model of opposition to Germans. Germans, who had been elites in eastern Europe (and even in the Russian Empire) were often seen by the national movements of emerging nation states as enemies, together with their religious affiliations. The secularisation that took place in the West in 1960s following the changing social attitudes, was carried on in the East with remarkably strong state policy support. By the end of the 1960s the church as a cultural entity had disappeared from the life of most Estonians – even rites of passage were no longer connected to traditional churches. The attempts of churches to contain secularisation were noticeable but inadequate.

In today's free society the Lutheran church has had both conservative and liberal reactions – on the one hand a tendency to keep traditions, to be morally conservative and to acquire the characteristics of a sect; on the other hand, to declare openness and to accept changes in the church, while keeping both factions in the same organisation. It is not uncommon for a mainstream church to harbour very different opinions and spiritualities, keeping the organisation together. One could think of many parallels, particularly in the worldwide Anglican and Lutheran communities.

There are two cultural communities in Estonian society: Estonian-speaking and Russian-speaking. The dominant confession for the Russian-speaking community is Orthodoxy. Orthodoxy has become the largest organised religious group in Estonia and is demographically well positioned for further growth. The Orthodox identity is connected with the self-understanding of Slavic nations that keeps the ties, however fragile, with Orthodoxy. However, the Orthodox community is also burdened by its complicated history, underlying its division into two canonical jurisdictions largely along ethnic lines – another story that is common for the post-Soviet area Orthodox communities.

Estonian legislation on religion and religious associations as legal entities reflects the population's lack of religious affiliations and the relegation of religion to the private sphere. The idea of state neutrality on religion was first articulated in the 1920 Estonian Constitution; one can now speak of legal egalitarianism on religious associations. In the policy domains of the rights of ethnic minorities and the legal recognition of same-sex families, the secularising intent of the European Union has been successful. In the longer-term perspective, its policy of "secularisation from above" tends to stir up reactions, which revitalise religious authority and create a new form of *religion-as-culture*.

We can therefore conclude that with secularisation one can see the transformation of religion against the backdrop of the weaknesses of established religious organisations. Rather one can speak more about the changes in forms of expression of religiosity than about the recession of religion more generally. A noteworthy competitor for a declining Christianity is the new spirituality that has been steadily growing for the last forty years. If we look closely at the religious landscape, one can see a religious turn. One-quarter to one-third of Estonians can be regarded as participants in New Age culture, with even more people in its sphere of influence. In this respect there is no clearer line between Western and Eastern Europe; statistics are roughly the same all over Europe. The reach of new spirituality is greater among the young and the educated. Almost half of Estonians who were asked expressed an interest in trying some New Age practice in the future. Deepening individualism and subjectivism tilt choices toward the self-spirituality of New Age. There is common ground between native faith (neo-paganism based on folk traditions) and the new spirituality in beliefs and values, particularly with regard to nature. The spiritual milieu has become an important carrier of socially shared values, as indicated, for example, by the growing popularity of the claim about the importance of personal spiritual growth. From the practitioners' position, spiritual teachings, techniques are commonly used in case of need and are seldom considered as distinctively religious nor perceived as a source of longer and stable obligation.

Does Estonia show the way for the rest of Europe, following its yet unique way or is it typical? There are many factors to consider when looking at a present situation generated by its past. In many ways Estonia has features that are perhaps not completely unique, but can be of interest when studying the complex religious landscape of contemporary European society. Estonia shares its features of religion and religiosity with most of Europe.

References

Aarelaid, A. (1998). Sovetid või eurooplased. In *Ikka kultuurile mõeldes* (pp. 77–236).Tallinn: Virgela.

Aarelaid-Tart, A. (2000). Topeltmõtlemise kujunemine sovetiajal. *Akadeemia*, 4, 755–773.

Agadjanian, A. (2015). Ethnicity, nation and religion: Current debates and the South Caucasian reality. In A. Agadjanian, A. Jödicke & E. van der Zweerde (Eds.), *Religion, Nation and Democracy in the South Caucasus* (pp. 22–37). Abingdon, New York: Routledge.

Agreement. (2015). Koostöökokkulepe Siseministeeriumi ja Eesti Kirikute Nõukogu vahel, 21. jaanuar 2015. Retrieved from https://www.siseministeerium.ee/sites/default/files/dokumendid/usuasjad/koostookokkulepe_siseministeerium_ja_ekn.pdf.

AK. (1920). Asutava Kogu protokollid /Protocols of Estonian Constituent Assembly/ ij (istungjärk/session), v (veerg/column), located in University of Tartu Library.

Aleksius II. (2009). *Õigeusk Eestimaal*. Tallinn: Revelex.

Altnurme, L. & Lyra, A. (2004). Tervendamine – misjoneeriv klientkultus. In *Mitut usku Eesti. Valik usundiloolisi uurimusi* (pp. 117–139). Tartu: Tartu Ülikooli Kirjastus.

Altnurme, L. (Ed.) (2004). *Mitut usku Eesti. Valik usundiloolisi uurimusi* /Multireligious Estonia/. Tartu: Tartu Ülikooli Kirjastus.

Altnurme, L. (2006). *Kristlusest oma usuni*. Dissertationes Theologiae Universitatis Tartuensis 9. Tartu: Tartu Ülikooli Kirjastus.

Altnurme, L. (Ed.) (2007). *Mitut usku Eesti II. Valik usundiloolisi uurimusi: kristluse eri*. Tartu: Tartu Ülikooli Kirjastus.

Altnurme, L. (2011). Changes in Mythic Patterns in Estonian Religious Life Stories. *Social Compass*, 58(1), 77–94. https://doi.org/10.1177/0037768610392725.

Altnurme, L. (2012). Mida võiks kirik teada eestimaalase individuaalsest religioossusest. In E. Jõks (Ed.), *Astu alla rahva hulka. Artikleid ja arutlusi Eesti elanikkonna vaimulaadist* (pp. 193–212).Tallinn: Eesti Kirikute Nõukogu.

Altnurme, L. (2013a). Kristluse tähenduse ja tähtsuse muutus eestlaste seas 1857–2010. *Tuna: ajalookultuuri ajakiri*, 4, 36–55.

Altnurme, L. (2013b). Uus vaimsus – mis see on? In M. Uibu (Ed.), *Mitut usku Eesti III: Uue vaimsuse eri* (pp. 18–36). Tartu: Tartu Ülikooli Kirjastus.

Altnurme, L. (2014). Usk ei sure välja. *Postimees*. Retrieved from https://arvamus.postimees.ee/2782584/lea-altnurme-usk-ei-sure-valja.

Altnurme, R. (1998). Eesti Evangeelne Luterlik Kirik Nõukogude Liidus. In S. Rutiku, R. Staats (Eds.). *Estland, Lettland und westliches Christentum. Eestimaa, Liivimaa ja lääne kristlus* (pp. 219–231). Kiel: Friedrich Wittig Verlag.

Altnurme, R. (2001). *Eesti Evangeeliumi Luteriusu Kirik ja Nõukogude riik 1944–1949.* Tartu: Tartu Ülikooli kirjastus.

Altnurme, R. (2006). Foreign Relations of the Estonian Evangelical Lutheran Church as a Means of Maintaining Contact With the Western World. *Kirchliche Zeitgeschichte / Contemporary Church History, 19*(1), 159–165. https://www.jstor.org/stable/43751750.

Altnurme, R. (Ed.) (2009). *History of Estonian Ecumenism.* Tallinn-Tartu: Estonian Council of Churches-University of Tartu.

Ammaturo, F. R. (2015). The 'Pink Agenda': Questioning and Challenging European Homonationalist Citizenship. *Sociology, 49*(6), 1151–1166. https://doi.org/10.1177/0038038514559324.

Ammerman, N. T. (2013). Spiritual But Not Religious? Beyond Binary Choices in the Study of Religion. *Journal for the Scientific Study of Religion, 52*(2), 258–278. https://doi.org/10.1111/jssr.12024.

Andersen, P. B.; Gundelach, P. & Lüchau, P. (2013). A Spiritual Revolution in Denmark? *Journal of Contemporary Religion, 28*(3), 385–400. https://doi.org/10.1080/13537903.2013.831646.

Annuk, E. (2003). Totalitarism ja/või kolonialismi pained. In *Võim ja kultuur* (pp. 13–39).Tartu: Eesti Kirjandusmuuseum.

Asamoah-Gyadu, J. K. (2008). Community. In D. Morgan (Ed.), *Key words in religion, media and culture* (pp. 56–68). New York: Routledge.

Aunver, J. (1953). *Eesti rahvakiriku ristitee.* Stockholm: EELK Komitee.

Avalik sõna ametivennale Th. Tallmeistrile. (1925). Meie Kirik, 24, 192.

Barkalaja, A. (2001, May 7). Kes suunab laste vabu valikuid. *Postimees.* Retrieved from https://arvamus.postimees.ee/1865695/kes-suunab-laste-vabu-valikuid?_ga=2.74456402.1994019185.1548501680-457702786.1394710816.

Baudrillard, J. (1998). *The Consumer Society: Myths and Structures.* London: Sage.

Bell, D. (1976). *The Cultural Contradictions of Capitalism.* New York: Basic Books.

Ben Porat, G. (2013). *Between state and synagogue: The secularization of Contemporary Israel.* Cambridge: Cambridge University Press.

Bender, E. L. (2014, April 25). Õigeusu tõus ja selle põhjused. *Kirik & Teoloogia.*

Ben-Nun Bloom, P.; Arikan, G. & Sommer, U. (2014). Globalization, Threat and Religious Freedom. *Political Studies, 62*(2), 273–291. https://doi.org/10.1111/1467-9248.12060.

Berg, E. & Kilp, A. (2017). Face to Face with Conservative Religious Values: Assessing the EU's Normative Impact in the South Caucasus. In A. Jödicke (Ed.), *Religion and Soft Power in the South Caucasus.* London; New York: Routledge.

Berger, P. L. (1969) [1967]. *The Sacred Canopy: Elements of a Sociological Theory of Religion.* New York: Anchor Books.

Berger, P. L. (1997). Epistemological Modesty: An interview with Peter Berger. *Christian Century, 114*(30), 972–978.

Berger, P. L. (1998). Conclusion: General Observations on Normative Conflicts and Mediation. In P. L. Berger (Ed.), *The Limits of Social Cohesion: Conflict and Mediation in Pluralist Societies* (pp. 352–372). Boulder, CO: Westview Pres.

Berger, P. L. (Ed., 1999). *The Desecularization of the World: Resurgent Religion and World Politics*. Grand Rapids: Eerdmans.

Berger, P. L. (2001). Reflections on the sociology of religion today. *Sociology of Religion*, 62(4), 443–454. https://doi.org/10.2307/3712435.

Berger, P. L. (2005). Religion and the West. *The National Interest*, 112–119.

Berger, P. L. (2014). *The Many Altars of Modernity: Toward a Paradigm for Religion in a Pluralist Age*. Boston; Berlin: De Gruyter.

Berger, P. L., Davie, G. & Fokas, E. (2008). *Religious America, Secular Europe? A Theme and Variations*. Farnham; Burlington: Ashgate.

Berghuijs, J.; Pieper, J. & Bakker, C. (2013). Being 'Spiritual' and Being 'Religious' in Europe: Diverging Life Orientations. *Journal of Contemporary Religion*, 28(1), 15–32. https://doi.org/10.1080/13537903.2013.750829.

Borowik, I.; Ančić, B. & Tyrała, R. (2013). Central and Eastern Europe. In S. Bullivant & M. Ruse (Eds.), *The Oxford Handbook of Atheism* (pp. 622–638). New York: Oxford University Press.

Brandt, A. (1928). Kiriku ja riigi vahekorrast Eestis. *Juriidiline ajakiri Õigus*, 2, 33–39.

Brown, C. G. (2005). *The Death of Christian Britain. Understanding secularisation 1800–2000*. London; New York: Routledge.

Bruce, S. (1999). Modernisation, Religious Diversity and Rational Choice in Eastern Europe. *Religion, State and Society*, 27(3–4), 265–275. https://doi.org/10.1080/096374999106476.

Bruce, S. (2000). The New Age and Secularization. In S. Sutcliff & M. Bowman (Eds.), *Beyond new age: Exploring alternative spirituality* (pp. 220–236). Edinburgh: Edinburgh University Press.

Bruce, S. (2001). Christianity in Britain, R. I. P. *Sociology of Religion*, 62(2), 191–203. https://doi.org/10.2307/3712455.

Bruce, S. (2002). *God is Dead: Secularization in the West*. Oxford: Blackwell.

Bruce, S. (2011). *Secularization: In Defence of an Unfashionable Theory*. Oxford: Oxford University Press.

Brüggemann, K. & Kasekamp, A. (2008). The Politics of History and the "War of Monuments" in Estonia. *Nationalities Papers*, 36(3), 425–448. https://doi.org/10.1080/00905990802080646.

Bruner, E. M. (1986). Experience and Its Expressions. In V. W. Turner & E. M. Bruner (Eds.), *The Anthropology of Experience* (pp. 3–32). Urbana, Chicago: University of Illinois Press.

Campbell, C. (2002) [1972]. The cult, the cultic milieu and secularization. In J. Kaplan & H. Lööw (Eds.), *The cultic milieu: Oppositional subcultures in an age of globalization* (pp. 12–25). Walnut Creek: Rowman Altamira.

Carol, S.; Helbling, M. & Michalowski, I. (2015). A Struggle over Religious Rights? How Muslim Immigrants and Christian Natives View the Accommodation of Religion in Six European Countries. *Social Forces, 9*(2), 647–671. https://doi.org/10.1093/sf/sov054.

Casanova, J. (1994). *Public Religions in the Modern World.* Chicago: University of Chicago Press.

Casanova, J. (2008). The Problem of Religion and the anxieties of European secular democracy. In G. Motzkin & Y. Fischer (Eds.), *Religion and Democracy in Contemporary Europe* (pp. 63–74). London: Alliance Publishing Trust.

Casanova, J. (2012). The politics of nativism: Islam in Europe, Catholicism in the United States. *Philosophy of Social Criticism, 38*(3–4), 485–495. https://doi.org/10.1177/0191453711435643.

Chaves, M. (1994). Secularization as Declining Religious Authority. *Social Forces, 72*(3), 749–774. https://doi.org/10.2307/2579779.

Christoffersen, L. (2006). Intertwinement: A New Concept for Understanding Religion-Law Relations. *Nordic Journal of Religion and Society, 19*(2), 107–126.

Cox, H. (1968). *The secular city: secularization and urbanization in theological perspective.* New York: Macmillan.

Cox, H. (1984). *Religion in the Secular City: Toward a Postmodern Theology.* New York: Simon & Schuster.

Crabtree, S. (2010). *Religiosity Highest in World's Poorest Nations.* Retrieved from https://news.gallup.com/poll/142727/religiosity-highest-world-poorest-nations.aspx.

Davie, G. (2002). *Europe: the Exceptional Case. Parameters of Faith in the Modern World.* London: Darton, Longman & Todd Ltd.

Davie, G. (2007). Vicarious Religion: A Methodological Challenge. In N. Ammerman (Ed.), *Everyday Religion. Observing Modern Religious Lives* (pp. 21–36). Oxford: Oxford University Press.

Davie, G. (2007). Vicarious Religion: A Methodological Challenge. In N. Ammerman (Ed.), *Everyday Religion. Observing Modern Religious Lives* (pp. 21–36). Oxford: Oxford University Press.

Dawson, A. (2011). Consuming the Self: New Spirituality as „Mystified Consumption". *Social Compass, 58*(3), 309–315. https://doi.org/10.1177/0037768611412137.

Day, A. (2013). *Believing in Belonging: Belief and Social Identity in the Modern World.* Oxford: Oxford University Press.

Demerath, N. J. (2000). The Rise of „Cultural Religion" in European Christianity: Learning from Poland, Northern Ireland, and Sweden. *Social Compass, 47*(1), 127–139. https://doi.org/10.1177/003776800047001013.

Dinham, A. & Jackson, R. (2012). Religion, welfare and education. In L. Woodhead & R. Catto (Eds.), *Religion and Change in modern Britain* (pp. 271–294). London: Routledge.

Dobbelaere, K. (1999). Towards an Integrated Perspective of the Processes Related to the Descriptive Concept of Secularization. *Sociology of Religion, 60*(3), 229–247. https://doi.org/10.2307/3711935.

Dobbelaere, K. (2006). Bryan Wilson's Contributions to the Study of Secularization. *Social Compass, 53*(2), 141–146. https://doi.org/10.1177/0037768606064293.

Dobbelaere, K. (2014). The Karel Dobbelaere lecture: From the study of religions to the study of meaning systems. *Social Compass, 61*(2), 219–233. https://doi.org/10.1177/0037768614524318.

Dogan, M. (1995). The decline of religious beliefs in Western Europe. *International Social Science Journal, 145*(September), 405–418.

Eek, L. (2015). Eestikeelse elanikkonna õigeusklikuks olemise põhjustest. In L. Eek (Ed.), *Mitut usku Eesti IV. Valik usundiloolisi uurimusi: õigeusu eri* (pp. 87–118). Tartu: Tartu Ülikooli Kirjastus.

Eek, L. (Ed.) (2015). *Mitut usku Eesti IV. Valik usundiloolisi uurimusi: õigeusu eri.* Tartu: Tartu Ülikooli Kirjastus.

Eek, L. (2017). *Tänapäeva eestikeelsete õigeusklike katehheesist ja uskumustest.* Dissertationes Theologiae Universitatis Tartuensis 33. Tartu: Tartu Ülikooli Kirjastus.

EELC (Estonian Evangelical Lutheran Church). (2019). Retrieved from www.eelk.ee.

EELK. (1937). = Eesti Evangeeliumi Luteri Usu Kiriku aruanne 1936. aasta kohta. Tallinn: Eesti Kirik.

EELK. (1938). = Eesti Evangeeliumi Luteri Usu Kiriku aruanne 1937. aasta kohta. Tallinn: Eesti Kirik.

EELKKA. (1930). (Eesti Evangeelse Luterliku Kiriku Konsistooriumi Arhiiv /Archives of Estonian Evangelical Lutheran Church) (1930). Eesti Evangeeliumi Luteri usu kiriku XII Kirikupäeva protokoll Tallinnas, 17., 18. ja 19. juunil 1930, Kiriku aruanne 1929, VII Kiriklik elu.

EELKKA. (1934). Eesti Evangeeliumi Luteri usu kiriku XVI Kirikupäeva protokoll Tallinnas, 19. ja 20. juunil 1934, Eesti Evangeeliumi Luteri usu kiriku aruanne 1933. a., 10.

EELKKA. (1947). Konsistooriumi protokollid 1947, Eesti NSV MN Esimees sm. Veimer, 22.10.1947.

Eesti II Hariduse kongress. (1918). Tartu 20–23 juuni, 1917. Tartu.

Eesti Kirikute Nõukogu. (2017). *Eesti Kirikute Nõukogu 2016. Issanda aasta tegevusaruanne.* Tallinn: Eesti Kirikute Nõukogu.

Eesti Riikline Statistika. (1924). *1922 a. rahvalugemise andmed. Vihk II. Üleriikline kokkuvõte. Tabelid. Resultats du recensement de 1922. Pour Toute la Republique. Tome II. Tableaux synoptiques.* Tallinn: Riigi Statistika Keskbüroo, Bureau central de statistique de l'Estonie.

Eesti Statistikaamet. (1995). *Eesti rahvastik rahvaloenduste andmetel I.* Tallinn. Eesti Statistikaamet

Ehala, M. (2009). The Bronze Soldier: Identity Threat and Maintenance in Estonia. *Journal of Baltic Studies, 40*(1), 139–158. https://doi.org/10.1080/01629770902722294.

ENSV ÜVT. (Ülemnõukogu ja Valitsuse Teataja) (1990). Eesti valitsemise ajutise korra alustest, 15, 247.

Esimene õhtu. (1933). *Esimene õhtu. Meie tänapäev ja ülesanded.* Tallinn: Tallinna Hiie Kirjastus.

Eurobarometer 225. (2005). Social Values, Science & Technology. Report. Retrieved from http://ec.europa.eu/commfrontoffice/publicopinion/archives/ebs/ebs_225_report_en.pdf.

EUU. (2016). Elust, usust ja usuelust 2015 tulemused tunnuste sugu ja rahvus alusel. Lisa 1. In Eerik Jõks (Ed.), *Kuhu lähed Maarjamaa? Quo Vadis Terra Mariana?* (pp. 435–486).Tallinn: Eesti Kirikute Nõukogu.

Ferrari, S. (2010). Civil Religions: Models and Perspectives. *The George Washington International Law Review, 41*(4), 749–763.

Foret, F. (2015). *Religion and politics in the European Union: secular canopy.* New York: Cambridge University Press.

Frank, A. (2010). Young Eastern Germans and the Religious and Ideological Heritage of their Parents and Grandparents. In E. Peperkamp & M. Rajtar (Eds.), *Religion and the secular in Eastern Germany, 1945 to the present* (pp. 147–165). Leiden; Boston: Brill.

Freedom House Report. (2016). Freedom in the World 2016. Freedom House. Retrieved from https://freedomhouse.org/report/freedom-world/freedom-world-2016.

Furseth, I. (2018). Introduction. In I. Furseth (Ed.) *Religious Complexity in the Public Sphere. Comparing Nordic Countries* (pp. 1–29). Cham: Springer Nature.

Furseth, I.; Ahlin, L.; Ketola, K.; Leis-Peters, A. & Sigurvinsson, B. R. (2018). Changing Religious Landscapes in the Nordic Countries. In I. Furseth (Ed.) *Religious Complexity in the Public Sphere. Comparing Nordic Countries* (pp. 31–80). Cham: Springer Nature.

Gauthier, F. (2020). (What is left of) secularization? Debate on Jörg Stolz's article on Secularization theories in the 21st century: ideas, evidence, and problems. *Social Compass, 67*(2), 309–314. https://doi.org/10.1177/0037768620917327.

Gavriļins, A. (1988). Pareizticīgās garīdzniecības loma latviešu un igauņu zemnieku pāriešanā pareizticībā 1845. –1848. gadā. *Latvijas PSR Zinātņu Akadēmijas Vēstis,* 11, 40–52.

Gavrilin, A. (1999). *Ocherki istorii Rizhskoi eparhii. 19 vek.* Riga: Filokaliya.

Gearon, L. (2012). European Religious Education And European Civil Religion. *British Journal of Educational Studies, 60*(2), 151–169. https://doi.org/10.1080/00071005.2012.671929.

Geertz, C. (1973). *The Interpretation of Cultures.* New York: Basic Books.

Gentile, E. (2000). The Sacralisation of Politics: Definitions, Interpretations and Reflections on the Question of Secular Religion and Totalitarianism.

REFERENCES

Totalitarian Movements and Political Religions, 1(1), 18–55. https://doi.org/10.1080/14690760008406923.

Habermas, J. & Ratzinger, J. (2006). *The Dialectics of Secularization: On Reason and Religion*, ed. Florian Schuller. San Francisco: Ignatius Press.

Habermas, J. (2006). Religion in the Public Sphere. *European Journal of Philosophy*, 14(1), 1–25. https://doi.org/10.1111/j.1468-0378.2006.00241.x.

Habermas, J. (2011). 'The Political': The Rational Meaning of a Questionable Inheritance of Political Theology. In E. Mendieta & J. VanAntwerpen (Eds.), *The Power of Religion in the Public Sphere* (pp. 15–33). New York: Columbia University Press.

Halman, L. (1995). Is there a moral decline? A crossnational inquiry into morality in contemporary society. *International Social Science Journal*, 67(3), 419–439. http://hdl.handle.net/10822/886719.

Hammer, O. (2010). I Did It My Way? Individual Choice and Social Conformity in New Age Religion. In S. Aupers & D. Houtman (Eds.), *Religions of Modernity: relocating the sacred to the self and the digital* (pp. 49–67). Leiden; Boston: Brill.

Hamplová, D. & Nešpor, Z. (2009). Invisible Religion in a "Non-believing" Country: The Case of the Czech Republic. *Social Compass*, 56(4), 581–597. https://doi.org/10.1177/0037768609345975.

Hansen, H. (2002). *Luterlased, õigeusklikud ja teised*. Tallinn.

Harless, G. C. A. (1869). *Geschichtsbilder aus der lutherischen Kirche Livlands vom Jahre 1845 an.* Leipzig: Duncker und Humboldt.

HDI. (2017). Human Development Reports. Retrieved from http://hdr.undp.org/en/composite/HDI.

Heelas, P. (1996). *The New Age Movement. The Celebration of the Self and the Sacralization of Modernity*. Oxford: Blackwell.

Heelas, P. & Woodhead, L. (2005). *The Spiritual Revolution: Why Religion is Giving Way to Spirituality*. Oxford: Blackwell.

Heelas, P. (2013). Eesti kui katselabor – ideaalne näide vaimsuse ja religiooni suundumuste uurimiseks. In M. Uibu (Ed.), *Mitut usku Eesti III: Uue vaimsuse eri* (pp. 167–187). Tartu: Tartu Ülikooli Kirjastus.

Heljas, M.-A. (2003). Eesti Apostlik Õigeusu Kirik: sünnilugu. *Kultuur ja Elu*, 4, 50–55.

Henry of Livonia. (2003). *The Chronicle of Henry of Livonia*. New York: Columbia University Press.

Hervieu-Léger, D. (1998). Secularization and Religious Modernity in Western Europe. In B. Misztal & A. Shupe (Eds.), *Religion, Mobilization and Social Action* (pp. 15–31). Westport: Praeger.

Hervieu-Léger, D. (2001). Individualism, the Validation of Faith, and the Social Nature of Religion in Modernity. In R. K. Fenn (Ed.), *The Blackwell Companion to Sociology of Religion* (pp. 161–175). Chichester: Blackwell.

Hetherington, K. (1994). The contemporary significance of Schmalenbach's concept of the Bund. *The sociological review*, *42*(1), 1–25. https://doi.org/10.1111/j.1467-954X.1994.tb02990.x.

Hildebrandt, A. (2014). Routes to decriminalization: A comparative analysis of the legalization of same-sex sexual acts. *Sexualities*, *17*(1–2), 230–253. https://doi.org/10.1177/1363460713511105.

Hjelm, T. (2018). Assessing the Influence of the Sacred Canopy: A Missed Opportunity for Social Constructionism? In T. Hjelm (Ed.), *Peter L. Berger and the Sociology of Religion. 50 years after the Sacred Canopy* (pp. 157–174). London; New York: Bloomsbury.

Höllinger, F. & Muckenhuber, J. (2019). Religiousness and existential insecurity: A cross-national comparative analysis on the macro- and micro-level. *International Sociology*, *34*(1), 19–37. https://doi.org/10.1177/0268580918812284.

Hölscher, L. (2001). *Datenatlas zur religiösen Geographie im protestantischen Deutschland. Von der Mitte des 19. Jahrhunderts bis zum Zweiten Weltkrieg*. 4 Bde., Berlin; New York: Walter de Gruyter.

Houtman, D. & Aupers, S. (2007). The Spiritual Turn and the Decline of Tradition: The Spread of Post-Christian Spirituality in 14 Western Countries 1981–2000. *Journal for the Scientific Study of Religion*, *46*(3), 305–320. https://doi.org/10.1111/j.1468-5906.2007.00360.x.

Hurd, E. S. (2006). Negotiating Europe: the politics of religion and the prospects for Turkish accession. *Review of International Studies*, *32*(2), 401–418. https://doi.org/10.1017/S026021050600708X.

Hurt, J. (1879). *Pildid isamaa sündinud asjust*. Tartu: Eesti Kirjameeste Seltsi Toimetused.

Hurt, J. (1907). *Elu valgus. Jutluseraamat*. Tallinn: August Buschi kirjastus.

Hurt, J. (1939a). Kiri `Sakala` väljaandjale 18. juuli 1878. In H. Kruus (Ed.), *Jakob Hurda kõned ja avalikud kirjad* (p. 202). Tartu: Eesti Kirjanduse Selts.

Hurt, J. (1939b). Kõne pedagoogilisel õhtul Tartus 1870. In H. Kruus (Ed.), *Jakob Hurda kõned ja avalikud kirjad* (pp. 80–94). Tartu: Eesti Kirjanduse Selts.

Hurt, J. (1989a). Eesti päevaküsimused 1874. In *J. Hurt, Kõned ja kirjad*. Loomingu Raamatukogu, 1–2, 43–61.

Hurts, J. (1989b). Kiri E.Ü.S.-ile 1878. J. Hurt, *Kõned ja kirjad*. Loomingu Raamatukogu, 1–2, 69–71.

Huss, B. (2014). Spirituality: The Emergence of a New Cultural Category and its Challenge to the Religious and the Secular. *Journal of Contemporary Religion*, *29*(1), 47–60. https://doi.org/10.1080/13537903.2014.864803.

Ilves, T. H. (1999). Sissejuhatus [Introduction]. In Samuel P. Huntington, *Tsivilisatsioonide kokkupõrge ja maailmakorra ümberkujunemine* (pp. 11–22). Tallinn: OÜ Fontese Kirjastus.

REFERENCES

Inglehart, R. (2021). *Religion's Sudden Decline: What's Causing it, and What Comes Next?* Oxford: Oxford University Press.

Jakelić, S. (2010). *Collectivistic Religions: Religion, Choice, and Identity in Late Modernity.* Farnham: Ashgate.

Jakobson, C. R. (1959). „Sakala" väljaandja avalik vastus kirikhärra J. Hurda teise kirja peale. In *Valitud teosed II* (pp. 165–180).Tallinn: Eesti Riiklik Kirjastus.

Jansen, E. (2004). Veel kord ärkamisaja kultuurimurrangust. In *Vaateid eesti rahvusluse sünniaegadesse* (pp. 60–102). Tartu: Ilmamaa.

Jansen, E. (2007). *Eestlane muutuvas ajas.* Tartu: Kirjastus Eesti Ajalooarhiiv.

Jansen, E. (2010). Usk ja kirik. In T. Karjahärm & T. Rosenberg (Eds.), *Eesti ajalugu V: pärisorjuse kaotamisest Vabadussõjani* (pp. 314–326). Tartu: Ilmamaa.

Jõesalu, K. (2006). Privaatse ja avaliku põimumisest Nõukogude Eesti eluilmas: postsotsialistlikke vaateid sotsiaalsetele suhetele nõukogude argielus. In *Eesti Rahva Muuseumi Aastaraamat XLIX* (pp. 91–124). Tartu: Eesti Rahva Muuseum.

Jõks, E. (2012). 'Elust, usust ja usuelust 2010 tulemused' võrdlus tunnuse sugu alusel. In E. Jõks (Ed.), *Astu alla rahva sekka. Artikleid ja arutlusi Eesti elanikkonna vaimulaadist* (pp. 283–317). Tallinn: Eesti Kirikute Nõukogu.

Jõks, E. (Ed.) (2012). *„Astu alla rahva hulka". Artikleid ja arutlusi Eesti elanikkonna vaimulaadist* [*Step Down among the People. Articles and Discussions on the Spiritual Inclinations of the Estonian Populace*]. Tallinn: Eesti Kirikute Nõukogu.

Jõks, E. (Ed.) (2016). *Kuhu lähed Maarjamaa? Quo vadis Terra Mariana?* Tallinn: Eesti Kirikute Nõukogu.

Käärde, K. (2006). *Naiste ordineerimise algus. EELK ja Laine Villenthal.* Bachelor thesis, manuscript, University of Tartu.

Kaasik, P. (2011). Psühhiaatrilise sundravi kuritarvitamisest Nõukogude Liidus. *Tuna: ajalookultuuri ajakiri*, 4, 79–96.

Kändler, T. (2003, April 29). Kas vajame kohustuslikku ateismiõpetust? *Postimees.* Retrieved from https://arvamus.postimees.ee/2016689/kas-vajame-kohustuslikku-ateismiopetust.

Kangilaski, J. (2002). Kohanemised marksismidega. In *Kohandumise märgid* (pp. 11–19). Underi ja Tuglase Kirjanduskeskus.

Kaplinski, J. (2001, March 31). Usuõpetus ja mõned küsimärgid. *Postimees*, 15.

Karjahärm, T. & Sirk, V. (1997). *Eesti haritlaskonna kujunemine ja ideed 1850-1917.* Tallinn: Eesti Entsüklopeediakirjastus.

Karjahärm, T. & Sirk, V. (2001). *Vaim ja võim. Eesti haritlaskond 1917-1940.* Tallinn: Argo.

Kesküla, K. (2009, June 18). "Kui nüüd Kalev koju jõuab ...", *Eesti Ekspress*, A1.

Ketola, M. (1996). Tallinnan ortodoksisen katedraalin purkuhanke vuonna 1928 – uskonnollista sortoa vai "kansallista terapiaa"? *Ortodoksia*, 45, 115–158.

Ketola, M. (2000). *The Nationality Question in the Estonian Evangelical Lutheran Church, 1918–1939.* Helsinki: Suomen Kirkkohistoriallinen Seura.

Ketola, M. (2003). Estonians, Baltic Germans and their Lutheran teachings about the Jews 1919–1945. *Kirchliche Zeitgeschichte/Contemporary Church History, 16*(1), 112–126. https://www.jstor.org/stable/43751681.

Ketola, M. (2009). The Baltic Churches and the Challenges of the Post-Communist World. *International journal for the Study of the Christian Church, 9*(3), 225–239. https://doi.org/10.1080/14742250903161888.

Kiivit, J. (1995). Eesti Evangeelne Luterlik Kirik peale Teist maailmasõda. In J. Gnadenteich, *Kodumaa kirikulugu. Usuõpetuse õpperaamat* (pp. 102–115). Tallinn: Logos.

Kilemit, L. & Nõmmik, U. (2004). Eesti elanike suhtumisest religiooni. In *Mitut usku Eesti. Valik usundiloolisi uurimusi* (pp. 10–36). Tartu: Tartu Ülikooli Kirjastus.

Kilp, A. (2009). Patterns of Lutheran Politics in a Post-Communist State: the Case of Estonia. *Kultura i Polityka, 6,* 66–77.

Kilp, A. (2011). Historical Reasons for the Decline of Religious Affiliation: Communism, Confession or Church's Relation with National Identity? *Studies in Church History, 35*(4), 171–200.

Kilp, A. (2012). *Church Authority in Society, Culture and Politics After Communism.* (Doctoral thesis). University of Tartu, Tartu.

Kilp, A. (2013). Lutheran and Russian Orthodox Church Buildings as Symbols of Cultural Identity in the Estonian Parliamentary Elections of 2011. *Religion, State and Society, 41*(3), 312–329. https://doi.org/10.1080/09637494.2013.839131.

Kilp, A. (2015). Religious Nationalism Blocking the Legal Recognition of Same-Sex Unions in the Baltic States. In S. Sremac & R. R. Ganzevoort (Eds.), *Religious and Sexual Nationalisms in Central and Eastern Europe* (pp. 113–133). Leiden; Boston: Brill.

Kilp, A. (2017). The Harmonization of Laws on Same-Sex Unions in Post-Communist Post-Accession Countries. In T. Hashimoto & M. Rhimes (Eds.), *Reviewing European union Accession: Unexpected Results, Spillover Effects, and Externalities* (pp. 183–203). Leiden; Boston: Brill. https://doi.org/10.1163/9789004352070_012.

Kiviorg, M. (2012). §40. In: Ü. Madise (Ed.), *The Constitution of the Republic of Estonia. Commented Edition* (pp. 436–437).Tallinn: Juura.

Kiviorg, M. (2016). *Law and Religion in Estonia.* Second Edition. Alphen aan den Rijn: Kluwer Law International.

Kivirähk, A. (2003, April 11). Köster jälle koolis. *Eesti Päevaleht.* Retrieved from http://epl.delfi.ee/news/arvamus/andrus-kivirahk-koster-jalle-koolis?id=50951931.

Klausen, J. (2009). Why religion has become more salient in Europe: four working hypotheses about secularization and religiosity in contemporary politics. *European Political Science, 8*(3), 289–300. https://doi.org/10.1057/eps.2009.14.

Kniss, F. (2003). Mapping the Moral Order: Depicting the Terrain of Religious Conflict and Change. In M. Dillon (Ed.), *Handbook of the Sociology of Religion* (pp. 331–347). Cambridge: Cambridge University Press.

REFERENCES

Knoblauch, H. (2008). Spirituality and popular religion in Europe. *Social Compass*, 55(2), 140–153.
Kõpp, J. (1940). *Kirikuvalitsemisõpetus.* Tartu: Akadeemilise Kooperatiivi Kirjastus.
Kriik, E. (2005, April 7). Usuõpetusele roheline tee. *Postimees*, 17.
Kruus, H. (1930). *Talurahva käärimine Lõuna-Eestis XIX sajandi 40-ndail aastail.* Tartu: Eesti Kirjanduse Seltsi Kirjastus.
Kukk, K. (2003). Mütologiseeritud ajaloo rollist eesti rahvuse arengus. *Vikerkaar*, 10–11, 98–107.
Kuutma, K. (2005). Vernacular Religions and the Invention of Identities Behind the Finno-Ugric Wall. *Temenos*, 41(1), 51–76. https://doi.org/10.33356/temenos.4802.
Lääne, M. (2009). Aleksander Nevski katedraali lugu. *Tuna: ajalookultuuri ajakiri*, 2, 148–156.
Laar, M. (2005). *Äratajad. Rahvuslik ärkamisaeg Eestis 19. sajandil ja selle kandjad.* Tartu: Eesti Ajalooarhiiv.
Laitin, D. (1998). *Identity in Formation: The Russian-Speaking Populations in the Near Abroad.* Ithaca: Cornell University Press.
Larsen, H. (2014). Normative Power Europe and the importance of discursive context: the European Union and the politics of religion. *Cooperation and Conflict*, 49(4), 419–437. https://doi.org/10.1177/0010836714532918.
Lauristin, M. & Vihalemm, P. (2017). Kultuurisuhte muutumine. In *Eesti ühiskond kiirenevas ajas* (pp. 223–250). Tartu: Tartu Ülikooli Kirjastus.
Leisman, N. (1907). *Õigeusu ajalugu Baltimaal uuemal ajal.* Riia.
LFRL. (2010). Survey „Life, Faith and the Religious Life" by Saar Poll.
LFRL. (2015). Survey „Life, Faith and the Religious Life" by Saar Poll.
Lõhmus, A. (2003, April 17). Toivo Maimets kardab, et kohustuslik usundiõpetus oleks Eestile häbiväärne. *Postimees*, 4.
Lõhmus, A. (2013, May 2). Eestist on saamas õigeusklik maa. *Maaleht*.
Lõhmus, M. (2004). "Esineb ideoloogiliselt ebatäpseid formuleeringuid ...". Avalike tekstide kontrolli mudelist totalitaarses süsteemis. *Akadeemia*, 4, 699–717.
Loorits, O. (1990). *Eesti rahvausundi maailmavaade.* Tallinn: Perioodika.
Luckmann T. (1963). *Das Problem der Religion in der modernen Gesellschaft. Institution, Person und Weltanschauung.* Freiburg im Breisgau: Rombach.
Luiga, G. E. (1930). Mis on meile teoloogias vastuvõetamatu? *Olion*, 8, 43–45.
Luik, K. (2012). *Vaimsete õpetuste usutavuse ja tähenduslikkuse loomine ajakirja Naised persoonilugudes.* Bachelor thesis, manuscript, University of Tartu.
Lynch, G. (2007). *The New Spirituality.* London; New York: I.B. Tauris.
Manchin, R. (2004). *Religion in Europe: Trust Not Filling the Pews.* Retrieved from https://news.gallup.com/poll/13117/religion-europe-trust-filling-pews.aspx.
Manners, I. (2002). Normative Power Europe: A Contradiction in Terms? *Journal of Common Market Studies*, 40(2), 235–258. https://doi.org/10.1111/1468-5965.00353.

Martin, D. (1978). *A General Theory of Secularization*. Oxford: Blackwell.

Martinelli, A. (2005). *Global Modernization: Rethinking the Project of Modernity*. London: Sage.

Masing, U. (1930). Vaatlusi maailmale teoloogi seisukohalt. *Olion*, 6, 8–10.

Masing, U. (1938). Eestipärasest ristiusust. *Protestantlik Maailm*, 1, 5–9.

McCormick, J. (2010). *Europeanism*. Oxford: Oxford University Press.

McCrea, R. (2010). *Religion and the Public Order of the European Union*. Oxford: Oxford University Press.

Mele, N. (2013). *The end of big: How the internet makes David the new Goliath*. New York: Macmillan, St. Martin's Press.

Meulemann, H. (1996). *Werte und Wertwandel. Zur Identität einer geteilten und wieder vereinten Nation*. München: Juventa.

Meulemann, H. (2003). Erzwungene Säkularisierung in der DDR – Wiederaufleben des Glaubens in Ostdeutschland? Religiöser Glaube in ost- und westdeutschen Alterskohorten zwischen 1991 und 1998. In Gärtner, C.; Pollack, D. & Wohlrab-Sahr, M. (Eds.). *Atheismus und religiöse Indifferenz* (pp. 271–289). Opladen: Leske+Budrich.

Ministry of the Interior. (2018). List of clergy with the right to contract marriage with civil validity as on 18 October 2017. Retrieved from https://www.siseministeerium.ee/sites/default/files/dokumendid/usuasjad/abielu_solmimise_oigust_omavate_vaimulike_nimekiri_seisuga_18.10.2017.pdf.

Mitchell, J. (2008). Narrative. In D. Morgan (Ed.), *Key Words in Religion, Media and Culture* (pp. 123–135). New York: Routledge.

Modood, T. (2010). Moderate secularism, religion as identity and respect for religion. *The Political Quarterly, 81*(1), 4–14. https://doi.org/10.1111/j.1467-923X.2010.02075.x.

Monsma, S. V. (1993). *Positive Neutrality: Letting Religious Freedom Ring*. Westport, CT: Greenwood Press.

Mõtte, E. (2007). Tudengite usulised otsingud kristlikus miljöös. In *Mitut usku Eesti II. Valik usundiloolisi uurimusi: kristluse eri* (pp. 127–149). Tartu: Tartu Ülikooli Kirjastus.

Mouzelis, N. (2012). Modernity and the Secularization Debate. *Sociology 46*(2), 207–223. https://doi.org/10.1177/0038038511428756.

MPEÕK. (2019). MPEÕK vaimulikkond. Retrieved from https://orthodox.ee/et/clergy-eocmp/.

Müller, T. (2020). Secularisation theory and its discontents: Recapturing decolonial and gendered narratives. Debate on Jörg Stolz's article on Secularization theories in the 21st century: ideas, evidence, and problems. *Social Compass, 67*(2), 315–322. https://doi.org/10.1177/0037768620917328.

Niitsoo, V. (1997). *Vastupanu 1955–1985*. Tartu: Tartu Ülikooli Kirjastus.

Norris, P. & Inglehart, R. (2004). *Sacred and Secular: Religion and Politics Worldwide*. Cambridge: Cambridge University Press.

Nowak, K. (1996). Staat ohne Kirche? Überlegungen zur Entkirchlichung der evangelischen Bevölkerung im Staatsgebiet der DDR. In G. Kaise & E. Frie (Eds.), *Christen, Staat und Gesellschaft in der DDR* (pp. 23–43). Frankfurt: Campus.

NS. (2010). Survey about new spirituality by Lea Altnurme & Saar Poll.

Pankhurst, J. G. & Kilp, A. (2013). Religion, the Russian Nation and the State: Domestic and International Dimensions: an Introduction. *Religion, State and Society, 41*(3), 226–243. https://doi.org/10.1080/09637494.2013.844592.

Papathomas, G. (2007). Eesti "õigeusu kiriklikku küsimust" ennetav kirikukoguline lahendus. In G. Papathomas (Ed.), *Õnnetus olla väike kirik väikesel maal: teoloogiline tõde Eesti Õigeusu Kiriku kohta* (pp. 35–82). Tallinn: Püha Platoni Seminar.

Pärkson, K. (2007). Muutustest tänapäeva kristlikus vaimsuses. In *Mitut usku Eesti II. Valik usundiloolisi uurimusi: kristluse eri* (pp. 150–200).Tartu: Tartu Ülikooli Kirjastus.

Partridge, C.H. (2004). *The Re-Enchantment of the West. Volume 1: Alternative Spiritualities, Sacralization, Popular Culture, and Occulture.* London: T & T Clark International.

Paul, T. (2003). Eesti kirik 1980-ndatel aastatel. In *Kirik keset küla.* Tartu: Ilmamaa.

Pekko, I. & Koppel, K. (2013). Püha Kolmainsus kui Ema-Isa-Laps: uus vaimsus ja luteri kirik. In M. Uibo (Ed.), *Mitut usku Eesti III: Valik usundiloolisi uurimusi: uue vaimsuse eri.* (pp. 139–166). Tartu: Tartu Ülikooli Kirjastus.

Peperkamp, E. & Rajtar, M. (2010). Introduction. In E. Peperkamp & M. Rajtar (Eds.), *Religion and the secular in Eastern Germany, 1945 to the present.* Leiden; Boston: Brill.

Perno Postimees ehk Näddalileht. (1857, June 5), 1, 1–2.

Pew Research Center. (2012). 'Global Religious Landscape', Religiously Unaffiliated. Retrieved from http://www.pewforum.org/2012/12/18/global-religious-landscape-unaffiliated/.

Pew Research Center. (2014). Russians Return to Religion, But Not to Church. Retrieved from http://www.pewforum.org/2014/02/10/russians-return-to-religion-but-not-to-church/.

Pew Research Center. (2017). Global Restrictions on Religion Rise Modestly in 2015, Reversing Downward Trend. Retrieved from http://www.pewforum.org/2017/04/11/global-restrictions-on-religion-rise-modestly-in-2015-reversing-downward-trend/.

Pickel, G. (2000). Konfessionslose in Ost- und Westdeutschland – ähnlich oder anders? In D. Pollack & G. Pickel (Eds.), *Religiöser oder kirchlicher Wandel in Ostdeutschland 1989–1999* (pp. 206–235). Opladen: Leske+Budrich.

Pickel, G. (2012). Religiosity and Bonding to the Church in East Germany in Eastern European Comparison – Is East Germany Still Following a Special Path? In G. Pickel & K. Sammet (Eds.), *Transformations of religiosity: religion and religiosity in Eastern Europe, 1989–2010* (pp. 135–154). Wiesbaden: Springer VS.

Pickel, G. (2014). Religion, Religiosität, Religionslosigkeit und religiöse Indifferenz. Religionssoziologische Perspektiven in vereinigten Deutschland. In M. Rose & M.

Wermke (Eds.), *Konfessionslosigkeit heute: zwischen Religiosität und Säkularität* (pp. 45–77). Leipzig: Evangelische Verlagsanstalt.

Pikkur, T. (1997, May 17). Anda inimestele vajalik ja päästev sõnum. *Eesti Kirik*, 18, 1.

PISA. (2018). PISA 2018 results. Retrieved from https://www.oecd.org/pisa/PISA-results_ENGLISH.png.

Plaat, J. (2001). *Usuliikumised, kirikud ja vabakogudused Lääne- ja Hiiumaal*. Tartu: Eesti Rahva Muuseum.

Plaat, J. (2011). Orthodoxy and Orthodox Sacral Buildings in Estonia from the 11th to the 19th centuries. *Folklore*, 1, 7–42. https://doi.org/10.7592/FEJF2011.47.plaat.

Plath, U. (2008). „Euroopa viimased metslased": eestlased saksa koloniaaldiskursuses 1770–1870. In *Rahvuskultuur ja tema teised* (pp. 37–64). Tallinn: Underi ja Tuglase Kirjanduskeskus.

Põld, P. (1917). Väited usuõpetuse korralduse kohta koolis. *Kasvatus ja Haridus*, 7–9, 189–191.

Pollack, D. (1999). The Situation of Religion in Eastern Germany after 1989. In P. J. Smith (Ed.), *After the Wall. Eastern Germany since 1989* (pp. 161–181). Boulder and Oxford: Westview Press.

Pollack, D. (2000). Der Wandel der religiös-kirchlichen Lage in Ostdeutschland nach 1989. In D. Pollack & G. Pickel (Eds.), *Religiöser oder kirchlicher Wandel in Ostdeutschland 1989–1999* (pp. 18–47). Opladen: Leske+Budrich.

Pollack, D. (2002). The change in religion and church in Eastern Germany after 1989: a research note. *Sociology of Religion*, 63(3), 373–387. https://doi.org/10.2307/3712475.

Pollack, D. & Müller, O. (2006). Religiousness in Central and Eastern Europe: Towards Individualization? In I. Borowik (Ed.), *Religions, Churches and Religiosity in Post-Communist Europe* (pp. 22–36). Krakow: Nomos.

Pollack, D. & Rosta, G. (2017). *Religion and Modernity: An International Comparison*. Oxford: Oxford University Press.

Polunov, A. (2001). The Orthodox Church in the Baltic Region and the Policies of Alexander III's Government. *Russian Studies in History*, 4, 66–76. https://doi.org/10.2753/RSH1061-1983390466.

Popp-Baier, U. (2010). From Religion to Spirituality. Megatrend in Contemporary Society or Methodological Artefact? A Contribution to the Secularization Debate from Psychology of Religion. *Journal of Religion in Europe*, 3, 34–67. https://doi.org/10.1163/187489209X478337.

Population Census. (2011). Population and Housing Census 2011. Demographic and ethno-cultural characteristics of the population. Religious Affiliation. Retrieved from http://pub.stat.ee/px-web.2001/Database/Rahvaloendus/REL2011/07Rahvastiku_demograafilised_ja_etno_kultuurilised_naitajad/09Usk/09Usk.asp.

Poska, J. (1968). *The Martyrdom of Bishop Platon*. Stockholm: Culture Fund of the Estonian Apostolic Orthodox Church.

REFERENCES

Pospielovsky, D. (1998). *The Orthodox Church in the History of Russia*. Yonkers: St. Vladimir's Seminary Press.

Possamai, A. (2000). A profile of New Agers: social and spiritual aspects. *Journal of Sociology, 36*(3), 364–377. https://doi.org/10.1177/144078330003600306.

Possamai, A. (2005). *In search of New Age spiritualities*. Aldershot: Ashgate.

Possamai, A. (2007). Producing and Consuming New Age Spirituality: The Cultic Milieu and the Network Paradigm. In D. Kemp & J. R. Lewis (Eds.), *Handbook of New Age* (pp. 151–165). Leiden, Boston: Brill.

Protocol. (2002). Eesti Vabariigi Valitsuse ja Eesti Kirikute Nõukogu ühishuvide protokoll, 17. oktoober 2002. Retrieved from https://www.siseministeerium.ee/sites/default/files/dokumendid/usuasjad/eesti_vabariigi_valitsuse_ja_eesti_kirikute_noukogu_uhishuvide_protokoll.pdf.

Püha Johannese Kool. (2019). About St. John the Evangelist School. Retrieved from http://pjk.ee/index.php/en/about.

Puttick, E. (2005). The Rise of Mind-Body-Spirit Publishing: Reflecting or Creating Spiritual Trends? *Journal of Alternative Spiritualities and New Age Studies, 1*(1), 129–149.

Raud, M. (1936). *Eesti algkooli lõpetaja. Algkooli lõpetajate teadmised usuõpetuse alal.* Haridus- ja Sotsiaalministeeriumi Koolivalitsuse väljaanne. Eesti Koolinõunikkude Ühingu toimetised nr. 30.

Raudsepp, A. (1998). *Riia vaimulik seminar 1846–1918*. Tartu: Eesti Kirjandusmuuseum.

Raudsepp, K. (1982). *Ristiga märgitud*. Toronto: Eesti Vaimulik Raamat.

Raudsepp, M. (2005). Eestlaste loodusesuhe keskkonnapsühholoogia vaatenurgast. In T. Maran & K. Tüür (Eds.), *Eesti looduskultuur* (pp. 379–420). Tartu: Eesti Kirjandusmuuseum.

Reiman, H. (1935). Kirikuelu 1930–34. *Eesti Statistika*, 158(1)–169(12).

Religio 2. (2017). Survey about religion by Kantar Emor.

Remmel, A. & Uibu, M. (2015). Outside Conventional Forms: Religion and Non-Religion in Estonia. *Religion and Society in Central and Eastern Europe, 8*(1), 5–20.

Remmel, A. (2011a). *Religioonivastane võitlus Eesti NSVs aastail 1957–1990. Tähtsamad institutsioonid ja nende tegevus*. Dissertationes Theologiae Universitatis Tartuensis 24. Tartu: Tartu Ülikooli Kirjastus.

Remmel, A. (2011b). Religiooniseaduste Kontrollimise Kaastöökomisjonid Nõukogude Eestis. *Ajalooline Ajakiri, 135*(1), 85–104.

Remmel, A. (2016). Eesti ühiskonna religioossusest ja sekulariseerumisest mittereligioossete eestlaste alusel. In E. Jõks (Ed.), *Kuhu lähed Maarjamaa? Quo vadis Terra Mariana?* (pp. 131–151). Tallinn: Eesti Kirikute Nõukogu.

Remmel, A. (2017). Religion, Interrupted? Observations on Religious Indifference in Estonia. In J. Quack & C. Schuh (Eds.), *Religious Indifference. New Perspectives From Studies on Secularization and Nonreligion* (pp. 123–142). Cham: Springer.

Rimestad, S. (2012). *The Challenges of Modernity to the Orthodox Church in Estonia and Latvia (1917–1940)*. Frankfurt: Peter Lang.

Rimestad, S. (2014). Orthodox churches in Estonia. In Leustean, L. (Ed.), *Eastern Christianity and Politics in the Twenty-First Century* (pp. 295–311). Abingdon/Oxon: Routledge.

Ringvee, R. (2011). *Riik ja religioon nõukogudejärgses Eestis 1991–2008*. Dissertationes Theologiae Universitatis Tartuensis 23. Tartu: Tartu Ülikooli Kirjastus.

Ringvee, R. (2013). Regulating religion in a neo-liberal context: the transformation of Estonia. In T. Martikainen & F. Gauthier (Eds.), *Religion in the Neo-Liberal Age. Political Economy and Modes of Governance* (pp. 143–160). Farnham: Ashgate.

Ringvee, R. (2013, June 14). Eesti õigeusu lugu. *Postimees*.

Ringvee, R. (2014). Religion: not declining but changing. What do the population censuses and surveys say about religion in Estonia? *Religion, 44*(3), 502–515. https://doi.org/10.1080/0048721X.2014.914635.

Ringvee, R. (2015a). Religious involvement in public sphere in a secular state: institutions, interests and attitudes. *International Review of Sociology, 25*(2), 252–261. https://doi.org/10.1080/03906701.2015.1039271.

Ringvee, R. (2015b). Jehovas Zeugen im Baltikum – ein historiografischer Überblick. In G. Besier, K. Stoklosa (Eds.), *Jehovas Zeugen in Europa – Geschichte und Gegenwart*. Band 2 (pp. 13–42). Berlin: LIT.

Ringvee, R. (2015c). *Annotated Legal Documents on Islam in Europe: Estonia*. Leiden; Boston: Brill.

Rinne, J. (2016). *Searching for Authentic Living Through Native Faith. The Maausk Movement in Estonia*. Södertörn Doctoral Dissertations 122. Stockholm: Elanders.

Risch, H. (1937). Die estnische apostolische-rechtgläubige Kirche. *Kyrios: Vierteljahresschrift für Kirchen- und Geistesgeschichte Osteuropas*, 2, 113–142.

Rittersporn, Gabor T.; Behrends, Jan C. & Rolf, Malte (2003). Open Spaces and Public Realm. In G. T. Rittersporn, M. Rolf & J.C. Behrends (Eds.), *Public Spheres in Soviet-Type Societies* (pp. 423–452). Frankfurt am Main: Peter Lang.

Rivers, J. (2007). Law, Religion and Gender Equality. *Ecclesiastical Law Journal, 9*(1), 24–52. https://doi.org/10.1017/S0956618X0700004X.

Rohtmets, P. & Salumäe, E. (2011). Eesti evangeelse luterliku vaba rahvakiriku asutamisest. *Akadeemia*, 6, 1135–1178.

Rohtmets, P. (2012). *Teoloogilised voolud Eesti Evangeeliumi Luteri Usu Kirikus aastatel 1917–1934*. Dissertationes Theologiae Universitatis Tartuensis 26. Tartu: Tartu Ülikooli Kirjastus.

Rohtmets, P. (2013, May 13). Usk rahvaloendusse. *Postimees*.

Rohtmets, P. & Ringvee, R. (2013). Religious Revival and the Political Activity of Religious Communities in Estonia during the Process of Liberation and the Collapse of the Soviet Union 1985–1991. *Religion, State and Society, 41*(4), 355–393. https://doi.org/10.1080/09637494.2013.855059.

Rohtmets, P. (2016). The international dimension of Estonian Lutheranism in the 20th century. *Nordost Archiv*, xxv, 136–166.

Rohtmets, P. & Tēraudkalns, V. (2016). Taking Legitimacy to Exile: Baltic Orthodox Churches and the Interpretation of the Concept of Legal Continuity during and after the Soviet Occupation of the Baltic States. *Journal of Church and State, 58*(4), 633–665. https://doi.org/10.1093/jcs/csv034.

Rohtmets, P. (2018). *Riik ja usulised ühendused*. Tallinn: Siseministeerium.

Rohtmets, P. & Altnurme, R. (2018). Luterlus. In R. Altnurme (Ed.), *Eesti kiriku- ja religioonilugu* (pp. 224–244). Tartu: Tartu Ülikooli Kirjastus.

Rohtmets, P. (2019, March 1). The Autocephaly of the Ukrainian Orthodox Church and the Future of the Eastern Orthodox Church. *International Centre for Defence and Security*. Retrieved from https://icds.ee/the-autocephaly-of-the-ukrainian-orthodox-church-and-the-future-of-the-eastern-orthodox-church.

Rose, S. (1998). An examination of the new age movement: Who is involved and what constitutes its spirituality. *Journal of Contemporary Religion, 13*(1), 5–22. https://doi.org/10.1080/13537909808580818.

Rousseau, J.-J. (1950). *The Social Contract and Discourses*. New York: E. P. Dutton.

RT. (Riigi Teataja) (1919). Maaseadus, 79/80, 156.

RT. (1920a). Eesti Vabariigi Põhiseadus, 113/114, 243.

RT. (1920b). Seisuste kaotamise seadus, 129–130, 254.

RT. (1922). Abielu seadus, 138, 88.

RT. (1925a). Matmispaikade seadus, 171/172, 86.

RT. (1925b). Perekonnaseisu seadus, 191/192, 110.

RT. (1925c). Usuühingute ja nende liitude seadus, 183/184, 96.

RT. (1933). Eesti Vabariigi Põhiseaduse muutmise seadus, 86, 628.

RT. (1934a). Kaitseseisukorra seadus, 22, 156.

RT. (1934b). Kirikute ja usuühingute seadus, 107, 840.

RT. (1937). Eesti Vabariigi Põhiseadus, 71, 590.

RT. (1990). Eesti NSV seadus kodanike ühenduste kohta, 1, 14.

RT. (1991). Eesti riiklikust iseseisvusest, 29, 338.

RT. (1992). Eesti Vabariigi Põhiseadus, 26, 349.

RT. (1993a). Kirikute ja koguduste seadus, I, 30, 510.

RT. (1993b). Maamaksuseadus, I, 24, 428.

RT. (1996). Mittetulundusühingute seadus, I, 42, 811.

RT. (1998). Erakooliseadus, 57, 859.

RT. (1999a). Eesti Vabariigi ja Püha Tooli vaheline kokkulepe katoliku kiriku õigusliku staatuse kohta Eesti Vabariigis, II, 7, 47.

RT. (1999b). Tulumaksuseadus, I, 101, 903.

RT. (2000). Vangistusseadus, I, 58, 376.

RT. (2001a). Loomakaitseseadus, I, 3, 4.

RT. (2001b). Võlaõigusseadus, I, 81, 487.

RT. (2002). Kirikute ja koguduste seadus, I, 24, 135.

RT. (2003). Kriminaalmenetluse seadustik, I, 27, 166.

RT. (2004). Soolise võrdõiguslikkuse seadus, I, 27, 181.

RT. (2008). Võrdse kohtlemise seadus, I, 56, 315.

RT. (2009a). Isikut tõendavate dokumentide seadus, I, 27, 166.

RT. (2009b). Perekonnaseadus, I, 60, 395.

RT. (2012a). Kaitseväeteenistuse seadus, I, 1.

RT. (2012b). Põllumajanduslooma religioossel eesmärgil tapmise erimeetodid, religioossel eesmärgil tapmise loa taotluse täpsemad sisu- ja vorminõuded ning religioossel eesmärgil tapmise läbiviimise nõuded ja kord /Special methods of religious slaughter of farm animals, more detailed substantive and formal requirements for religious slaughter and requirements and procedure for religious slaughter/, I, 53.

RT. (2014). Kooseluseadus, I, 1.

RT. (2017). Perekonnaseisutoimingute seadus, I, 78.

RTE. (2014). Survey about religious trends in Estonia by Lea Altnurme & Kantar Emor.

Ruutsoo, R. (2000). Sotsiaalteaduste võimalused: demokraatia diskursus ja diskursiivne demokraatia annekteeritud Eestis. In *Kõnelev ja kõneldav inimene* (pp. 24–62). Tallinn: TPÜ Kirjastus.

Ryan, D. C. (2007). Religious conversion and the problem of commitment in Livland province, 1850s–1860s. *Ajalooline Ajakiri*, 3/4, 369–392.

Saar, A. (2010). Changes in Estonia's value judgements in 1990–2008. In M. Lauristin; M. Heidmets & R. Vetik (Eds.), *Estonian Human Development Report 2009* (pp. 109–113). Tallinn: Estonian Cooperation Assembly.

Saar, A. (2012). Eestimaalane ja tema usk sotsioloogi pilgu läbi. In E. Jõks (Ed.), *Astu alla rahva hulka. Artikleid ja arutlusi Eesti elanike vaimulaadist* (pp. 49–75). Tallinn: Eesti Kirikute Nõukogu.

Saard, R. (2000). *Eesti rahvusest pastorkonna väljakujunemine ja vaba rahvakiriku projekti loomine 1870–1917*. Helsinki: Suomen Kirkkohistoriallinen Seura.

Saard, R. (2007). Eestlane ja luterlus II. *Akadeemia*, 7, 1424–1451.

Saard, R. (2008). Eesti Apostlik-Õigeusu Kiriku algusaastad. *Akadeemia*, 7, 1543–1572.

Saard, R. (2014, February 21). Eesti elanike religioossusest ning tervest ja ebatervest religioonis. *Kirik & Teoloogia*.

Salo, V. (2000). *Riik ja kirik 1940–1991*. Brampton: Maarjamaa.

Salumaa, E. (1938). Meie usu- ja kirikuelu välisorientatsioonist. *Akadeemia*, 5, 306–310.

Salumaa, E. (2010). *Tüüb pandud aastaile õlale*. Tallinn: Eesti Päevaleht/Akadeemia.

Salupere, M. (2001). Sissejuhatus: Johann Voldemar Jannseni päevaraamatud. In *Diarium. Johann Voldemar Jannseni Pärnu päevik* (pp. 9–23). Pärnu: Pärnu Muusem.

Saluste, M. (2011). *Uue vaimsuse kirjanduse retseptsioon*. Master's thesis, manuscript, University of Tartu.

Samarin, Yu. (1889). *Sochineniya Yu. F. Samarina. T. 7. Pis'ma iz Rigi i istorija Rigi*. Moskva: D. Samarin.

Samoldin, A. (2007). *Usuelu Eestis Saksa okupatsiooni ajal aastail 1941–1944*. Bachelor thesis, manuscript, University of Tartu.

Schanda, B. (2003). Religion and State in the Candidate Countries to the European Union – Issues Concerning Religion and State in Hungary. *Sociology of Religion, 64*(3), 333–348. https://doi.org/10.2307/3712488.

Schihalejev, O. & Ringvee, R. (2017). Silent Religious Minorities in Schools in Estonia. In A. Sjöborg & H.-G. Ziebertz (Eds.), *Religion, Education and Human Rights. Theoretical and Empirical Perspectives* (pp. 63–76). Cham: Springer.

Schildermann, H. (2014). Religiosität und Säkularität in Europa: empirisch-theologische Perspektiven. In M. Rose & M. Wermke (Eds.), *Konfessionslosigkeit heute: zwischen Religiosität und Säkularität* (pp. 29–44). Leipzig: Evangelische Verlagsanstalt.

Schlesinger, P. & Foret, F. (2006). Political Roof and Sacred Canopy? Religion and the EU Constitution. *European Journal of Social Theory, 9*(1), 59–81. https://doi.org/10.1177/1368431006060463.

Schmidt, T. & Wohlrab-Sahr, M. (2003). Still the Most Areligious Part of the World: Developments in the Religious Field in Eastern Germany since 1990. *International Journal of Practical Theology, 7*, 86–100.

Schvak, T. (2015). Eesti õigeusu kiriku lugu 19. sajandist tänaseni. In L. Eek (Ed.), *Mitut usku Eesti IV. Valik usundiloolisi uurimusi: õigeusu eri* (pp. 40–86). Tartu: Tartu Ülikooli Kirjastus.

Schvak, T. (2016). Die orthodoxe Kirche im protestantischen Estland der Zwischenkriegszeit. *Nordost-Archiv: Zeitschrift für Regionalgeschichte, 25*, 92–113.

Segato, R. L. (2008). Closing Ranks: Religion, Society and Politics Today. *Social Compass, 55*(2), 203–215. https://doi.org/10.1177/0037768608089740.

Selart, A. (2003). Muistne vabadusvõitlus. *Vikerkaar,* 10–11, 108–120.

Selart, A. (2009) The Orthodox Monastery in Tartu during the Livonian War. *Tuna: ajalookultuuri ajakiri. Special issue on the history of Estonia,* 46–55.

Shimazono, S. (1999). "New Age Movement" or "New Spirituality Movements and Culture"? *Social Compass, 46*(2), 121–133. https://doi.org/10.1177/003776899046002002.

Siemer, K. (2003). Võim, indiviid ja kohanemine elulugudes: vanemad eestlased elust Nõukogude Eestis. In E. Kõresaar, T. Anepaio (Eds.), *Mälu kui kultuuritegur: etnoloogilisi perspektiive* (pp. 124–149). Tartu: Tartu Ülikooli Kirjastus.

Smith, D. E. (1974). Religion and Political Modernization: Comparative Perspectives. In D. E. Smith (Ed.), *Religion and Political Modernization: Comparative Perspectives* (pp. 3–28). New Haven, MA, London: Yale University Press.

Sommerville, J. (2002). Stark's Age of Faith Argument and the Secularization of Things: A Commentary. *Sociology of Religion, 63*(3), 361–372. https://doi.org/10.2307/3712474.

Sõtšov, A. (2001). *Eesti Apostlik-Õigeusu Kirik 1940–1945*. Bachelor thesis, manuscript, University of Tartu.

Sõtšov, A. (2004). *Eesti õigeusu piiskopkonna halduskorraldus ja vaimulikkond aastail 1945–1953*. Master's thesis, manuscript, University of Tartu.

Sõtšov, A. (2008). *Eesti õigeusu piiskopkond nõukogude religioonipoliitika mõjuväljas 1954–1964*. Tartu: Tartu Ülikooli Kirjastus.

Spohn, W. (2003). Multiple Modernity, Nationalism and Religion: A Global Perspective. *Current Sociology, 51*(3–4), 265–286. https://doi.org/10.1177/0011392103051003007.

Stark, R. (1999). Secularization, R.I.P. *Sociology of Religion, 60*(3), 249–273. https://doi.org/10.2307/3711936.

Statistikaamet. (2000). Rahva ja eluruumide loendus 2000. RL231: Rahvastik religiooni suhtumise, usu ja rahvuse järgi. Retrieved from http://pub.stat.ee/px-web.2001/Database/Rahvaloendus/REL2000/17Usk/17Usk.asp.

Statistikaamet. (2011). Rahva ja eluruumide loendus 2011. RL0454: Vähemalt 15-aastased usu, soo, vanuserühma, rahvuse ja maakonna järgi. Retrieved from http://pub.stat.ee/px-web.2001/Database/Rahvaloendus/REL2011/07Rahvastiku_demograafilised_ja_etno_kultuurilised_naitajad/09Usk/09Usk.asp.

Stolz, J.; Könemann, J.; Schneuwly Purdie, M.; Englberger, T. & Krüggeler, M. (2016). *(Un)believing in Modern Society. Religion, Spirituality, and Religious-Secular Competition*. London; New York: Routledge.

Stolz, J. (2020a). Secularization theories in the twenty-first century: Ideas, evidence, and problems. Presidential address. *Social Compass, 67*(2), 282–308. https://doi.org/10.1177/0037768620917320.

Stolz, J. (2020b). Secularization research and its competitors: A response to my critics. *Social Compass, 67*(2), 337–346. https://doi.org/10.1177/0037768620917331.

Stolz, J.; Pollack, D. & De Graaf, N. D. (2020). Can the State Accelerate the Secular Transition? Secularization in East and West Germany as a Natural Experiment. *European Sociological Review, 36*(4), 626–642. https://doi.org/10.1093/esr/jcaa014.

Storm, I. (2011). 'Christian nations'? Ethnic Christianity and Anti-Immigration Attitudes in Four Western European Countries. *Nordic Journal of Religion and Society, 24*(1), 75–96.

Sutcliff, S. & Bowman, M. (Eds.) (2000). *Beyond New Age: Exploring Alternative Spirituality*. Edinburgh: Edinburgh University Press.

Sutcliffe S. J. (2004). The Dynamics of Alternative Spirituality. Seekers, Networks, and "New Age". In James R. Lewis (Ed.), *The Oxford Handbook of New Religious Movements* (pp. 466–490). Oxford: Oxford University Press.

Swatos, W. H. & Christiano, K. J. (1999). Secularization Theory: The Course of a Concept. *Sociology of Religion, 60*(3), 209–228. https://doi.org/10.2307/3711934.

Taagepera, R. (2007). Estonia's Constitutional Assembly, 1991–1992. *Journal of Baltic Studies, 25*(3), 211–232. https://doi.org/10.1080/01629779400000141.

Tamm, E. (2001). *Moodsad kirikud: Eesti 1920.–1930. aastate sakraalarhitektuur.* Tallinn: Eesti Arhitektuurimuuseum.

Tamm, M. (2003). Monumentaalne ajalugu. Mida me teame ajaloost? *Vikerkaar*, 10–11, 60–68.

Tammjärv, M. (2016). "Juhtkiri: Liiga kaugele üle piiri on ohtlik". *Müürileht*. Retrieved from https://www.muurileht.ee/juhtkiri-liiga-kaugele-ule-piiri-on-ohtlik/.

Tarand, K. (2013, May 3). Lojaalsuskonflikt. *Sirp*.

Taylor, C. (2007). *A Secular Age*. Cambridge (Mass.); London: Belknap Press of Harvard University Press.

The Council of the European Union (2013). EU Guidelines on the promotion and protection of freedom of religion or belief, Luxembourg, 24 June 2013. Retrieved from http://www.consilium.europa.eu/uedocs/cms_Data/docs/pressdata/EN/foraff/137585.pdf.

Therborn, G. (1999). *The Ideology of Power and the Power of Ideology*. London; New York: Verso.

Thomas, S. M. (2005). *The Global Resurgence of Religion and the Transformation of International Relations: The Struggle for the Soul of the Twenty-First Century*. New York: Palgrave.

Tiit, E.-M. (2011). *Eesti rahvastik. Viis põlvkonda ja kümme loendust.* Tallinn: Statistikaamet.

TNS Emor. (2014). Survey about the support to the law of cohabitation by TNS Emor.

TNS Opinion & Social (2010). Special Eurobarometer 341 / Wave 73.1. Retrieved from http://ec.europa.eu/public_opinion/archives/ebs/ebs_341_en.pdf.

Tobien, A. (1911). *Die Agrargesetzgebung Livlands im 19. Jahrhundert. Bd 2. Die Vollendung der Bauerbefreiung*. Riga: Löffler.

Tomka, M. (1998). Contradictions of secularism and the preservations of the sacred. Four contexts of religious change in communism. In R. Laermans; B. Wilson & J. Billiet (Eds.), *Secularization and Social Integration* (pp. 177–189). Leuven: Leuven University Press.

Tomka, M. (2006). Catholics and Protestants in Post-Communist Europe. In I. Borowik (Ed.), *Religions, Churches and Religiosity in Post-Communist Europe* (pp. 37–51). Krakow: Nomos.

Tschannen, O. (1991). The Secularization Paradigm: A Systematization. *Journal for the Scientific Study of Religion, 30*(4), 395–415. https://doi.org/10.2307/1387276.

Uibu, M. & Saluste, M. (2013). Lugejate virtuaalne kogukond: Kirjandus ja ajakirjandus vaimsete-esoteeriliste ideede kandja ja levitajana. In M. Uibu (Ed.), *Mitut usku Eesti: Uue vaimsuse eri* (pp. 79–106). Tartu: Tartu Ülikooli Kirjastus.

Uibu, M. (2011). *Seekers of the 'Alternative': Making Sense of the Self and the World Through Spiritual Practices in Estonia*. Master's thesis, manuscript, Central European University.

Uibu, M. (2012). Creating Meanings and Supportive Networks on the Spiritual Internet Forum "The Nest of Angels". *Journal of Ethnology and Folkloristics*, 6(2), 69–86.

Uibu, M. (2012). Võitlus teaduse nimel. *Ajalooline Ajakiri, 141/142* (3/4), 337–357.

Uibu, M. (2015). Elu tõelise olemuse tunnetamine, moodsa aja religioon või umbluu – uue vaimsuse erinevad nimetamis- ja käsitlusviisid Eestis. *Usuteaduslik Ajakiri* 69(2), 99–121.

Uibu, M. (2016). Reemerging religiosity: the mainstreaming of new spirituality in Estonia. *Journal of Baltic Studies*, 47(2), 257–274. https://doi.org/10.1080/01629778.2015.1113432.

Uibu, M. (2016). *Religiosity as cultural toolbox: a study of Estonian new spirituality*. Dissertationes Theologiae Universitatis Tartuensis 32. Tartu: University of Tartu Press.

Uibu, M. (Ed.) (2013). *Mitut usku Eesti III. Valik usundiloolisi uurimusi: uue vaimsuse eri.* Tartu: Tartu Ülikooli Kirjastus.

Undusk, J. (2003). Retooriline sund Eesti Nõukogude ajalookirjutuses. In *Võim ja kultuur* (pp. 41–68). Tartu: Eesti Kirjandusmuuseum.

Undusk, J. (2016). Ideetud eestlased. In J. Undusk, *Eesti kirjanike ilmavaatest* (pp. 792–808) Tartu: Ilmamaa.

Utriainen, T.; Hovi T. & Broo, M. (2012). Combining choice and destiny: identity and agency within post-secular well-being practices. In P. Nynäs; M. Lassander & T. Utriainen (Eds.), *Post-secular society* (pp. 187–216). New Brunswick: Transactions Publishers.

Vaher, B. (2003, April 30). Usundiõpetuse debatist agnostiku pilguga. *Postimees*. Retrieved from https://arvamus.postimees.ee/2017005/usundiopetusdebatist-agnostiku-pilguga.

Vahtre, L. (2002). *Elu-olu viimasel vene ajal*. Tallinn: Kirjastuskeskus.

Valk, P. (1997). *Ühest heledast laigust Eesti kooli ajaloos*. Tallinn: Logos.

Valk, P. (2009). *Religiooniõpetus – Mis? Miks? Kuidas?* Tartu: Tartu Ülikooli Kirjastus.

van Dijk, T. A. (2005). *Ideoloogia. Multidistsiplinaarne käsitlus*. Tartu: Tartu Ülikooli Kirjastus.

Van Hove, H. (1999). L'émergence d'un 'marché spirituel'. *Social Compass*, 46(2), 161–172. https://doi.org/10.1177/003776899046002005.

Västrik, E.-H. (2015). In Search of Genuine Religion: The Contemporary Estonian Maausulised Movement and National Discourse. In K. Rountree (Ed.), *Contemporary Pagan and Native Faith Movements in Europe: Colonialist and Nationalist Impulses* (pp. 130–153). Oxford: Berghahn.

Veingold, A. (2003, March 15). Filosoofia tagasi koolidesse! *Postimees.* Retrieved from https://arvamus.postimees.ee/2017401/filosoofia-tagasi-koolidesse.

Velliste, A. (Ed.) (2011). *Usk vabadusse: artikleid ja mälestusi Eesti Evangeelse Luterliku Kiriku osast Eesti iseseisvuse taastamisel.* Tallinn: EELK Konsistoorium.

Versteeg, P. & Roeland, J. (2014). Fieldwork on Experience: Spirituality, Individuality and Authority. In A. Droogers & A. van Harskamp (Eds.), *Methods for the Study of Religious Change* (pp. 101–111). Sheffield; Bristol: Equinox.

Vihuri, V. (2007). *Hugo Bernhard Rahamägi, Eesti Evangeelse Luterliku Kiriku teine piiskop 1934–1939.* Dissertationes Theologiae Universitatis Tartuensis 11. Tartu: Tartu Ülikooli Kirjastus.

Vihuri, V. (2008). Piiskop Rahamägi ja luterlik kirik vaikival ajastul. *Ajalooline Ajakiri*, 125(3), 215–244.

Viilma, U. (2016). Kristluse homsest päevast Eestis – millised on ristirahva võimalused. In E. Jõks (Ed.), *Kuhu lähed Maarjamaa? Quo vadis terra Mariana?* (pp. 419–432). Tallinn: Tallinna Raamatutrükikoda.

Viilma, U. (2017). *Advent Reflection – Homily of Archbishop Urmas Viilma on 30 November 2017 in Tallinn Cathedral.* Retrieved from https://eelk.ee/en/uudised/advent-reflection-homily-of-archbishop-urmas-viilma-on-30-november-2017-in-tallinn-cathedral/.

Viires, A. (2001). Eestlaste ajalooteadvus 18.-19. sajandil. *Tuna: ajalookultuuri ajakiri*, 3, 20–36.

Voas, D. (2008). The continuing secular transition. In D. Pollack & D. Olson (Eds.), *The Role of Religion in Modern Societies* (pp. 25–48). New York: Routledge.

Voas, D. (2009). The rise and fall of fuzzy fidelity in Europe. *European Sociological Review* 25(2), 155–168. https://doi.org/10.1093/esr/jcn044.

Voas, D. (2020). Is the secularization research programme progressing? Debate on Jörg Stolz's article on Secularization theories in the 21st century: ideas, evidence, and problems. *Social Compass*, 67(2), 323–329. https://doi.org/10.1177/0037768620917329.

Walters, P. (2002). Notes on Autocephaly or Phyletism. *Religion, State and Society*, 4, 357–364. https://doi.org/10.1080/09637490120103320.

Weber, M. (1946). Religious Rejections of the World and Their Directions. In H. H. Gerth & C. W. Mills (Eds.), *Max Weber: Essays in Sociology* (pp. 323–359). New York: Oxford University Press.

Weber, M. (1958). *The Protestant Ethic and the Spirit of Capitalism.* New York: Charles Scribner's Sons.

Wilkins-Laflamme, S. (2020). Exploring further debates in the secularization paradigm. Debate on Jörg Stolz's article on Secularization theories in the 21st century: ideas, evidence, and problems. *Social Compass*, 67(2), 330–336. https://doi.org/10.1177/0037768620917330.

Williams, R. H. (1996). Religion as Political Resource: Culture or Ideology. *Journal for the Scientific Study of Religion, 35*(4), 368–378. https://doi.org/10.2307/1386412.

Wilson, B. (1982). *Religion in Sociological Perspective*. Oxford: Oxford University Press.

Wohlrab-Sahr, M. & Karstein, U. & Schmidt-Lux, T. (2009). *Forcierte Säkularität. Religiöser Wandel und Generationendynamik im Osten Deutschlands*. Frankfurt am Main: Campus.

Wohlrab-Sahr, M.; Schmidt-Lux, T. & Karstein, U. (2008). Secularization as Conflict. *Social Compass, 55*(2), 127–139. https://doi.org/10.1177/0037768608089734.

Wohlrab-Sahr, M. (2010). Dealing with Two Masters' Commands – Explorations of the Complexities of Religious Life under a Dictatorial Regime. In E. Peperkamp & M. Rajtar (Eds.), *Religion and the secular in Eastern Germany, 1945 to the present* (pp. 209–219). Leiden; Boston: Brill.

Woodhead, L. (2010). Real Religion and Fuzzy Spirituality? Taking Sides in the Sociology of Religion. In D. Houtman & S. Aupers (Eds.), *Religions of Modernity: Relocating the Sacred to the Self and the Digital* (pp. 31–48). Leiden; Boston: Brill. https://doi.org/10.1163/ej.9789004184510.i-273.13.

Woodhead, L. (2012). Introduction. In L. Woodhead & R. Catto (Eds.), *Religion and Change in modern Britain* (pp. 1–33). London: Routledge.

Woodhead, L. (2013). Tactical and Strategic Religion. In N. Dessing; N. Jeldtoft; J. Nielsen & L. Woodhead (Eds.), *Everyday Lived Islam in Britain* (pp. 9–22). Aldershot: Ashgate.

Wuthnow, R. (2001). Spirituality and spiritual practice. In R. K. Fenn (Ed.), *The Blackwell Companion to Sociology of Religion* (pp. 306–320). Chichester: Blackwell.

Yad Vashem. The Righteous Among the Nations Database, "Masing Uku & Eha (Tuulemaa)". Retrieved from http://db.yadvashem.org/righteous/family.html?language=en&itemId=4043741†FM_ListOfIllustrations_Entry.

Zetterberg, S. (2009). *Eesti ajalugu*. Tallinn: Tänapäev.

Zorgdrager, H. (2013). Homosexuality and hypermasculinity in the public discourse of the Russian Orthodox Church: an affect theoretical approach. *International Journal of Philosophy and Theology, 74*(3), 214–239. https://doi.org/10.1080/21692327.2013.829649.

Zuckerman, P. (2008). *Society without God: what the least religious nations can tell us about contentment*. New York; London: New York University Press.

Index

abortion   19, 43
aesthetics   72
agrarian culture, agriculture   5, 20
Alexander (Paulus)   51
Alexander III   48
Alexy (Ridiger)   53, 77
alienation   143, 147
alternative (lifestyle, thinking)   6, 8, 15, 20, 21, 24, 88, 89, 92, 101, 116, 120, 121, 125n, 126, 129
America   133
Amish   132
angels   125, 127
Anglican   151 (see also Church of England)
animal rights   63
Annist, August   14
Annuk, Eve   17
anti-Christian   8, 113, 115, 145
anticlerical(ism)   1, 6, 9, 14, 60, 82, 143, 144
anti-religious
    attitudes   101, 145
    politics, propaganda   17, 18, 22, 95
art(s)   23, 25, 87, 88, 92, 95, 104, 109
Asad, Talal   139
association of congregations   65, 69
Asson, Emma   10
Ast, Karl   10
astrology   119
atheism   1, 6, 13, 16, 39, 40, 44, 52, 60, 86, 87, 95, 101, 111, 113, 115, 116, 132, 144, 145
autocephaly   49
autonomy
    individual   80, 126
    of the Orthodox church   49, 53
    political   7, 78
    religious   62, 64, 83

Baltic German
    colonial discourse   89
    cultural influence   48
    nobility   7, 8, 14, 23, 30, 32, 33, 46, 143
Baltic states   47, 55, 60, 140
baptism(s)   21, 22, 31, 32, 40, 42, 47, 61, 62, 97, 99
Baptists   13, 39, 68, 69

baptismal movement   22, 23
behaviour   6, 9, 16, 32, 72, 80, 81, 92, 112, 122, 129
belief   3, 5, 9, 15, 41, 44, 47, 58, 61–64, 68, 70, 72–73, 84–91, 93–94, 97, 99–107, 110–116, 118, 120, 122, 123, 127–129, 133, 135–136, 141, 142, 144, 146, 152
believer   18, 21, 29, 46, 102, 109, 111, 114, 119, 128, 142, 150
    Orthodox   48–54, 94
belonging   13, 68, 76, 79, 80, 97, 119, 122–124, 127–129, 147
Berger, Peter L.   75, 131, 133, 134, 136
Bible   5–7, 13, 25, 29, 97, 98
births   6, 26, 31
blasphemy   6
Bolsheviks   9, 15, 49n
boundary, -ies   8, 13, 14, 21, 79, 80, 108, 118, 121, 125n, 129
breathwork   43, 104–106
Brethren   4 (See also Moravian church)
'bringers of culture'   59
Brown, Callum   92, 142
Bruce, Steve   132, 133
Buddhism   53, 88, 91, 95
burial   24, 31, 146 (see also funeral)
Byelorussians   47

Campbell, Colin   124
canonical jurisdiction(s)   49, 51, 53–55, 57, 60, 151
Casanova, José   132, 133, 141
cells of religiosity   2
census   13, 32, 45–47, 57, 59, 79, 91, 94, 99, 144
changes of political regime   4, 40, 62, 133
chaplaincy   69, 70
charismatic and Pentecostal Christian groups   62, 69, 132
China   135, 143
christianisation   5, 7, 15, 96, 110
Christian Democratic Party   40, 84
Christiano, Kevin J.   132
Church of England   33 (see also Anglican)
church in exile   23, 37, 50, 51, 53

church tithes (membership tax)   13, 30, 35, 143
civil religion   76
clergy   6–8, 14, 18, 23, 31–33, 36–40, 42–43, 48, 49, 51–54, 56, 59, 60, 62, 66–69
cohabitation act (law)   26, 81–84, 100
collectivisation   20, 39
collectivism   21
collectivist religion   79
colonial church   7
colonial discourse   89, 137
Commissioner of Religious Affairs   38, 60, 61
communism, -t   16, 30, 75, 76, 82, 137, 143, 145, 146
communion   32, 43, 50n
conceptualisation   5, 8, 19, 77, 96, 119, 122
confessional secrecy   66, 68
confirmation (rite)   6, 16, 18, 19, 32, 34, 37–39, 61, 62, 99
congregation   22, 31, 33–39, 48–50, 62, 63, 65–70, 95, 97–101, 105, 112
conscientious objection   64
consciousness   5, 7, 14, 134
conservative Christians   18, 21, 26, 27, 33, 34, 36, 42–44, 100, 151
Conservative People's Party   84
consistory, -ia   7, 18, 38, 39, 60
constitution   13, 35, 58–61, 64, 65, 68, 70, 151
Constitutional Assembly   61
consumerism   72
convent   56
convert   45, 50, 115
cosmic justice   99
court   35, 40, 53, 63, 66
Cox, Harvey   132
creation of the world   9
cultural Christianity   79
cultural homogeneity   84
culture (general)   3, 9, 10, 14–16, 17, 23, 25, 73, 74, 80, 86, 87, 91, 97, 117, 133, 137
   agrarian   20
   Christian   11, 19, 91, 99, 103
   Estonian   77, 78, 97, 98
   European   27, 44, 87, 90, 101, 134
   folk   17
   irreligious   147
   mainstream   121
   national   71

New Age   88, 89, 93, 94, 103–108, 110, 112–114, 116, 151
   of churchlessness   147
   Orthodox   83
   peasant   89
   political   76, 79
   popular   121
   physical   92
   Protestant   8
   religion-as-   151
   religious   103
   Russian   48, 79
   secular   76, 85, 103
   spiritual   5
   western   18, 92
   Western European   74, 75
Cyprus   75
Czechia   138, 140, 142–146, 148, 150
Czechoslovak Hussite Church   143 (see also Hussite)

Davie, Grace   26, 100, 133
Dawson, Andrew   107
de-christianisation   1, 2, 51
defence forces   65, 66, 69
de-institutionalisation   1, 72
democratic   11, 30, 32, 74, 143
demographic process   45, 46, 54, 57, 151
Denmark   74, 140, 141
desecularisation   76, 132, 139
destiny   102, 106, 111, 112 (see also fate)
deterioration   11
differentiation   72, 132, 134
discrimination   81, 83, 146
discursive power   92, 98
disenchantment   121, 131
diversity   6, 42, 43, 84, 142
divine   6, 8, 9, 125
divorce   19, 31, 60
Dobbelaere, Karel   133, 134
dogma   10, 13, 76, 88
doubt   5, 6, 9, 100

eastern religious philosophies   21
East(ern) Germany (see also German Democratic Republic)   136–139, 145–147
eco-movement   88

INDEX

Ecumenical Patriarchate of
    Constantinople 49, 51, 53, 56, 60
education 15, 17, 19, 25, 29, 33, 41, 48, 52, 54,
    56, 66–68, 70, 73, 86, 92, 95, 101–103,
    107–109, 111, 114, 117, 134–136, 140, 143,
    145, 147, 149
Eek, Liina 94
egalitarian 58, 59, 70
Eilart, Anton 38
elite 8, 15, 82–84, 96, 144, 145, 150 (see
    also ruler)
emancipation 19, 22, 72
emic 103
enlightener, -ment 7, 14, 18
enthusiasm 22, 61
environment 6, 43, 49, 72, 87, 90, 103, 110,
    113, 116
Eparchy of Riga 48, 49n
equality 58, 63, 64, 67, 81, 148
eroticism 72
esoteric (religion), esotericism 21, 88, 107,
    108, 134
Estland, Estonia (province) 8, 46
Estonian Apostolic Orthodox Church
    (EAOC) 49–51, 53–56, 59–60, 69
Estonian Centre Party 55, 77, 78
Estonian Council of Churches (ECC) 41, 69,
    70, 78, 83, 93
Estonian Evangelical Lutheran Church
    (EELC) 18, 20–23, 30–46, 52, 56, 58–
    63, 68, 69, 78, 84, 95, 99, 115, 143–145, 151
Estonian Metropolitanate 51, 53–55
Estonian National Independence Party 40
Estonianness 14, 77–79
ethnic, ethnicity 14, 27, 46–57, 71, 75–79, 83,
    84, 86, 92, 96, 115, 150, 151
etic 103
Eugene (Reshetnikov) 54
Europe 2, 9, 23, 24, 27, 28, 41, 72–77, 80–82,
    84–86, 91, 96, 97, 100, 119, 120, 129, 132–
    134, 137, 140, 141, 143–145, 147, 148, 150–152
European culture 27, 44, 101, 134
European Union (EU) 63, 67, 71, 74–77, 80–
    82, 96, 151
European values 83, 87, 89
Eurosecularism 71, 74, 75
Eusebius (Grozdov) 50
evolutionary theory 9

Facebook 122, 126, 129
faith 5–9, 17, 24, 43, 65, 89, 90, 93, 97, 98,
    101–104, 110, 111, 132, 135, 150
    native 89–91, 94, 95, 98, 108–110, 114,
    116, 152
    Orthodox 94
    own 111, 113, 114
    Russian 48–52
faith healers 99 (see also healers)
family 12, 16, 19, 21, 26, 32, 36, 51, 67, 81–85,
    97, 99, 100, 103, 105, 106, 108, 109, 142
fate 102, 111, 112 (see also destiny)
feminisation 18, 19
feminism 142
feng shui 92
Finke, Roger 133
Finland 33, 39, 140, 141, 150
Finno-Ugric 89
Fokas, Effie 133
folk culture 17, 89, 110, 114, 152
forced secularisation 60, 142, 143, 146
Founding Assembly 9–11
fragmentation 72, 120, 129
framework of meaning 8
France 30, 139
Frank, Anja 148
free congregations 4, 7, 13, 21, 99
freedom 5, 14, 34, 46, 61, 62, 64, 66, 102,
    113, 120
    of religion 10, 13, 35, 39, 58, 61, 63, 64,
    68, 70, 74
fundamentalism 90, 132, 139
funeral 16, 141 (see also burial)
Furseth, Inger 140, 142

Gallup 1
Gauthier, François 136
Geertz, Clifford 127
gender 19, 22, 26, 63, 67, 80, 81, 83, 92, 100,
    101, 109, 114, 137, 148
General Synod 39, 59
generation 11, 19, 20–22, 25, 39, 47, 51, 52, 92,
    94, 95, 97, 104, 115, 135, 144, 148
German Democratic Republic 16, 145 (see
    also East Germany)
Germans 14, 15, 17, 23, 27, 36, 37, 51, 56, 145,
    150 (see also Baltic German)
globalisation 81, 87, 89, 138

goal-orientedness   12
God   4–6, 8, 10, 11, 14, 23, 32, 47, 74, 93, 97, 99, 101, 102, 104, 111, 112, 118, 127, 142, 146
  Mother of   55n, 78
gospel   7, 8
Great Britain   39
Great Northern War   48
Gregorian calendar   49
guarantor of rules   8, 11

Habermas, Jürgen   133, 134, 137
Hammer, Olav   126
Hamplová, Dana   143
hard work   12, 29
healer   41, 89, 107, 118, 123 (see also faith healer)
Heelas, Paul   91, 95, 129, 141
Hervieu-Léger, Danièle   125n
Hetherington, Kevin   124
Hinduism   88, 91, 95
hippie movement   88
historical   1, 14–16, 23, 29, 30, 34, 42, 47, 69, 73, 90, 91, 95, 96, 131–133, 136, 139, 140, 143, 145–150
  critical approach   33
  reasons   50, 86, 118, 131, 133, 143
historically   41, 62, 72, 77, 137
history   2, 4, 6, 11, 14, 17, 21, 25, 41, 45, 47, 48, 57, 58, 76–78, 85, 91, 94, 95, 125, 129, 142, 143, 151
Hitler, Adolf   36
holistic   87, 141, 142
Höllinger, Franz   135, 138
Hölscher, Lucian   147
homosexuality   26, 43, 81–84, 100 (see also LGBTI persons)
Hong Kong   143
horoscopes   41, 99, 125n (see also astrology)
human being   8, 11, 102
Human Development Index (HDI)   135, 138
humanitarian aid   22
Hurt, Jakob   6–7, 12–14
Hussite   145
hypocrisy   25

Iannaccone, Laurence R.   133
Iceland   141

ideology   1, 3–5, 8–10, 12–17, 19–25, 27–28, 40–41, 70, 72–74, 76, 82, 84, 86, 89, 90, 96, 105, 113, 120, 129, 150
Ilves, Toomas Hendrik   77
imagination   13, 25, 86, 102
immigrants   23, 52, 84, 85
immigration   1, 2, 141
individual   3, 13, 16, 18, 19, 22, 27, 28, 61, 62, 64–67, 72, 74, 76, 80, 81, 87, 88, 90–93, 100, 105, 110, 115, 116, 120, 123–126, 128, 133–135, 138, 140
  religiosity   2, 4, 6, 29, 75, 76, 88, 91, 95, 99, 110–112, 114, 115, 120, 129
  secularisation   135, 141 (see also inner secularisation)
individualisation   1, 18, 43, 75, 87, 102, 126, 138–140, 143, 145, 148, 149
individualism   13, 116, 123, 126, 128, 138, 152
industrial   2, 86, 89
industrialisation   1, 2, 52, 145
Inglehart, Ronald   135, 142
inner secularisation   2, 146 (see also individual secularisation)
inner self   127
insecurity   22, 135, 142
institutional religion   1, 6, 8, 15, 27, 30, 31, 33, 35, 41–44, 47, 49, 53, 61–66, 68–74, 77, 80–82, 99, 100, 104, 108, 110, 113–115, 118–119, 124n, 126–129, 137
intellectual   1, 7, 13, 14, 21, 103, 109, 120
International Social Survey Programme (ISSP)   144
Islam   27, 91, 95, 101, 131, 133 (see also Muslim)
Ivan the Terrible   48

Jakobson, Carl Robert   7, 8, 14
Jannsen, Johann Voldemar   4, 5
Japan   143
Jehovah's Witnesses   59
Jesus   97, 98
Jews   13, 37, 132
Julian calendar   49
Jürjo, Villu   40

Kaplinski, Jaan   25
Karjahärm, Toomas   14
Keskküla, Kalev   24

INDEX

KGB 39, 53
Khrushchev, Nikita 39
Kiivit, Jaan 39
Kiviorg, Merilin 69
Kõpp, Johan 14, 37, 38, 56
Kukk, Jakob 34, 35
Kulbusch, Paul (Platon) 49

Lakatos, Imre 137, 138
Landeskirche 33
Latvia 39, 46, 48, 60, 76, 144
Lazar (Gurkin) 54
left-wing 8, 19, 26, 113
legislation 1, 30, 35, 52, 59–60, 62, 63, 64n, 66, 67, 69, 70, 75, 82, 151
legitimacy 5, 120
Lenin, Vladimir 16
Lepp-Utuste, Marta 13
LGBTI persons 81 (see also homosexuality)
liberalism 1, 6, 9, 13, 16, 26, 43, 59, 62, 70, 74, 75, 80, 82, 83, 86, 87, 90, 103, 137
liberal theology 33, 42, 44, 151
life force 119, 142
lifestyle 83, 87, 102, 120, 122, 125n
literature 17, 20, 33, 55, 87, 88, 95, 97, 98, 104, 106, 109, 112, 113, 121, 138
Lithuania 60
Livonia 8
Lõhmus, Maarja 16
Loorits, Oskar 89
Luckmann, Thomas 132
Luiga, Georg Eduard 34
Lutheran church 7, 29
    identity 29
    values 12
Lutheranism 4, 8, 13, 23, 24, 29, 33, 34, 45, 46, 50, 56, 77, 79, 84, 94, 97, 98

Maavalla Koda 90, 108
magic(al) 5, 6, 14, 41, 106–108
mainstream 1, 41, 79, 89, 116, 120, 121, 125n, 151
mainstreaming 119, 121, 128
majority 4, 11, 45, 48, 49, 53, 69, 83, 91, 99, 108, 115, 122, 123, 137
    church 29, 32, 62, 69, 141
Malta 75, 82
marginalisation 3, 4, 15, 22, 29, 60

marital relations 19
market 62, 70, 75, 86, 118, 125n, 128, 137
marriage, 6, 12, 26, 31, 64, 67, 69, 80, 83, 99
Martin, David 133, 136, 139
martial arts 53
Martna, Mihkel 12, 18
marxism 1, 10, 14–17, 27, 150
Masing, Uku 14, 33, 34, 37, 89
mass conversion 45, 46, 48
materialism 7, 8, 41, 86, 92, 118, 119, 125, 127 (see also scientific-materialist worldview)
meaning 1, 3, 4, 8, 17, 20–22, 26, 27, 60, 72, 79, 96, 103, 104, 107, 109, 111, 119, 125, 127, 128
media 34, 92, 116, 117, 120–122, 124–129
meditation 62, 89, 99, 104–106, 112, 114
memory 6, 17, 77, 85
    collective 73
    cultural 25–28
mentally ill 18
Merkel, Garlieb Helwig 14
meso-level 2, 3, 133
Methodists 13, 39, 68, 69
Meulemann, Heiner 146
mind-body duality 107
minority 26, 47, 53, 55, 57, 76, 77, 79, 84, 100, 137, 141, 151
mission 20, 44, 47, 102
Molotov-Ribbentrop Pact 60
monastery 48, 54, 56, 65
Moravian church 145 (see also Brethren)
moral
    (counter)arguments 12, 26
    formation 11
    hero 6
    ideal 12
    norm 12, 26, 28, 72, 80, 100
    panic 11
    Protestant 12
morality 12, 15, 18–20, 22, 25, 26, 28, 36, 43, 66, 81, 100, 134
Moscow Patriarchate 51, 53, 56, 57 (see also Patriarch of Moscow)
Mõtsnik, Harri 40
Mstislav Mstislavich 47
Muckenhuber, Johanna 135, 138
Muslim 85, 132, 141 (see also Islam)

Müller, Tobias   137
multiculturalism   77
myth   7, 14–16, 27, 74, 89, 102, 133, 150
mythology   24, 103

narrative   3, 5, 14–17, 23, 24, 27, 34, 46, 90, 93, 98, 110, 114, 116, 120, 127, 128, 150
national
   awakening   4, 22, 48
   cause   35
   character   28
   church   29
   culture   71, 76
   discourse   23, 48
   identity   1, 17, 23, 27, 47, 51, 73, 76, 89, 97, 136, 150
   ideology   8, 13, 15, 24, 25, 27, 86
   movement   6–8, 14, 15, 17, 78, 134, 140, 143, 145, 148, 150
   myth   7, 14
   mythology   24
   narrative   14, 15, 17, 23, 24, 27, 90, 98, 110, 114, 150
   religion   77, 78
   self-image   107
   sentiment   33
   stance   33
   unity   35
National Christian Party   30
nationalism   1, 6, 7, 9, 12, 13, 14, 15, 19–23, 27, 28, 33, 73, 76, 77, 86, 89, 90, 95, 96, 110, 113, 145, 150
nationality   6, 33, 53, 84
nationally minded   6–9, 12, 83, 90
National Socialist regime   37
native faith   24, 89–91, 94, 95, 98, 108–111, 114, 116, 152
natural place   109
natural sciences   6, 8, 15, 19, 88
nature   5, 89, 90, 109, 110, 112, 116, 152
nature religion   90, 91, 114, 145
neoliberalism   62, 70
neopagan   13, 24 (see also new paganism)
Nešpor, Zdeněk R.   143, 144
New Age   22, 43, 53, 87–89, 92–94, 103–108, 110, 112–114, 116, 118, 120–124, 127, 129, 151, 152 (see also new spirituality)
new paganism   89 (see also neopagan)

new spirituality   2, 41, 43, 87–89, 91–95, 97–101, 103–108, 110–119, 121–124, 129, 136, 151, 152 (see also New Age)
non-believers   143 (see also nones and non-religious)
nonconformism   18, 20, 22
nones   122, 141, 144 (see also non-believers and non-religious)
non-religious   44, 47, 57, 72, 73, 82, 87, 96, 100–103, 105, 107, 113, 116, 118, 134n, 143 (see also non-believers and nones)
Norris, Pippa   135, 142
North Korea   143
Norway   141
Novgorod   47, 53n

occultism   87, 88, 148
'one's own religion'   111, 113, 114
opposition   6–9, 15, 19, 21, 23, 25, 27, 28, 42, 79, 82, 88–90, 95, 101, 104, 107, 108, 112, 114, 124, 139, 150
organised church   7
Orthodoxy   13, 45–48, 50–53, 75, 79, 151
   Russian   4, 7, 8, 23, 94, 96
out-of-church movement   143

pagan   13, 18, 24, 110
   association Hiis   60
Pähn, August   38, 39
Pajula, Kuno   40
pantheism   7
paranormal phenomena   41
parish   31, 35, 42, 50–56 (see also congregation)
parliament   9, 30, 31, 35, 40, 59, 60, 62, 63, 77–79, 82–84
Patriarch of Moscow   48, 53, 77
Päts, Konstantin   35
peasants   4–6, 29, 34, 89, 96
Pentecostalism   131
Peperkamp, Esther   146
personal experience   88
Peter the Great   48
petition   12, 24
Pickel, Gert   147, 148
pietism   5, 6
PISA (Program for International Student Assessment)   86, 135, 149

INDEX

Ploompuu, Johan 11
pluralism 2, 9, 120, 125, 134–136, 140
Poland 48, 75, 146
Põld, Harald 33
political 1, 8–10, 15, 30, 40, 42, 45, 49, 53, 55, 56, 60, 62, 53, 70, 72–74, 76, 78–80, 84, 133, 134, 146, 147
   correctness 77
   history 4, 47
politicisation 79
politics 1, 3, 4, 15–17, 19, 22, 27, 53, 71–74, 77, 84, 92
   of nativism 85
Pollack, Detlef 146
Pope 7, 134n
population 2, 3, 13, 20, 34, 44–47, 51, 52, 56, 58, 59, 70, 75, 77, 79, 84, 91, 94, 101, 103, 115, 122, 141–144, 147, 148, 151
positivist worldview 8, 15, 19
Possamai, Adam 124
post-Communist 62, 73, 75, 76
power 4, 6, 8–10, 14, 15, 16, 18, 36, 47, 59, 60, 62, 72, 80, 81, 92, 98, 99, 102, 110, 112, 114, 122, 123, 125, 129, 144
public function 30, 134
practice
praying 6, 29, 41, 43, 55, 97, 98, 101
predetermination 99
President 35, 60, 62, 53, 77, 78 (see also State Elder)
privilege 5, 8, 59, 70, 127, 147
propaganda 10, 18, 40, 52, 101
Pro Patria party (Isamaa) 83
psychology 88, 102, 103, 110
public discourse 3, 78
Pühtitsa convent in Kuremäe 56

Rahamägi, Hugo Bernhard 32, 35–37
Rajtar, Malgorzata 146
Ränk, Gustav 15
'ratherism' 95, 123
rational choice theory 133
Ratzinger, Joseph (Benedict XVI) 134n
rebellion 7
reconceptualisation 19
referendum 12, 13, 59, 61
reflection 6, 69
Reform party 83

refugee 23, 26, 43, 100
Register of Religious Associations 63, 65, 66
regulation 31, 58, 59, 63, 65–68, 124, 135, 136, 138, 140, 148
Reiki 104–106, 118
reincarnation 41, 99, 107, 112, 141, 142, 144
religion-as-culture 85, 151
religiosity 1, 2, 25, 27, 29, 32, 44, 47, 76, 87, 88, 91, 94, 95–97, 99, 110–112, 114, 115, 118–120, 122, 129, 132, 135, 136, 138–140, 142, 143, 145–148, 151, 152
religious
   authority 71–73, 76, 79, 82, 133, 151
   boom 22, 28, 61
   change 62, 94 (see also religious turn)
   commitment 47, 50n, 51, 118, 127
   complexity 142
   dynamics 2
   education 20, 39, 67, 95, 107, 143, 144
   headgear 68
   ideas 1
   identity 1, 23, 50, 51, 76, 79, 109
   instruction 9–13, 15, 18, 20, 24–26
   knowledge 6
   language 6, 111, 118
   leaders 1, 63, 78
   lobbying 58
   modernisation 75
   participation 79, 118, 123
   pluralism 2, 136
   policy 71
   preference 13, 91
   slaughtering 63
   socialisation 20, 143, 147, 148
   society 75
   symbol 24, 79, 80
   traditions 9, 20, 58, 59, 62, 74, 78, 80, 82, 84, 119, 120, 132, 134
   transformation 137, 138
   transition 139
   turn 91, 92, 103, 115–117, 151 (see also religious change)
Remmel, Atko 95
repentance 8, 11, 23
representation 3, 4, 8, 9, 15, 18, 21, 22
research programme 137, 138
resistance 17, 21, 22, 37, 40
resource 4, 12, 43, 89, 115, 125

responsibility (sense of)   8, 11, 12, 18, 31, 61, 62, 144
Res Publica party   83
revolution
   Islamic   131
   October   16
   Russian   9
   Singing   22, 23, 89
   sixties discourse   142
   spiritual   91, 121, 141
right-wing   30
Rinne, Jenny   108
ritual   5, 6, 13, 15–17, 26, 32, 35, 41, 66, 79, 106, 119, 123, 125n, 141, 146, 148, 150
Rivers, Julian   81
Roman Catholic church   41, 56, 65, 69, 132, 141, 145, 148
Romania   75
ruler   8, 10, 96, 99 (see also elite)
rural population   2
Russian Empire   4, 8, 31, 34, 48, 50, 59, 150
Russian Orthodox Church (ROC)   46–49, 51–55
Russians   2, 23, 28, 47–57, 77–79, 83, 96, 97, 151
russification   7, 17, 48
Rüütel, Arnold   77

Saar, Andrus   113
Saard, Riho   23
sacralisation   72, 73, 80, 107, 121
Salum, Vello   40
salvation   7, 126
same-sex relationships   26, 63, 81–83, 151
Savisaar, Edgar   55n, 78
Scandinavia   29, 33, 84, 141, 142, 150
schism   53, 54
Schmalenbach, Herman   124
school   5, 6, 9–12, 15, 18, 20, 24–26, 31, 48, 55, 62, 67, 68, 95, 107, 110, 115, 147
scientific knowledge   8
scientific-materialist worldview   8, 86, 92, 119, 125
scientism   148
secularism   71, 74, 75, 133, 144, 145, 148
secularity   1, 62, 75, 137, 142
secularisation   1–3, 20, 28, 29, 32, 42, 51, 58, 71–73, 75, 76, 79, 80, 84, 86, 119, 121, 131–151
secular   19, 21, 27, 30, 31, 74, 76, 78, 79, 82, 85, 86, 92, 95, 101–104, 107, 109, 117–119, 121

competition   135, 136, 140, 143, 149
society   2, 30, 58, 70, 94, 119, 122
thinking   5–7
transition   135–140
seekers   21, 113, 126, 127
self-creation   88
self-spirituality   88, 103–105, 110, 116, 152
self-understanding   14, 142, 151
Semper, Johannes   10
separation of church and state   30, 64, 68, 69, 74
sermon   23, 32, 35, 40
sexual chastity   12
sexuality   19, 71, 80–83, 102
Singing Revolution   22, 23, 89
Sirk, Väino   14
situationality   118, 119, 122–124, 130
skepticism   24, 89, 116
sobriety   12
social   8, 12, 18, 21, 22, 26–28, 30, 32, 36, 42, 43, 45, 49, 50, 53, 60, 66, 70, 72, 73, 76, 80–84, 89, 93, 96, 100, 110, 115, 116, 118, 120, 122, 123, 126–128, 132, 134, 136, 139, 146, 150
   changes   1, 2, 32, 62, 100, 126, 142
   Darwinism   9
   democracy   10, 12, 83, 143
   interaction   3
   media   116, 122, 126
   structures   1
   world   3
socialism   9, 15, 17, 21, 30, 86, 146, 148
Sõtšov, Andrei   52n
Soviet
   bloc   136, 140, 146, 147
   period   1, 15, 19, 22, 62, 141
   state religion   16
   Union   15, 37, 52, 53, 60, 82, 89, 132
Spencer, Herbert   9
spiritual
   revolution   91, 121, 141
   but not religious   44, 89, 91, 101, 103, 105, 106, 111
   development   88, 104, 113, 114
   humanism   95
   milieu   1, 118, 121–128, 130, 134, 152
sports   92, 102, 117
Stalin, Joseph   19, 39
Stark, Rodney   132, 133

state church   10, 35, 46, 60, 62, 64, 68
State Elder   59, 60 (see also President)
statue of the Bronze Soldier   77
stereotypes   3, 18, 25, 101–103, 115
stigmatisation   18, 96, 120
Stolz, Jörg   135, 136, 138, 139
struggle   6, 9, 14, 15, 17–19, 27, 44, 76, 90, 96, 150
subculture   41, 105, 132
superstition   7, 107
Supreme Council   61
syncretism   88, 95, 97, 111, 112, 118–120
Swatos, William H.   132
Sweden   37, 48, 140–143, 146, 148, 150
Swedish era   5

Taara religion   13
talisman   107
Tallmeister, Theodor   33
Tammsaare, Anton Hansen   29
Tantra   118
Taoism   53, 88
Taylor, Charles   133, 137
teaching   7, 9, 13, 24, 87, 88, 98, 100, 102–105, 107, 110, 112, 118, 120, 122, 125, 127, 128, 152
theological
    academy   54
    conservatism   34, 43
    education   38, 68
    faculty   60, 62
    institute   56
    research   33
    seminary   48
theology   14, 25, 33–35, 37, 56
thrift   12
Tikhon   49
towns   2, 34, 43, 52
Tõnisson, Jaan   11
transcendental   148
Transcendental Meditation   62 (see also meditation)
transformation   2, 128, 137, 138, 150, 151
translation of the Bible   29
transnational   90
tribal cultures   88
truth   3, 17, 97, 107

Ukraine   27, 54
Ukrainians   47

ultra-orthodox Jews   132
Uluots, Jüri   12
Undusk, Jaan   96
uniformity   21
University of Tartu   60, 62, 94, 118n
understanding   1, 3, 4, 8–10, 12, 14–16, 19, 22, 24, 26, 41, 45, 48, 51, 77, 84, 90, 93, 96, 98, 107, 116, 118, 121, 122, 125, 130, 131, 133, 134n, 137
urbanisation   1, 2, 20, 34, 52, 89, 145
urban population   1, 20
user-generated content   125, 126

Vällik, Martin   24
value   3, 4, 12–15, 18, 19, 21, 25–29, 32–34, 43, 72, 74, 80–83, 86–90, 103, 107, 110, 116, 120–123, 125, 126, 128, 129, 138, 142, 152
Veimer, Arnold   18
vernacular   50, 126, 127, 129
Viilma, Urmas   41
Villenthal, Laine   38
vicarious religion   26, 27, 94, 100, 116
Vladimir Mstislavich   47
Voas, David   135–138
Volkskirche (people's church)   56

Weber, Max   121, 131, 133
welfare   66, 102, 136, 142
Wilkins-Laflamme, Sarah   138, 139
Wohlrab-Sahr, Monika   147, 148
women's
    emancipation   19, 22, 92
    ordination   43
    religiosity   142
Woodhead, Linda   91, 119, 141
World Values survey   1, 82
World War II   14, 15, 51–53, 60, 77

Yaroslav the Wise   47
yoga   53, 89, 99, 104–106, 121

13th century   5, 7
19th century   2, 5, 6, 9, 14, 27, 33, 34, 45, 47, 48, 50n, 73, 76, 89, 96, 143, 146
20th century   2, 6, 8, 9, 13, 18, 19, 25, 29, 34, 41, 86, 137, 150
1960ies   18, 19, 26, 28, 38, 39, 80, 87, 88, 92, 131, 132, 142, 143, 150, 151